Everyday Data Structures

A practical guide to learning data structures simply and easily

William Smith

BIRMINGHAM - MUMBAI

Everyday Data Structures

First published: March 2017

Production reference: 1080317

Published by Packt Publishing Ltd.
Livery Place
35 Livery Street
Birmingham
B3 2PB, UK.
ISBN 978-1-78712-104-1

www.packtpub.com

Credits

Author

William Smith

Reviewer

Aditya Abhay Halabe

Commissioning Editor

David Barnes

Acquisition Editor

Shweta Pant

Content Development Editor

Zeeyan Pinheiro

Technical Editors

Pavan Ramchandani

Pratish Shetty

Copy Editor

Pranjali Chury

Project Coordinator

Vaidehi Sawant

Proofreader

Safis Editing

Indexer

Aishwarya Gangawane

Graphics

Abhinash Sahu

Production Coordinator

Shraddha Falebhai

About the Author

William Smith has been writing software since 1988, but he began his professional career in the environmental field with degrees in Environmental Science and Business Administration. While working in this field, William continued writing software as a hobbyist before returning to the University of Maryland for a degree in Computer Science.

William currently works as an independent software engineer and author. He is the owner of Appsmiths LLC, a development and consulting firm concentrating on mobile application and game development using native tools as well as cross-platform tools, such as Xamarin and Monogame.

William lives in rural West Virginia with his beautiful wife and four sons, where they enjoy hunting, fishing, and camping as a family.

About the Reviewer

Aditya Abhay Halabe is a full-stack web application developer at Springer Nature's technology division. His primary technology stack includes Scala, Java, Graph, and document store databases, micro-web services, multiple frameworks, and extreme programming practices. He is passionate about his work and likes to take on new challenges and responsibilities. Previously, Aditya worked as a consultant with Oracle and as a developer with John Deere Ltd.

www.PacktPub.com

For support files and downloads related to your book, please visit www.PacktPub.com.

Did you know that Packt offers eBook versions of every book published, with PDF and ePub files available? You can upgrade to the eBook version at www.PacktPub.com and as a print book customer, you are entitled to a discount on the eBook copy. Get in touch with us at service@packtpub.com for more details.

At www.PacktPub.com, you can also read a collection of free technical articles, sign up for a range of free newsletters and receive exclusive discounts and offers on Packt books and eBooks.

https://www.packtpub.com/mapt

Get the most in-demand software skills with Mapt. Mapt gives you full access to all Packt books and video courses, as well as industry-leading tools to help you plan your personal development and advance your career.

Why subscribe?

- Fully searchable across every book published by Packt
- Copy and paste, print, and bookmark content
- On demand and accessible via a web browser

Customer Feedback

Thanks for purchasing this Packt book. At Packt, quality is at the heart of our editorial process. To help us improve, please leave us an honest review on this book's Amazon page at `https://www.amazon.com/dp/1787121046`.

If you'd like to join our team of regular reviewers, you can email us at `customerreviews@packtpub.com`. We award our regular reviewers with free eBooks and videos in exchange for their valuable feedback. Help us be relentless in improving our products!

Table of Contents

Preface

Quite often, as software developers, when presented with a new task or challenge, we find ourselves grabbing code fragments or patterns that we are most familiar with. We typically make this choice because those fragments and patterns represent the shortest path between two points, namely, the client's requirements and a deadline (also known as payday). However, this approach sometimes prevents us from learning new skills and ideas that will make us better and more efficient developers.

This book was written to give aspiring, new, or relatively inexperienced but busy developers an opportunity to step back and examine some of the fundamental concepts regarding data types and data structures. To that, we will examine how these types and structures are built, how they function, and how we can leverage them in our everyday applications. By doing so, we will gain new knowledge, skills, abilities and, hopefully, get some new ideas on how to leverage these basic components.

What this book covers

Chapter 1, *Data Types: Foundational Structures*, is a very brief overview of basic data types that comprise of data structures. This will be a rapid overview as even new programmers will already be familiar with some or most of these components. Attention will be paid to applications for each type, best practices, and a high-level comparison of any variations between platforms.

Chapter 2, *Arrays: Foundational Collections*, introduces you to the array data structure. This discussion will include specific details of the structure, including the typical applications, as well as specific concerns for each language. This is an important foundation chapter, as many of the subsequent data structures are built using arrays.

Chapter 3, *Lists: Linear Collections*, covers the specific details of the list data structure, including the most common functions associated with lists, typical applications for lists, and specific concerns for each language.

Chapter 4, *Stacks: LIFO Collections*, introduces you to the stack data structure. In this chapter, the reader will learn the specific details of the structure including the most common functions associated with stacks, typical applications for stacks, and specific concerns for each language.

Chapter 5, *Queues: FIFO Collections*, talks about the specific details of the queue data structure, including the most common functions associated with queues, typical applications for queues, and specific concerns for each language.

Chapter 6, *Dictionaries: Keyed Collections*, delves into the specific details of the dictionary data structure, including the most common functions associated with dictionaries, typical applications for dictionaries, and specific concerns for each language.

Chapter 7, *Sets: No Duplicates*, discusses the specific details of the set data structure, including the foundations of set theory; the most common functions associated with sets, typical applications for sets, and specific concerns for each language.

Chapter 8, *Structures: Complex Types*, explores the specific details of structures or the struct data structure, including most common functions associated with structs, typical applications for structs, and specific concerns for each language.

Chapter 9, *Trees: Non-Linear Structures*, talks about the specific details of the abstract tree structure with particular emphasis on the binary tree. This discussion will include an examination of the most common functions associated with trees, typical applications for trees, and specific concerns for each language.

Chapter 10, *Heaps: Ordered Trees*, delves into the specific details of the heap data structure, including the most common functions associated with heaps, typical applications for heaps, and specific concerns for each language.

Chapter 11, *Graphs: Values with Relationships*, introduces the specific details of the graph data structure, including the most common functions associated with graphs, typical applications for graphs, and specific concerns for each language.

Chapter 12, *Sorting: Bringing Order Out of Chaos*, is an advanced chapter that focuses on the concept of sorting. This concept will be introduced by examining several common and popular sorting algorithms, with particular attention being paid to operational cost, common applications, and concerns accompanying each algorithm.

Chapter 13, *Searching: Finding What You Need*, is also an advanced chapter that focuses on the concept of searching for data within a data structure. This concept will be introduced by examining several common and popular searching algorithms, with particular attention being paid to operational cost, common applications, and concerns for each language.

What you need for this book

In order for you to take full advantage of this book, you will need a modern computer. The code examples in this book are broad enough that you can use a Mac, PC, or even a Linux machine. Ultimately, you will also need a functioning development environment, such as Visual Studio, XCode, Eclipse, or NetBeans, that can run on your chosen development machine.

Who this book is for

This book is for anyone who wants to improve their knowledge and skills in fundamental programming concepts related to data structures. More specifically, this book is for new or self-taught programmers or programmers who range in experience from relatively new to having three or four years of experience. This book focuses on the four languages most commonly used in mobile software development, so the audience also includes those interested in mobile software development. The reader should have a basic understanding of programming, including how to create console applications, and how to use an Integrated Development Environment, or IDE, for their preferred development language

Conventions

In this book, you will find a number of text styles that distinguish between different kinds of information. Here are some examples of these styles and an explanation of their meaning.

Each chapter of this book will also include a case study, or similar code example, that will be broken down and detailed to explain how the data structure is applied. As such, this book is full of code examples.

A block of code is set as follows:

```
public boolean isEmpty()
{
    return this._commandStack.empty();
}
```

When we wish to draw your attention to a particular part of a code block, the relevant lines or items are set in bold:

```
func canAddUser(user: EDSUser) -> Bool
{
    if (_users.contains(user))
    {
        return false;
```

```
    } else {
        return true;
}
```

New terms and **important words** are shown in bold. Words that you see on the screen, for example, in menus or dialog boxes, appear in the text like this: "The first validation method, isFull(), checks if our stack has reached its capacity."

We will also discuss algorithms and mathematical concepts related to algorithms in this text. Whenever operational cost values written in Big-O notation are shown they appear as follows: "This is small consolation, however, because the selection sort algorithm still has an $O(n^2)$ complexity cost."

Likewise, when mathematical formulas and algorithms are used, they will appear as follows: "Our algorithm will find the smallest value in S[0...4], which in this case is 3, and place it at the beginning of S[0...4]."

Warnings or important notes appear in a box like this.

Tips and tricks appear like this.

Reader feedback

Feedback from our readers is always welcome. Let us know what you think about this book-what you liked or disliked. Reader feedback is important for us as it helps us develop titles that you will really get the most out of. To send us general feedback, simply e-mail feedback@packtpub.com, and mention the book's title in the subject of your message. If there is a topic that you have expertise in and you are interested in either writing or contributing to a book, see our author guide at www.packtpub.com/authors.

Customer support

Now that you are the proud owner of a Packt book, we have a number of things to help you to get the most from your purchase.

Downloading the example code

You can download the example code files for this book from your account at `http://www.p acktpub.com`. If you purchased this book elsewhere, you can visit `http://www.packtpub.c om/support` and register to have the files e-mailed directly to you.

You can download the code files by following these steps:

1. Log in or register to our website using your e-mail address and password.
2. Hover the mouse pointer on the **SUPPORT** tab at the top.
3. Click on **Code Downloads & Errata**.
4. Enter the name of the book in the **Search** box.
5. Select the book for which you're looking to download the code files.
6. Choose from the drop-down menu where you purchased this book from.
7. Click on **Code Download**.

Once the file is downloaded, please make sure that you unzip or extract the folder using the latest version of:

- WinRAR / 7-Zip for Windows
- Zipeg / iZip / UnRarX for Mac
- 7-Zip / PeaZip for Linux

The code bundle for the book is also hosted on GitHub at `https://github.com/PacktPubl ishing/Everyday-Data-Structures`. We also have other code bundles from our rich catalog of books and videos available at `https://github.com/PacktPublishing/`. Check them out!

Errata

Although we have taken every care to ensure the accuracy of our content, mistakes do happen. If you find a mistake in one of our books-maybe a mistake in the text or the code-we would be grateful if you could report this to us. By doing so, you can save other readers from frustration and help us improve subsequent versions of this book. If you find any errata, please report them by visiting `http://www.packtpub.com/submit-errata`, selecting your book, clicking on the **Errata Submission Form** link, and entering the details of your errata. Once your errata are verified, your submission will be accepted and the errata will be uploaded to our website or added to any list of existing errata under the Errata section of that title.

To view the previously submitted errata, go to `https://www.packtpub.com/books/content/support` and enter the name of the book in the search field. The required information will appear under the **Errata** section.

Piracy

Piracy of copyrighted material on the Internet is an ongoing problem across all media. At Packt, we take the protection of our copyright and licenses very seriously. If you come across any illegal copies of our works in any form on the Internet, please provide us with the location address or website name immediately so that we can pursue a remedy.

Please contact us at `copyright@packtpub.com` with a link to the suspected pirated material.

We appreciate your help in protecting our authors and our ability to bring you valuable content.

Questions

If you have a problem with any aspect of this book, you can contact us at `questions@packtpub.com`, and we will do our best to address the problem.

1
Data Types: Foundational Structures

Calling data types *foundational structures* may seem like a bit of a misnomer, but not when you consider that developers use data types to build their classes and collections. So, before we examine proper data structures, it's a good idea to quickly review data types, as these are the foundation of what comes next. This chapter is meant to review the most common and most important fundamental data types from the 10,000-foot view. If you already have a strong grasp of these basic concepts, feel free to skim through this chapter or even skip it entirely as you see fit.

In this chapter, we will cover the following topics:

- Numeric data types
- Casting, Narrowing, and Widening
- 32-bit and 64-bit architecture concerns
- Boolean data types
- Logic operations
- Order of operations
- Nesting operations
- Short-circuiting
- String data types
- Mutability of strings

Numeric data types

A detailed description of all the numeric data types in each of the following four languages, C#, Java, Objective-C, and Swift, could easily encompass a book of its own. Here, we will review only the most common numeric type identifiers for each language. The simplest way to evaluate these types is based on the underlying size of the data, using examples from each language as a framework for the discussion.

> **Compare apples to apples!**
> When you are developing applications for multiple mobile platforms, you should be aware that the languages you use could share a data type identifier or keyword, but under the hood, those identifiers may not be equal in value. Likewise, the same data type in one language may have a different identifier in another. For example, examine the case of the 16-bit unsigned integer, sometimes referred to as an `unsigned short`. Well, it's called an `unsigned short` in Objective-C. In C#, we talk about a `ushort`, while Swift calls it a `UInt16`. Java's only provision for the 16-bit unsigned integer, on the other hand, is `char` although this object would typically not be used for numeric values. Each of these data types represents a 16-bit unsigned integer; they just use different names. This may seem like a small point, but if you are developing apps for multiple devices using each platform's native language, for the sake of consistency, you will need to be aware of these differences. Otherwise, you may risk introducing platform-specific bugs that are extremely difficult to detect and diagnose.

Integer types

Integer data types are defined as representing whole numbers and can be either **signed** (negative, zero, or positive values) or **unsigned** (zero or positive values). Each language uses its own identifiers and keywords for integer types, so it is easiest to think in terms of memory length. For our purpose, we will only discuss the integer types representing 8-, 16-, 32-, and 64-bit memory objects.

8-bit data types, or **bytes** as they are more commonly referred to, are the smallest data types that we will examine. If you have brushed up on your binary math, you will know that an 8-bit memory block can represent 2^8, or 256 values. Signed bytes can range in value from -128 to 127, or $-(2^7)$ to $(2^7) - 1$. Unsigned bytes can range in value from 0 to 255, or 0 to (2^8) -1.

A 16-bit data type is often referred to as a **short**, although that is not always the case. These types can represent 2^{16} values. Signed shorts can range in value from $-(2^{15})$ to $(2^{15}) - 1$. Unsigned shorts can range in value from 0 to $(2^{16}) - 1$.

A 32-bit data type is most commonly identified as an integer, although it is sometimes identified as a **long**. Int types can represent 2^{32} values. Signed integers can range in values from -2^{31} to $2^{31} - 1$. Unsigned integers can range in values from 0 to $(2^{32}) - 1$.

Finally, a 64-bit data type is most commonly identified as a long, although Objective-C identifies it as a **long long**. Long types can represent 2^{64} values. Signed long types can range in values from $-(2^{63})$ to $(2^{63}) - 1$. Unsigned long types can range in values from 0 to $(2^{63}) - 1$.

Note that these values happen to be consistent across the four languages we will work with, but some languages will introduce slight variations. It is always a good idea to become familiar with the details of a language's numeric identifiers. This is especially true if you expect to be working with cases that involve the identifier's extreme values.

C#

C# refers to integer types as **integral types**. The language provides two mechanisms for creating 8-bit types, `byte` and `sbyte`. Both containers hold up to 256 values, and the unsigned byte ranges from 0 to 255. The signed byte provides support for negative values and, therefore, ranges from -128 to 127:

```
// C#
sbyte minSbyte = -128;
byte maxByte = 255;
Console.WriteLine("minSbyte: {0}", minSbyte);
Console.WriteLine("maxByte: {0}", maxByte);

/*
  Output
  minSbyte: -128
  maxByte: 255
*/
```

Interestingly, C# reverses its pattern for longer bit identifiers. Instead of prefixing signed identifiers with s, as in the case of `sbyte`, it prefixes unsigned identifiers with u. So, for 16-, 32-, and 64-bit identifiers, we have `short`, `ushort`; `int`, `uint`; `long`, and `ulong` respectively:

```
short minShort = -32768;
ushort maxUShort = 65535;
Console.WriteLine("minShort: {0}", minShort);
Console.WriteLine("maxUShort: {0}", maxUShort);

int minInt = -2147483648;
uint maxUint = 4294967295;
Console.WriteLine("minInt: {0}", minInt);
Console.WriteLine("maxUint: {0}", maxUint);

long minLong = -9223372036854775808;
ulong maxUlong = 18446744073709551615;
Console.WriteLine("minLong: {0}", minLong);
Console.WriteLine("maxUlong: {0}", maxUlong);

/*
  Output
  minShort: -32768
  maxUShort: 65535
  minInt: -2147483648
  maxUint: 4294967295
  minLong: -9223372036854775808
  maxUlong: 18446744073709551615
*/
```

Java

Java includes integer types as a part of its primitive data types. The Java language only provides one construct for 8-bit storage, also identified as a `byte`. It is a signed data type, so it will represent values from -127 to 128. Java also provides a wrapper class called `Byte`, which wraps the primitive value and provides additional constructor support for parsable strings, or text, which can be converted to a numeric value such as the text 42. This pattern is repeated in the 16-, 32-, and 64-bit data types:

```
//Java
byte myByte = -128;
byte bigByte = 127;

Byte minByte = new Byte(myByte);
Byte maxByte = new Byte("128");
System.out.println(minByte);
System.out.println(bigByte);
```

```
System.out.println(maxByte);

/*
  Output
  -128
  127
  127
*/
```

Java shares identifiers with C# for all of integer data type, which means it also provides the byte, short, int, and long identifiers for 8-, 16-, 32-, and 64-bit types. One exception to the pattern in Java is the char identifier, which is provided for unsigned 16-bit data types. It should be noted, however, that the char data type is typically only used for ASCII character assignment and not for actual integer values:

```
//Short class
Short minShort = new Short(myShort);
Short maxShort = new Short("32767");
System.out.println(minShort);
System.out.println(bigShort);
System.out.println(maxShort);
int myInt = -2147483648;
int bigInt = 2147483647;

//Integer class
Integer minInt = new Integer(myInt);
Integer maxInt = new Integer("2147483647");
System.out.println(minInt);
System.out.println(bigInt);
System.out.println(maxInt);
long myLong = -9223372036854775808L;
long bigLong = 9223372036854775807L;

//Long class
Long minLong = new Long(myLong);
Long maxLong = new Long("9223372036854775807");
System.out.println(minLong);
System.out.println(bigLong);
System.out.println(maxLong);

/*
  Output
  -32768
  32767
  32767
  -2147483648
  2147483647
```

```
        2147483647
        -9223372036854775808
        9223372036854775807
        9223372036854775807
*/
```

In the preceding code, take note of the `int` type and `Integer` class. Unlike the other primitive wrapper classes, `Integer` does not share the same name as the identifier it is supporting.

Also, note the `long` type and its assigned values. In each case, the values have the suffix `L`. This is a requirement for `long` literals in Java because the compiler interprets all numeral literals as 32-bit integers. If you want to explicitly specify that your literal is larger than 32-bit, you must append the suffix `L`. Otherwise, the compiler will honk at you. This is not a requirement, however, when passing a string value into the `Long` class constructor:

```
Long maxLong = new Long("9223372036854775807");
```

Objective-C

For 8-bit data, Objective-C provides the `char` data type in both signed and unsigned formats. As with other languages, the signed data type ranges from -127 to 128, while the unsigned data type ranges from 0 to 255. Developers also have the option to use Objective-C's fixed-width counterparts named `int8_t` and `uint8_t`. This pattern is repeated in the 16-, 32-, and 64-bit data types. Finally, Objective-C also provides an object-oriented wrapper class for each of the integer types in the form of the `NSNumber` class:

The difference between the `char` or the other integer data type identifiers and their fixed-width counterparts is an important distinction. With the exception of char, which is always precisely 1 byte in length, every other integer data type in Objective-C will vary in size, depending on the implementation and underlying architecture. This is because Objective-C is based on C, which was designed to work at peak efficiency with various types of underlying architectures. Although it is possible to determine the exact length of an integer type at runtime, at compile, you can only be certain that `short <= int <= long <= long long`.

This is where **fixed-width integers** come in handy. If more rigid control over the number of bytes is required, the `(u)int<n>_t` data types allow you to denote integers that are precisely 8-, 16-, 32-, or 64-bit in length.

```
//Objective-C
char number = -127;
```

```
unsigned char uNumber = 255;
NSLog(@"Signed char number: %hhd", number);
NSLog(@"Unsigned char uNumber: %hhu", uNumber);
//fixed width
int8_t fixedNumber = -127;
uint8_t fixedUNumber = 255;
NSLog(@"fixedNumber8: %hhd", fixedNumber8);
NSLog(@"fixedUNumber8: %hhu", fixedUNumber8);

NSNumber *charNumber = [NSNumber numberWithChar:number];
NSLog(@"Char charNumber: %@", [charNumber stringValue]);

/*
  Output
  Signed char number: -127
  Unsigned char uNumber: 255
  fixedNumber8: -127
  fixedUNumber8: 255
  Char charNumber: -127
*/
```

In the preceding example, you can see that, when using the `char` data types in code, you must specify the `unsigned` identifier, such as `unsigned char`. However, `signed` is the default and may be omitted, which means the `char` type is equivalent to `signed char`. This pattern applies to each of the integer data types in Objective-C.

Larger integer types in Objective-C include `short` for 16-bit, `int` for 32-bit, and `long long` for 64-bit. Each of these has a fixed-width counterpart following the `(u)int<n>_t` pattern. Supporting methods are also available for each type within the `NSNumber` class:

```
//Larger Objective-C types
short aShort = -32768;
unsigned short anUnsignedShort = 65535;
NSLog(@"Signed short aShort: %hd", aShort);
NSLog(@"Unsigned short anUnsignedShort: %hu", anUnsignedShort);

int16_t fixedNumber16 = -32768;
uint16_t fixedUNumber16 = 65535;
NSLog(@"fixedNumber16: %hd", fixedNumber16);
NSLog(@"fixedUNumber16: %hu", fixedUNumber16);

NSNumber *shortNumber = [NSNumber numberWithShort:aShort];
NSLog(@"Short shortNumber: %@", [shortNumber stringValue]);

int anInt = -2147483648;
unsigned int anUnsignedInt = 4294967295;
NSLog(@"Signed Int anInt: %d", anInt);
```

```
    NSLog(@"Unsigned Int anUnsignedInt: %u", anUnsignedInt);

    int32_t fixedNumber32 = -2147483648;
    uint32_t fixedUNumber32 = 4294967295;
    NSLog(@"fixedNumber32: %d", fixedNumber32);
    NSLog(@"fixedUNumber32: %u", fixedUNumber32);

    NSNumber *intNumber = [NSNumber numberWithInt:anInt];
    NSLog(@"Int intNumber: %@", [intNumber stringValue]);

    long long aLongLong = -9223372036854775808;
    unsigned long long anUnsignedLongLong = 18446744073709551615;
    NSLog(@"Signed long long aLongLong: %lld", aLongLong);
    NSLog(@"Unsigned long long anUnsignedLongLong: %llu",
anUnsignedLongLong);

    int64_t fixedNumber64 = -9223372036854775808;
    uint64_t fixedUNumber64 = 18446744073709551615;
    NSLog(@"fixedNumber64: %lld", fixedNumber64);
    NSLog(@"fixedUNumber64: %llu", fixedUNumber64);

    NSNumber *longlongNumber = [NSNumber numberWithLongLong:aLongLong];
    NSLog(@"Long long longlongNumber: %@", [longlongNumber stringValue]);

    /*
      Output
      Signed short aShort: -32768
      Unsigned short anUnsignedShort: 65535
      fixedNumber16: -32768
      fixedUNumber16: 65535
      Short shortNumber: -32768
      Signed Int anInt: -2147483648
      Unsigned Int anUnsignedInt: 4294967295
      fixedNumber32: -2147483648
      fixedUNumber32: 4294967295
      Int intNumber: -2147483648
      Signed long long aLongLong: -9223372036854775808
      Unsigned long long anUnsignedLongLong: 18446744073709551615
      fixedNumber64: -9223372036854775808
      fixedUNumber64: 18446744073709551615
      Long long longlongNumber: -9223372036854775808
    */
```

Swift

The Swift language is similar to others, in that, it provides separate identifiers for signed and unsigned integers, for example `Int8` and `UInt8`. This pattern applies to each of the integer data types in Swift, making it possibly the simplest language in terms of remembering which identifier applies to which type:

```
//Swift
var int8 : Int8 = -127
var uint8 : UInt8 = 255
print("int8: \(int8)")
print("uint8: \(uint8)")

/*
  Output
  int8: -127
  uint8: 255
*/
```

In the preceding example, I have explicitly declared the data type using the `:Int8` and `:UInt8` identifiers to demonstrate explicit declaration. In Swift, it is also acceptable to leave these identifiers out and allow Swift to infer the types dynamically at runtime:

```
//Larger Swift types
var int16 : Int16 = -32768
var uint16 : UInt16 = 65535
print("int16: \(int16)")
print("uint16: \(uint16)")

var int32 : Int32 = -2147483648
var uint32 : UInt32 = 4294967295
print("int32: \(int32)")
print("uint32: \(uint32)")

var int64 : Int64 = -9223372036854775808
var uint64 : UInt64 = 18446744073709551615
print("int64: \(int64)")
print("uint64: \(uint64)")

/*
  Output
  int16: -32768
  uint16: 65535
  int32: -2147483648
  uint32: 4294967295
  int64: -9223372036854775808
  uint64: 18446744073709551615
*/
```

Why do I need to know this?

You may ask, Why do I need to know the ins and outs of these data types? Can't I just declare an `int` object or some similar identifier and move on to writing the interesting code? Modern computers and even mobile devices provide nearly unlimited resources, so it's not a big deal, right?

Well, not exactly. It is true that, in many circumstances in your daily programming experience, any integer type will do. For example, looping through a list of license plates issued at **Department of Motor Vehicles** (**DMV**) offices across the state of West Virginia on any given day may yield anything from a few dozen to perhaps a few hundred results. You could control the `for` loop's iterations using a `short` or you could use `long long`. Either way, the loop will have very little impact on the performance of your system.

However, what if you're dealing with a set of data where each discrete result in that set can fit in a 16-bit type, but you choose a 32-bit identifier just because that's what you're used to? You've just doubled the amount of memory required to manage that collection. This decision wouldn't matter with 100 or maybe even 100,000 results. However, when you start working with very large sets of data, with hundreds of thousands or even millions of discrete results, such design decisions can have a huge impact on system performance.

Single precision float

Single precision floating point numbers, or **floats** as they are more commonly referred to, are 32-bit floating point containers that allow storing values with much greater precision than integer types, typically to six or seven significant digits. Many languages use the `float` keyword or identifier for single-precision float values, and that is the case for each of the four languages we are discussing.

You should be aware that floating point values are subject to rounding errors because they cannot represent base-10 numbers exactly. The arithmetic of floating point types is a fairly complex topic, the details of which will not be pertinent to the majority of developers on any given day. However, it is still a good practice to familiarize yourself with the particulars of the underlying science as well as the implementation in each language.

 As I am by no means an expert on the subject, this discussion will only scratch the surface of the science behind these types, and we will not even begin to cover the arithmetic. There are others who truly are experts in this area, however, and I highly recommend you review some of their work listed in the *Additional resources* section at the end of this chapter.

C#

In C#, the `float` keyword identifies 32-bit floating point values. The C# `float` data type has an approximate range of -3.4×10^{38} to $+3.4 \times 10^{38}$ and a precision of six significant digits:

```
//C#
float piFloat = 3.14159265358979323846264338327f;
Console.WriteLine("piFloat: {0}", piFloat);

/*
  Output
  piFloat: 3.141593
*/
```

When you examine the preceding code, you will notice that the `float` value assignment has the `f` suffix. This is because, like other C-based languages, C# treats real numeric literals on the right-hand side of assignments as a **double** (discussed later) by default. If you leave the `f` or `F` suffix off the assignment, you will receive a compilation error, because you are trying to assign a double point precision value to a single point precision type.

Also, note the rounding error in the last digit. We populated the `piFloat` object with pi presented out to 30 significant digits. However, `float` can only retain six significant digits, so the software rounded off everything after that. When pi is calculated out to six significant digits, we get 3.141592, but our `float` value is now 3.141593 due to this limitation.

Java

As with C#, Java uses the **float** identifier for floating point values. In Java, a `float` has an approximate range of -3.4×10^{38} to $+3.4 \times 10^{38}$ and a precision of six or seven significant digits:

```
//Java
float piFloat = 3.14159265358979323846264643383279f;
System.out.println(piFloat);

/*
  Output
  3.1415927
*/
```

When you examine the preceding code, you will notice that the float value assignment has the f suffix. This is because, like other C based languages, Java treats real numeric literals on the right side of assignments as a double by default. If you leave the f or F suffix off the assignment, you will receive a compilation error because you are trying to assign a double-point precision value to a single-point precision type.

Objective-C

Objective-C uses the float identifier for floating point values. In Objective-C, a float has an approximate range of -3.4×10^{38} to $+3.4 \times 10^{38}$ and a precision of 6 significant digits:

```
//Objective-C
float piFloat = 3.14159265358979323846264338327f;
NSLog(@"piFloat: %f", piFloat);

NSNumber *floatNumber = [NSNumber numberWithFloat:piFloat];
NSLog(@"floatNumber: %@", [floatNumber stringValue]);

/*
  Output
  piFloat: 3.141593
  floatNumber: 3.141593
*/
```

When you examine the preceding code, you will notice that the float value assignment has the f suffix. This is because, like other C-based languages, Objective-C treats real numeric literals on the right-hand side of assignments as a double by default. If you leave the f or F suffix off of the assignment, you will receive a compilation error because you are trying to assign a double-point precision value to a single-point precision type.

Also, note the rounding error in the last digit. We populated the piFloat object with pi presented out to 30 significant digits, but float can only retain six significant digits, so the software rounded off everything after that. When pi is calculated out to six significant digits, we get 3.141592, but our float value is now 3.141593 due to this limitation.

Swift

Swift uses the float identifier for floating point values. In Swift, a float has an approximate range of -3.4×10^{38} to $+3.4 \times 10^{38}$ and a precision of six significant digits:

```
//Swift
var floatValue : Float = 3.14159265358979323846264338279
print("floatValue: \(floatValue)")

/*
  Output
```

```
    floatValue: 3.141593
*/
```

When you examine the preceding code, you will notice that the float value assignment has the `f` suffix. This is because, like other C-based languages, Swift treats real numeric literals on the right-hand side of assignments as a double by default. If you leave the `f` or `F` suffix off of the assignment, you will receive a compilation error because you are trying to assign a double-point precision value to a single-point precision type.

Also, note the rounding error in the last digit. We populated the `floatValue` object with pi presented out to 30 significant digits, but float can only retain six significant digits, so the software rounded off everything after that. When pi is calculated out to six significant digits, we get 3.141592, but our float value is now 3.141593 due to this limitation.

Double precision float

Double precision floating point numbers, or **doubles** as they are more commonly referred to, are 64-bit floating point values that allow storing values with much greater precision than the integer types, typically to 15 significant digits. Many languages use the double identifier for double precision float values and that is also the case for each of the four languages we are discussing.

In most circumstances, it will not matter whether you choose `float` over `double` unless memory space is a concern, in which case you will want to choose `float` whenever possible. Many argue that `float` is more performant than double under most conditions, and generally speaking, this is the case. However, there are other conditions where `double` will be more performant than `float`. The reality is that the efficiency of each type is going to vary from case to case, based on criteria that are too numerous to detail in the context of this discussion. Therefore, if your particular application requires truly peak efficiency, you should research the requirements and environmental factors carefully and decide what is best for your situation. Otherwise, just use whichever container will get the job done and move on.

C#

In C#, the `double` keyword identifies 64-bit floating point values. The C# `double` has an approximate range of $\pm 5.0 \times 10^{-324}$ to $\pm 1.7 \times 10^{308}$ and a precision of 14 or 15 significant digits:

```
//C#
double piDouble = 3.14159265358979323846264338327;
double wholeDouble = 3d;
Console.WriteLine("piDouble: {0}", piDouble);
Console.WriteLine("wholeDouble: {0}", wholeDouble);

/*
   Output
   piDouble: 3.14159265358979
   wholeDouble: 3
*/
```

When you examine the preceding code, you will notice that the `wholeDouble` value assignment has the d suffix. This is because, like other C-based languages, C# treats real numeric literals on the right-hand side of assignments as integers by default. If you were to leave the d or D suffix off the assignment, you will receive a compilation error because you are trying to assign an integer value to a double-point precision type.

Also, note the rounding error in the last digit. We populated the `piDouble` object using pi out to 30 significant digits, but double can only retain 14 significant digits, so the software rounded off everything after that. When pi is calculated out to 15 significant digits, we get 3.141592653589793, but our float value is now 3.14159265358979 due to this limitation.

Java

In Java, the `double` keyword identifies 64-bit floating-point values. The Java `double` has an approximate range of $\pm 4.9 \times 10^{-324}$ to $\pm 1.8 \times 10^{308}$ and a precision of 15 or 16 significant digits:

```
double piDouble = 3.14159265358979323846264338327 9;
System.out.println(piDouble);

/*
   Output
   3.141592653589793
*/
```

When you examine the preceding code, note the rounding error in the last digit. We populated the piDouble object using pi out to 30 significant digits, but double can only retain 15 significant digits, so the software rounded off everything after that. When pi is calculated out to 15 significant digits, we get 3.1415926535897932, but our float value is now 3.141592653589793 due to this limitation.

Objective-C

Objective-C also uses the double identifier for 64-bit floating point values. The Objective-C double has an approximate range of $2.3E^{-308}$ to $1.7E^{308}$ and a precision of 15 significant digits. Objective-C takes accuracy a step further by providing an even more precise version of double called the **long double**. The long double identifier is used for an 80 bit storage container with a range of $3.4E^{-4932}$ to $1.1E^{4932}$ and a precision of 19 significant digits:

```
//Objective-C
double piDouble = 3.14159265358979323846264338327;
NSLog(@"piDouble: %.15f", piDouble);

NSNumber *doubleNumber = [NSNumber numberWithDouble:piDouble];
NSLog(@"doubleNumber: %@", [doubleNumber stringValue]);

/*
  Output
  piDouble: 3.141592653589793
  doubleNumber: 3.141592653589793
*/
```

In our preceding example, note the rounding error in the last digit. We populated the piDouble object using pi out to 30 significant digits, but double can only retain 15 significant digits, so the software rounded off everything after that. When pi is calculated out to 15 significant digits, we get 3.1415926535897932, but our float value is now 3.141592653589793 due to this limitation.

Swift

Swift uses the double identifier for 64-bit floating-point values. In Swift, a double has an approximate range of $2.3E^{-308}$ to $1.7E^{308}$ and a precision of 15 significant digits. Note that, according to Apple's documentation for Swift, when either float or double types will suffice, double is recommended:

```
//Swift
var doubleValue : Double = 3.14159265358979323846264338327 9
print("doubleValue: \(doubleValue)")

/*
```

```
  Output
  doubleValue: 3.14159265358979
*/
```

In our preceding example, note the rounding error in the last digit. We populated the `doubleValue` object using pi out to 30 significant digits, but double can only retain 15 significant digits, so the software rounded off everything after that. When pi is calculated out to 15 significant digits, we get 3.141592653589793, but our `float` value is now 3.14159265358979 due to this limitation.

Currency

Due to the inherent inaccuracy found in floating point arithmetic, grounded in the fact that they are based on binary arithmetic, floats, and doubles cannot accurately represent the base-10 multiples we use for currency. Representing currency as a `float` or `double` may seem like a good idea at first as the software will round off the tiny errors in your arithmetic. However, as you begin to perform more and complex arithmetic operations on these inexact results, your precision errors will begin to add up and result in serious inaccuracies and bugs that can be very difficult to track down. This makes float and double data types insufficient for working with currency where perfect accuracy for multiples of 10 is essential. Luckily, each of the languages we are discussing provides a mechanism to work with currency, and other arithmetic problems require high precision in based-10 values and calculations.

C#

C# uses the `decimal` keyword for precise floating-point values. In C#, `decimal` has a range of $\pm1.0 \times 10^{-28}$ to $\pm7.9 \times 10^{28}$ with a precision of 28 or 29 significant digits:

```
  var decimalValue =
NSDecimalNumber.init(string:"3.141592653589793238462643383279")
  print("decimalValue \(decimalValue)")

  /*
    Output
    piDecimal: 3.1415926535897932384626433833
  */
```

In the preceding example, note that we populated the `decimalValue` object with pi out to 30 significant digits, but the framework rounded this off to 28 significant digits.

Java

Java provides an object-oriented solution to the currency problem in the form of the `BigDecimal` class:

```
    BigDecimal piDecimal = new
BigDecimal("3.14159265358979323846264338327 9");
    System.out.println(piDecimal);

    /*
      Output
      3.14159265358979323846264338327 9
    */
```

In the preceding example, we are initializing the `BigDecimal` class using a constructor that takes a string representation of our decimal value as a parameter. When the program runs, the output proves that the `BigDecimal` class did not lose any of our intended precision, returning pi to 30 significant digits.

Objective-C

Objective-C also provides an object-oriented solution to the currency problem in the form of the `NSDecimalNumber` class:

```
    //Objective-C
    NSDecimalNumber *piDecimalNumber = [[NSDecimalNumber alloc]
initWithDouble:3.14159265358979323846264338327];
    NSLog(@"piDecimalNumber: %@", [piDecimalNumber stringValue]);

    /*
      Output
      piDecimalNumber: 3.141592653589793792
    */
```

Swift

Swift also provides an object-oriented solution to the currency problem, and it is the same class used in Objective-C, the `NSDecimalNumber` class. The Swift version is initialized slightly differently, but it retains the same functionality as its Objective-C counterpart:

```
    var decimalValue =
NSDecimalNumber.init(string:"3.14159265358979323846264338327 9")
    print("decimalValue \(decimalValue)")

    /*
      Output
      decimalValue 3.14159265358979323846264338327 9
```

```
*/
```

Note that precision, in both the Objective-C and Swift examples, is retained out to 30 significant digits, proving that the NSDecimalNumber class is superior for working with currency and other base-10 values.

> In the spirit of full disclosure, there is a simple and arguably more elegant alternative to using these custom types. You could just use int or long for your currency calculations and count in cents rather than dollars:
> //C# long total = 316;
> //$3.16

Typecasting

In the realm of computer science, **type conversion** or **typecasting** means to converting an instance of one object or data type into another. For example, let's say you make a call to a method that returns an integer value but you need to use that value in another method that requires a long value as the input parameter. Since an integer value by definition exists within the realm of allowable long values, the int value can be redefined as a long.

Such conversions can be done through either implicit conversion, sometimes called **coercion**, or explicit conversion, otherwise known as **casting**. To fully appreciate casting, we also need to understand the difference between **static** and **dynamic** languages.

Statically versus dynamically typed languages

A statically typed language will perform its **type checking** at compile time. This means that, when you try to build your solution, the compiler will verify and enforce each of the constraints that apply to the types in your application. If they are not enforced, you will receive an error and the application will not build. C#, Java, and Swift are all statically typed languages.

Dynamically typed languages, on the other hand, do most or all of their type checking at run time. This means that the application might build just fine, but could experience a problem while it is actually running if the developer wasn't careful in how he wrote the code. Objective-C is a dynamically typed language because it uses a mixture of statically typed objects and dynamically typed objects. The plain C objects used for numeric values discussed earlier in this chapter are all examples of statically typed objects, while the Objective-C classes NSNumber and NSDecimalNumber are both examples of dynamically typed objects. Consider the following code example in Objective-C:

```
double myDouble = @"chicken";
NSNumber *myNumber = @"salad";
```

The compiler will throw an error on the first line, stating `Initializing 'double' with an expression of incompatible type 'NSString *'`. That's because `double` is a plain C object, and it is statically typed. The compiler knows what to do with this statically typed object before we even get to the build, so your build will fail.

However, the compiler will only throw a warning on the second line, stating `Incompatible pointer types initializing 'NSNumber *' with an expression of type 'NSString *'`. That's because `NSNumber` is an Objective-C class, and it is dynamically typed. The compiler is smart enough to catch your mistake, but it will allow the build to succeed (unless you have instructed the compiler to treat warnings as errors in your build settings).

Although the forthcoming crash at runtime is obvious in the previous example, there are cases where your app will function perfectly fine despite the warnings. However, no matter what type of language you are working with, it is always a good idea to consistently clean up your code warnings before moving on to new code. This helps keep your code clean and avoids any runtime errors which can be difficult to diagnose.

On those rare occasions where it is not prudent to address the warning immediately, you should clearly document your code and explain the source of the warning so that other developers will understand your reasoning. As a last resort, you can take advantage of macros or pre-processor (pre-compiler) directives that can suppress warnings on a line-by-line basis.

Implicit and explicit casting

Implicit casting does not require any special syntax in your source code. This makes implicit casting somewhat convenient. Consider the following code example in C#:

```
int a = 10;
double b = a++;
```

In this scenario, since a can be defined as both an `int` and a `double`, the cast to type `double` is perfectly acceptable because we have defined both types manually. However, since implicit casts do not necessarily define their types manually, the compiler cannot always determine which constraints apply to the conversion and therefore will not be able to check these constraints until runtime. This makes the implicit cast also somewhat dangerous. Consider the following code example also in C#:

```
double x = "54";
```

This is an implicit conversion because you have not told the compiler how to treat the string value. In this case, the conversion will fail when you try to build the application, and the compiler will throw an error for this line, stating `Cannot implicitly convert type 'string' to 'double'`. Now, consider the explicitly cast version of this example:

```
double x = double.Parse("42");
Console.WriteLine("40 + 2 = {0}", x);

/*
  Output
  40 + 2 = 42
*/
```

This conversion is explicit and therefore type-safe, assuming that the string value is *parsable*.

Widening and narrowing

When casting between two types, an important consideration is whether the result of the change is within the range of the target data type. If your source data type supports more bytes than your target data type, the cast is considered to be a **narrowing conversion**.

Narrowing conversions are either casts that cannot be proven to always succeed or casts that are known to possibly lose information. For example, casting from a float to an integer will result in loss of information (precision in this case), as the result will be rounded off to the nearest whole number. In most statically typed languages, narrowing casts cannot be performed implicitly. Here is an example by borrowing from the C# single-precision and double-precision examples earlier in this chapter:

```
//C#
piFloat = piDouble;
```

In this example, the compiler will throw an error, stating `Cannot implicitly convert type 'double' to 'float'. And explicit conversion exists (Are you missing a cast?)`. The compiler sees this as a narrowing conversion and treats the loss of precision as an error. The error message itself is helpful and suggests an explicit cast as a potential solution for our problem:

```
//C#
piFloat = (float)piDouble;
```

We have now explicitly cast the double value `piDouble` to a `float`, and the compiler no longer concerns itself with loss of precision.

If your source data type supports fewer bytes than your target data type, the cast is considered to be a **widening conversion**. Widening conversions will preserve the source object's value, but may change its representation in some way. Most statically typed languages will permit implicit widening casts. Let's borrow again from our previous C# example:

```
//C#
piDouble = piFloat;
```

In this example, the compiler is completely satisfied with the implicit conversion and the app will build. Let's expand the example further:

```
//C#
piDouble = (double)piFloat;
```

This explicit cast improves readability, but does not change the nature of the statement in any way. The compiler also finds this format to be completely acceptable, even if it is somewhat more verbose. Beyond improved readability, explicit casting when widening adds nothing to your application. Therefore, it is your preference if you want to use explicit casting when widening is a matter of personal preference.

Boolean data type

Boolean data types are intended to symbolize binary values, usually denoted by 1 and 0, `true` and `false`, or even YES and NO. Boolean types are used to represent truth logic, which is based on Boolean algebra. This is just a way of saying that Boolean values are used in conditional statements, such as `if` or `while`, to evaluate logic or repeat an execution conditionally.

Equality operations include any operations that compare the value of any two entities. The equality operators are:

- == implies equal to
- != implies not equal to

Relational operations include any operations that test a relation between two entities. The relational operators are:

- > implies greater than
- >= implies greater than or equal to
- < implies less than
- <= implies less than or equal to

Logic operations include any operations in your program that evaluate and manipulate Boolean values. There are three primary logic operators, namely AND, OR, and NOT. Another, slightly less commonly used operator, is the **exclusive or**, or XOR operator. All Boolean functions and statements can be built with these four basic operators.

The AND operator is the most exclusive comparator. Given two Boolean variables A and B, AND will return true if, and only if, both A and B is true. Boolean variables are often visualized using tools called **truth tables**. Consider the following truth table for the AND operator:

A	B	A ^ B
0	0	0
0	1	0
1	0	0
1	1	1

This table demonstrates the AND operator. When evaluating a conditional statement, 0 is considered to be false, while any other value is considered to be true. Only when the value of both A and B is true, is the resulting comparison of A ^ B also true.

The OR operator is the inclusive operator. Given two Boolean variables A and B, OR will return `true` if either A or B is `true`, including the case when both A and B are `true`. Consider the following truth table for the OR operator:

A	B	A v B
0	0	0
0	1	1
1	0	1
1	1	1

Next, the NOT A operator is `true` when A is `false`, and `false` when A is `true`. Consider the following truth table for the NOT operator:

A	!A
0	1
1	0

Finally, the XOR operator is `true` when either A or B is `true`, but not both. Another way to say it is, XOR is `true` when A and B are different. There are many occasions where it is useful to evaluate an expression in this manner, so most computer architectures include it. Consider the following truth table for XOR:

A	B	A XOR B
0	0	0
0	1	1
1	0	1
1	1	0

Operator precedence

Just as with arithmetic, comparison and Boolean operations have **operator precedence**. This means the architecture will give a higher precedence to one operator over another. Generally speaking, the Boolean order of operations for all languages is as follows:

- Parentheses
- Relational operators
- Equality operators
- Bitwise operators (not discussed)
- NOT
- AND
- OR
- XOR
- Ternary operator
- Assignment operators

It is extremely important to understand operator precedence when working with Boolean values, because mistaking how the architecture will evaluate complex logical operations will introduce bugs in your code that you will not understand how to sort out. When in doubt, remember that, as in arithmetic parentheses, take the highest precedence and anything defined within them will be evaluated first.

Short-circuiting

As you recall, AND only returns `true` when both of the operands are `true`, and OR returns `true` as soon as one operand is `true`. These characteristics sometimes make it possible to determine the outcome of an expression by evaluating only one of the operands. When your applications stops evaluation immediately upon determining the overall outcome of an expression, it is called **short-circuiting**. There are three main reasons why you would want to use short-circuiting in your code.

First, short-circuiting can improve your application's performance by limiting the number of operations your code must perform. Second, when later operands could potentially generate errors based on the value of a previous operand, short-circuiting can halt execution before the higher risk operand is reached. Finally, short-circuiting can improve the readability and complexity of your code by eliminating the need for nested logical statements.

C#

C# uses the `bool` keyword as an alias of `System.Boolean` and stores the values `true` and `false`:

```
//C#
bool a = true;
bool b = false;
bool c = a;

Console.WriteLine("a: {0}", a);
Console.WriteLine("b: {0}", b);
Console.WriteLine("c: {0}", c);
Console.WriteLine("a AND b: {0}", a && b);
Console.WriteLine("a OR b: {0}", a || b);
Console.WriteLine("NOT a: {0}", !a);
Console.WriteLine("NOT b: {0}", !b);
Console.WriteLine("a XOR b: {0}", a ^ b);
Console.WriteLine("(c OR b) AND a: {0}", (c || b) && a);

/*
  Output
  a: True
  b: False
  c: True
  a AND b: False
  a OR b: True
  NOT a: False
  NOT b: True
  a XOR b: True
  (c OR b) AND a: True
*/
```

Java

Java uses the `boolean` keyword for the primitive Boolean data type. Java also provides a `Boolean` wrapper class for the same primitive type:

```
//Java
boolean a = true;
boolean b = false;
boolean c = a;

System.out.println("a: " + a);
System.out.println("b: " + b);
System.out.println("c: " + c);
System.out.println("a AND b: " + (a && b));
System.out.println("a OR b: " + (a || b));
```

```java
System.out.println("NOT a: " + !a);
System.out.println("NOT b: " + !b);
System.out.println("a XOR b: " + (a ^ b));
System.out.println("(c OR b) AND a: " + ((c || b) && a));

/*
  Output
  a: true
  b: false
  c: true
  a AND b: false
  a OR b: true
  NOT a: false
  NOT b: true
  a XOR b: true
 (c OR b) AND a: true
*/
```

Objective-C

Objective-C uses the BOOL identifier to represent Boolean values:

```objc
//Objective-C
BOOL a = YES;
BOOL b = NO;
BOOL c = a;

NSLog(@"a: %hhd", a);
NSLog(@"b: %hhd", b);
NSLog(@"c: %hhd", c);
NSLog(@"a AND b: %d", a && b);
NSLog(@"a OR b: %d", a || b);
NSLog(@"NOT a: %d", !a);
NSLog(@"NOT b: %d", !b);
NSLog(@"a XOR b: %d", a ^ b);
NSLog(@"(c OR b) AND a: %d", (c || b) && a);

/*
  Output
  a: 1
  b: 0
  c: 1
  a AND b: 0
  a OR b: 1
  NOT a: 0
  NOT b: 1
  a XOR b: 1
  (c OR b) AND a: 1
*/
```

```
*/
```

As it happens, Boolean data types give Objective-C yet another opportunity to prove it is more complex than its counterparts. The language does not provide one identifier or class to represent logic values. It provides five. For the sake of simplicity (and because my editor won't give me the extra pages), we're only going to use BOOL in this text. If you want to know more, I encourage you to check out the *Additional resources* section at the end of this chapter.

Swift

Swift uses the `Bool` keyword for the primitive Boolean data type:

```swift
//Swift
var a : Bool = true
var b : Bool = false
var c = a

print("a: \(a)")
print("b: \(b)")
print("c: \(c)")
print("a AND b: \(a && b)")
print("a OR b: \(a || b)")
print("NOT a: \(!a)")
print("NOT b: \(!b)")
print("a XOR b: \(a != b)")
print("(c OR b) AND a: \((c || b) && a)")

/*
   Output
   a: true
   b: false
   c: true
   a AND b: false
   a OR b: true
   NOT a: false
   NOT b: true
   a XOR b: true
   (c OR b) AND a: true
*/
```

In the preceding example, the Boolean object c is not explicitly declared as Bool, but it is implicitly typed as a Bool. In Swift terms, the data type has been *inferred* in this case. Also, note that Swift does not provide a specific XOR operator, so if you need that comparison, you should use the (a != b) pattern.

Objective-C nil values

In Objective-C, the value `nil` also evaluates to `false`. Although other languages must handle NULL objects with care, Objective-C will not crash when it attempts to perform an operation on a nil object. Speaking from personal experience, this can be somewhat confusing for developers who learned C# or Java before learning Objective-C, and thus expect an unhandled NULL object to crash their app. However, it is common for Objective-C developers to use this behavior to their advantage. Many times, simply checking whether an object is `nil` logically confirms whether an operation was successful, saving you from writing tedious logical comparisons.

Strings

Strings are not precisely data types, although as developers we very often treat them as such. In actuality, strings are simply objects whose value is text; under the hood, strings contain a sequential collection of read-only `char` objects. This read-only nature of a string object makes strings **immutable**, which means the objects cannot be changed once they have been created in memory.

It is important to understand that changing any immutable object, not just a string, means your program is actually creating a new object in memory and discarding the old one. This is a more intensive operation than simply changing the value of an address in memory and requires more processing. Merging two strings together is called **concatenation**, and this is an even more costly procedure as you are disposing of two objects before creating a new one. If you find that you are editing your string values frequently, or frequently concatenating strings together, be aware that your program is not as efficient as it could be.

Strings are strictly immutable in C#, Java, and Objective-C. It is interesting to note that the Swift documentation refers to strings as mutable. However, the behavior is similar to Java, in that, when a string is modified, it gets copied on assignment to another object. Therefore, although the documentation says otherwise, strings are effectively immutable in Swift as well.

C#

C# uses the string keyword to declare string types:

```
//C#
string one = "One String";
Console.WriteLine("One: {0}", one);

String two = "Two String";
Console.WriteLine("Two: {0}", two);

String red = "Red String";
Console.WriteLine("Red: {0}", red);

String blue = "Blue String";
Console.WriteLine("Blue: {0}", blue);

String purple = red + blue;
Console.WriteLine("Concatenation: {0}", purple);

purple = "Purple String";
Console.WriteLine("Whoops! Mutation: {0}", purple);
```

Java

Java uses the system class String to declare string types:

```
//Java
String one = "One String";
System.out.println("One: " + one);

String two = "Two String";
System.out.println("Two: " + two);

String red = "Red String";
System.out.println("Red: " + red);

String blue = "Blue String";
System.out.println("Blue: " + blue);

String purple = red + blue;
System.out.println("Concatenation: " + purple);

purple = "Purple String";
System.out.println("Whoops! Mutation: " + purple);
```

Objective-C

Objective-C provides the `NSString` class to create string objects:

```
//Objective-C
NSString *one = @"One String";
NSLog(@"One: %@", one);

NSString *two = @"Two String";
NSLog(@"Two: %@", two);

NSString *red = @"Red String";
NSLog(@"Red: %@", red);

NSString *blue = @"Blue String";
NSLog(@"Blue: %@", blue);

NSString *purple = [[NSArray arrayWithObjects:red, blue, nil]
componentsJoinedByString:@""];
NSLog(@"Concatenation: %@", purple);

purple = @"Purple String";
NSLog(@"Whoops! Mutation: %@", purple);
```

When you examine the Objective-C example, you might wonder why we have all that extra code for creating the purple object. That code is necessary because Objective-C does not provide a shortcut mechanism for concatenating strings like the other three languages we're using. So, in this scenario, I have chosen to place the two strings into an array and then call the `NSArray` method `componentsJoinedByString:`. I could have also chosen to use the `NSMutableString` class, which provides a method for concatenating strings. However, since we're not discussing mutable string classes in any of our selected languages, I have opted not to use that approach.

Swift

Swift provides the `String` class to create string objects:

```
//Swift
var one : String = "One String"
print("One: \(one)")

var two : String = "Two String"
print("Two: \(two)")

var red : String = "Red String"
print("Red: \(red)")

var blue : String = "Blue String"
```

```
print("Blue: \(blue)")

var purple : String = red + blue
print("Concatenation: \(purple)")

purple = "Purple String";
print("Whoops! Mutation: \(purple)")

/*
  Output from each string example:
  One: One String
  Two: Two String
  Red: Red String
  Blue: Blue String
  Concatenation: Red StringBlue String
  Whoops! Mutation: Purple String
*/
```

Summary

In this chapter, you learned about the basic data types available to a programmer in each of the four most common mobile development languages. Numeric and floating point data type characteristics and operations are as dependent on the underlying architecture as on the specifications of the language. You also learned about casting objects from one type to another and how the type of cast is defined as either a widening cast or a narrowing cast depending on the size of the source and target data types in the conversion. Next, we discussed Boolean type and how it is used in comparators to affect program flow and execution. In this, we discussed operator order of precedence and nested operations. You also learned how to use short-circuiting to improve your code's performance. Finally, we examined the String data type and what it means to work with mutable objects.

2
Arrays: Foundational Collections

Quite often, our applications need to store multiple pieces of user data or objects in memory at runtime. One solution is to define multiple fields (properties) in our various classes to store each of our required data points. Unfortunately, even when working with the simplest workflows, this approach quickly becomes ineffective. We will either have too many fields to work with, or we simply won't have any way of anticipating all of the dynamic requirements for our project at compile time.

One solution to this problem is to use an array. Arrays are simple collections of data, and they are one of the most common data structures you will encounter in your day-to-day programming experience due to the fact that many other data structures are built on top of them.

Arrays are containers that hold a fixed number of items of a particular type. The size of an array in C and its descendant languages are determined when the array is created, and the length remains fixed from that point forward. Each item in an array is called an **element**, and each element can be accessed by its index number. Generally speaking, an array is a collection of data items that can be selected by indices that are determined at runtime.

In this chapter, we will cover the following topics:

- Definition
- Mutable arrays versus immutable arrays
- Example applications for arrays
- Linear searches
- Primitive arrays
- Object arrays
- Mixed arrays
- Multidimensional arrays
- Jagged arrays

> Note that arrays in most languages use what is known as a **zero-based index**, meaning that the first item in the array has an index of 0, the second has an index of 1, and so on.
>
> **Off-by-one errors** occur when the source code attempts to access an item at a given index that is one point away from the actual item you intended to access. This type of mistake is common to new and experienced programmers alike and can very often be the source of **Index is out of range** or **Index is out of bounds** runtime errors.

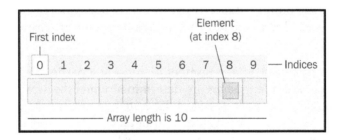

Compile time and runtime

In compiled programming languages (as opposed to interpreted languages), the difference between compile time and runtime is simply the difference between when an application is compiled and when it is run. During compiling, the high-level source code that the developer has written is fed into another program (usually called a compiler, oddly enough). The compiler checks whether the source code has the proper syntax, confirms type constraints are enforced, optimizes the code, and then produces an executable in a low-level language that the target architecture can utilize. If a program succeeds in compiling, we know that the source code is well formed and the resulting executable can be started. Note that developers will sometimes use the term *compile time* to include the actual process of writing the source code, although this is semantically incorrect.

During runtime, the compiled code runs in the execution environment, but it can still experience errors. For example, attempting to divide by zero, dereferencing null memory pointers, running out of memory, or attempting to access resources that do not exist could all potentially crash your application if your source code does not handle these scenarios gracefully.

Mutable versus immutable arrays

Typically, languages that are based on the C language share many of the same fundamental characteristics. For example, in C the size of a plain array cannot be changed once the array has been created. Since the four languages we are examining here are all based on C, the arrays we will be working with also have a fixed length in. However, although the size of an array cannot be changed, the contents of the structure can change after the array is created.

So, are arrays mutable or immutable? In terms of mutability, we say that *plain C arrays are immutable* because the structure itself cannot change once it has been created. For this reason, it is typically a bad idea to use a plain C array for anything other than static datasets. This is because, whenever the dataset changes, your program will need to copy the modified data into a new array object and dispose of the old one, which are both costly operations.

Most of the array objects you will be working with in higher-level languages are not plain C arrays, but rather wrapper classes created for the developer's convenience. Array wrapper classes encapsulate the complexities of the underlying data structure in favor of methods that handle the heavy lifting behind the scenes and properties that expose the characteristics of the dataset.

> Whenever a language provides a wrapper class for a particular type or data structure, you should take advantage of it. These are more convenient than writing your own implementation, and typically more reliable.

Case study: users logged in to a web service

Business problem: A developer has created an application that logs mobile users in to a particular web service. Due to limitations in the server hardware, the web service can only permit 30 connected users at any given time. Therefore, the developer needs a way to track and limit the number of mobile device users who have connected to the service. In order to avoid duplicate users being permitted to log in and overload the service, a simple count of the connections is insufficient, as the developer will have no way of differentiating between the owners of each connection. Maintaining an array of objects representing a logged-in user is chosen as a core component of the solution.

C#

```
using System;
//...
User[] _users;
public LoggedInUserArray ()
{
    User[] users = new User[0];
    _users = users;
}
```

There are a few important pieces of the preceding example we need to make note of. First, we are storing our User instances in a private class field called _users. Next, the constructor is instantiating a new array of User objects. Finally, we are instantiating the array to be 0 items in length and then assigning that collection to our private backer field. This is because our array doesn't have any users assigned to it yet, and we don't want to further complicate this code by trying to keep track of null values. In a real-world example, you might choose to instantiate and assign the private backer field all in one line:

```
_users = new User[0];
```

The former example is more verbose and, therefore, more readable. However, using the more succinct example takes up less space. Either approach will work. Next we'll look at a method that allows us to add `User` objects to the array:

```
bool CanAddUser(User user)
{
    bool containsUser = false;
    foreach (User u in _users)
    {
        if (user == u)
        {
            containsUser = true;
            break;
        }
    }

    if (containsUser)
    {
        return false;
    } else {
        if (_users.Length >= 30)
        {
            return false;
        } else {
            return true;
        }
    }
}
```

Here, we introduced a private method for some form of **validation**. The purpose of this method is to determine whether adding a user to the array is a valid operation at this time. First, we declared a `bool` variable called `containsUser`. We'll use this flag to signal whether or not the array already contains the `User` object being passed in. Next, we performed a `for` loop to check every object in the array against the passed in `User` object. If we find a match, we set the `containsUser` flag to `true` and break out of the `for` loop to save processor time. If `containsUser` is `true`, we know that the user object was found, and adding another copy would be a violation of our specified business rules. So, the method returns `false`. If the user does not exist in the array, execution continues.

Next, we checked whether the array already contains 30 or more items by evaluating its `Length` property. If `true`, we return `false` because the array is full according to our business rules and adding more would be a violation. Otherwise, we return `true` and program execution can continue:

```
public void UserAuthenticated(User user)
{
    if (this.CanAddUser(user))
    {
        Array.Resize(ref _users, _users.Length + 1);
        _users[_users.Length - 1] = user;
        Console.WriteLine("Length after adding user {0}: {1}", user.Id,
_users.Length);
    }
}
```

This method is called once the user has been authenticated, which is the only time we want to add a user to the user rolls. In this method, we validated the add user operation by calling the `CanAddUser()` method. If the `CanAddUser()` method returns `true`, method execution continues. First, we used the `Array` wrapper class' `Resize()` method to grow the array by one and make room for our new addition. Next, we assigned the new `User` object to the last position in the resized array. Finally, we performed some simple housekeeping by logging the user id and new length of the _users array to the console:

```
public void UserLoggedOut(User user)
{
    int index = Array.IndexOf(_users, user);
    if (index > -1)
    {
        User[] newUsers = new User[_users.Length - 1];
        for (int i = 0, j = 0; i < newUsers.Length - 1; i++, j++)
        {
            if (i == index)
            {
                j++;
            }
            newUsers[i] = _users[j];
        }
        _users = newUsers;
    }
    else
    {
        Console.WriteLine("User {0} not found.", user.Id);
    }
    Console.WriteLine("Length after logging out user {0}: {1}",
user.Id, _users.Length);
```

```
    }
```

This method is called when a previously authenticated user has been logged out of the web service. It uses the array wrapper class' `IndexOf()` method to determine whether the passed-in `User` object exists in the array. Since the `IndexOf()` returns `-1` if no matching object can be found, this method confirms that the value of `i` is equal to `-1`. If the value of `index` is equal to `-1` we perform some housekeeping in the form of a console message stating this user ID is not currently logged in. Otherwise, we begin the process of deleting an object from an array.

First, we have to create a temporary array that is one element shorter than the old array. Next, we loop from 0 to the length of the new array, with `i` marking the position in the new array and `j` marking the position in the old array. If `i` equals the position of the item we want to remove, we increment `j` to skip past that element in the old array. Finally, we assign a user we intend to keep from the correct position in the old array to the new array. Once we're done iterating over the array, we assign the new list to the `_users` property. After this, we perform some simple housekeeping by logging the deleted user ID and new length of the `_users` array to the console.

Java

```
User[] _users;

public LoggedInUserArray()
{
    User[] users = new User[0];
    _users = users;
}
```

There are a few important pieces of the preceding example we need to make note of. First, we are storing our `User` instances in a private class field called `_users`. Next, the constructor is instantiating a new array of `User` objects. Finally, we are instantiating the array as 0 items in length and then assigning that collection to our private backer field. This is because our array doesn't have any users assigned to it yet, and we don't want to further complicate this code by trying to keep track of null values. In a real-world example, you might choose to instantiate and assign the private backer field all in one line:

```
_users = new User[0];
```

The former example is more verbose and, therefore, more readable. However, using the more succinct example takes up less space. As with C#, either approach will work:

```java
boolean CanAddUser(User user)
{
    boolean containsUser = false;
    for (User u : _users)
    {
        if (user.equals(u))
        {
            containsUser = true;
            break;
        }
    }

    if (containsUser)
    {
        return false;
    } else {
        if (_users.length >= 30)
        {
            return false;
        } else {
            return true;
        }
    }
}
```

Here, we are introducing a private method for some sort of validation. The purpose of this method is to determine whether adding a user to the array is a valid operation at this time. First, we declared a `boolean` variable called `containsUser`. We'll use this flag to signal whether or not the array already contains the `User` object being passed in. Next, we performed a `for` loop to check every object in the array against the passed-in `User` object. If we find a match, we set the `containsUser` flag to `true` and break out of the `for` loop to save processor time. If `containsUser` is true, we know the user object was found, and adding another copy would be a violation of our specified business rules. So, the method returns `false`. If the user does not exist in the array, execution continues.

Next, we check whether the array already contains 30 or more items by evaluating its `Length` property. If `true`, we return `false` because the array is full according to our business rules, and adding more would be a violation. Otherwise, we return `true`, and program execution can continue:

```csharp
public void UserAuthenticated(User user)
{
    if (this.CanAddUser(user))
```

```
    {
        _users = Arrays.copyOf(_users, _users.length + 1);
        _users[_users.length - 1] = user;
        System.out.println("Length after adding user " + user.GetId() +
": " + _users.length);
    }
}
```

This method is called once the user has been authenticated, which is the only time we want to add a user to the user rolls. In this method, we validated the add user operation by calling the CanAddUser() method. If CanAddUser() returns true, the method execution continues. First, we used the Arrays wrapper class' copyOf() method to create a new copy of the array that is one element larger, making room for our new addition. Next, we assign the new User object to the last position in the resized array. Finally, we performed some simple housekeeping by logging the user id and the new length of the _users array to the console:

```
public void UserLoggedOut(User user)
{
    int index = -1;
    int k = 0;
    for (User u : _users)
    {
        if (user == u)
        {
            index = k;
            break;
        }
        k++;
    }

    if (index == -1)
    {
        System.out.println("User " + user.GetId() + " not found.");
    }
    else
    {
        User[] newUsers = new User[_users.length - 1];
        for (int i = 0, j = 0; i < newUsers.length - 1; i++, j++)
        {
            if (i == index)
            {
                j++;
            }
            newUsers[i] = _users[j];
        }
```

```
            _users = newUsers;
        }

        System.out.println("Length after logging out user " + user.GetId()
    + ": " + _users.length);
        }
```

This method is called when a previously authenticated user has been logged out of the web service. First, it loops through the _users array to locate a matching object to the User object that has been passed in. We instantiate the index value to –1 so that, if no matching object can be found, this value does not change. This method next confirms that the value of index is equal to –1. If true, we perform some housekeeping by logging in to the console this user id is not currently logged in. Otherwise, we begin the process of deleting the object from the _users array.

First, we have to create a temporary array that is one element shorter than the old array. Next, we loop from 0 to the length of the new array, with i marking the position in the new array and j marking the position in the old array. If i equals the position of the item we want to remove, we increment j to skip past that element in the old array. Finally, we assign a user we intend to keep from the correct position in the old array to the new array. Once we're done looping, we assign the new list to the _users property. After this, we perform some simple housekeeping by logging the deleted user id and new length of the _users array to the console.

Objective-C

Working with a primitive C array in Objective-C is considerably different than in C# or Java, predominantly because Objective-C does not provide methods for working *directly* with the primitive type. However, Objective-C does provide the NSArray wrapper class, which we will use in our code example here:

```
@interface EDSLoggedInUserArray()
{
    NSArray *_users;
}

-(instancetype)init
{
    if (self = [super init])
    {
        _users = [NSArray array];
    }
    return self;
}
```

First, our Objective-C class interface defines an **ivar** property for our array. Next, our initializer instantiates the _users object using the [NSArrayarray] convenience initializer:

```
- (BOOL) canAddUser: (EDSUser *) user
{
    BOOL containsUser = [_users containsObject:user];

    if (containsUser)
    {
        return false;
    }
    else
    {
        if ([_users count] >= 30)
        {
            return false;
        }
        else
        {
            return true;
        }
    }
}
```

The canAddUser: method also serves as internal validation in our Objective-C example. The purpose of this method is to determine whether adding a user to the array is a valid operation at this time. Since we're working with NSArray, we have access to the containsUser: method, which can immediately determine whether the passed-in User object exists in the _users array. Don't be fooled by the simplicity of this code, however, because, under the NSArray hood, the containsUser: method looks something like this:

```
BOOL containsUser = NO;
for (EDSUser *u in _users) {
    if (user.userId == u.userId)
    {
        containsUser = YES;
        break;
    }
}
```

If that code looks familiar, it should because it is nearly identical in function to our previous C# and Java examples. The containsObject: method exists for our convenience, and it performs the heavy lifting for us behind the scenes. Again, if the user object is found, adding another copy is a violation of our specified business rules, and the method returns false. If the user does not exist, execution continues.

Next, we check whether the array already contains 30 or more items by evaluating its `count` property. If `true`, we return `false` because the array is full according to our business rules, and adding more would be a violation. Otherwise, we return `true`, and program execution can continue:

```
- (void) userAuthenticated: (EDSUser *) user
{
    if ([self canAddUser:user])
    {
        _users = [_users arrayByAddingObject:user];
        NSLog(@"Length after adding user %lu: %lu", user.userId,
[_users count]);
    }
}
```

This method is called once the user has been authenticated, which is the only time we want to add a user to the user rolls. In this method, we validated the add user operation by calling `canAddUser:`. If `canAddUser:` returns `true`, the method execution continues. We use the `NSArray` class' `arrayByAddingObject:` method to create a new copy of the array that includes our new `User` object. Last, we performed some simple housekeeping by logging the user id and new length of the `_users` array to the console:

```
- (void) userLoggedOut: (EDSUser *) user
{
    NSUInteger index = [_users indexOfObject:user];
    if (index == NSNotFound)
    {
        NSLog(@"User %lu not found.", user.userId);
    }
    else
    {
        NSArray *newUsers = [NSArray array];
        for (EDSUser *u in _users)
        {
            if (user != u)
            {
                newUsers = [newUsers arrayByAddingObject:u];
            }
        }
        _users = newUsers;
    }
    NSLog(@"Length after logging out user %lu: %lu", user.userId, [_users
count]);
}
```

This method is called when a previously authenticated user has been logged out of the web service. First, it uses the `NSArray indexOfObject:` array to get an index for any object matching the `User` object that has been passed in. If the object is not found, the method returns `NSNotFound`, which is equivalent to `NSIntegerMax`.

This method next confirms that the value of `index` is equal to `NSNotFound`. If `true`, we perform some housekeeping by logging in to the console to which this user id is not currently logged in. Otherwise, we begin the process of deleting the object from the `_users` array.

Unfortunately, `NSArray` does not provide a method for deleting an object from the underlying immutable array, so we need to get a little creative. First, we create a temporary array object called `newUsers` to hold all the `User` objects that we want to keep. Next, we loop through the `_users` array, checking each object to see whether it matches the `User` we want to delete. If there is no match, we add it to the `newUsers` array in the same way we added a new user to `_users` when a user is authenticated. If the `User` object matches, we simply skip it, effectively deleting it from the final array of objects. As you can imagine, this procedure is very costly, and this pattern should be avoided if at all possible. Once the loop is complete, we assign the new array to the `_users` property. Finally, we perform some simple housekeeping by logging the deleted user id and the new count of the `_users` array to the console.

Swift

Working with a primitive C array in Swift is very similar to doing so in C# or Java, in that it provides the `Array` class, which we will use in our code example here:

```
var _users: Array = [EDSUser]()
```

We only need one class property to support our array of users. Swift arrays are type-dependent just as in C# and Java, and we must declare the type when declaring the array property. Note the difference in how Swift initializes arrays by surrounding the type name or object class name with the subscription operator, rather than appending the operator to the name:

```
func canAddUser(user: EDSUser) -> Bool
{
    if (_users.contains(user))
    {
        return false;
    }
    else
    {
        if (_users.count >= 30)
```

```
                {
                        return false;
                }
                else
                {
                        return true;
                }
        }
}
```

The `canAddUser:` method also serves as internal validation. The purpose of this method is to determine whether adding a user to the array is a valid operation at this time. First, we're using the `Array.contains()` method to determine whether the user we want to add already exists in the array. If the user object is found, adding another copy is a violation of our specified business rules, and the method returns `false`. If the user does not exist, execution continues.

Next, we use the `count` property of the _users array to check that the total number of objects within the array is not greater than or equal to 30. If `true`, we return `false` because the array is full according to our business rules, and adding more would be a violation. Otherwise, we return `true`, and program execution can continue:

```
public func userAuthenticated(user: EDSUser)
{
        if (self.canAddUser(user))
        {
                _users.append(user)
        }
        print("Length after adding user \(user._userId): \
(_users.count)");
}
```

Again, this method is called once the user has been authenticated, which is the only time we want to add a user to the user rolls. In this method, we validate the add user operation by calling the `canAddUser()` method. If `canAddUser()` returns `true`, the method execution continues, and we add the user to the array using the `Array.append()` method. Last, we perform some simple housekeeping by logging the user id and new length of the _users array to the console:

```
public func userLoggedOut(user: EDSUser)
{
        if let index = _users.indexOf(user)
        {
                _users.removeAtIndex(index)
        }
        print("Length after logging out user \(user._userId):
```

```
\(_users.count)")
   }
```

Finally, to remove a user during logout, we first need to determine whether the object exists in the array and get its index within the array. Swift allows us to simultaneously declare the `index` variable, perform this check, and assign a value to `index`. If this check returns `true`, we call `Array.removeAtIndex()` to take the `user` object out of the array. Finally, we perform some simple housekeeping by logging the deleted user ID and the new count of the `_users` array to the console.

Separation of concerns

When you examine the previous examples, you might wonder what happens to all those `User` objects we have been adding once we are done with them. If so, great catch! If you look closely, you will see we have not instantiated or modified a single `User` object in this example-only the array that was contained the objects. This is by design.

In object-oriented programming, the concept of **separation of concerns** dictates that computer programs should be broken up into distinct operational features that overlap as little as possible. For example, a class named `LoggedInUserArray`, which operates as a wrapper to an underlying array structure, should only manipulate its array's operations and have little bearing on objects within the array. In this case, the inner workings and details of the `User` class objects that are passed in are not the `LoggedInUserArray` class's concern.

Once each `User` is removed from the array, the object goes on its merry way. If the application retains no other references to the `User` object, some form of **garbage collection** will eventually dispose it off from memory. Either way, the `LoggedInUserArray` class is not responsible for garbage collection and remains agnostic concerning these types of detail.

Advanced topics

Now that we have seen how arrays are used in common practice, let's examine a few advanced topics relating to arrays: search patterns and variations on the basic types of objects that can be stored in an array.

Linear search

When learning about data structures, it is impossible to avoid discussing the subjects of **searching** and **sorting**. Without the ability to search a data structure, the data would be fairly useless to us. Without the ability to sort the data set for use in a particular application, the data would be extremely tedious to manage.

The steps or process we follow to perform a search or a sort of a particular data structure are called an **algorithm**. The performance or the complexity of an algorithm in computer science is measured using the **big O notation**, which is derived from the function $f(n) = O(g(n))$, read as *f of n equals big oh of g of n*. In the simplest terms, **big O** is the terminology we use to describe the worst case for how long an algorithm takes to run. For example, if we know the index of the object we are searching for in an array, it takes only one comparison to locate and retrieve that object. Therefore, the worst case requires one comparison, and the cost of the search is $O(1)$.

Although we will examine searching and sorting in much greater detail later, for now, we will examine **linear searching,** or sequential searching, which is the simplest and least efficient pattern for searching a collection. Iteration means repeating a process over and over again. With a linear search, we iterate sequentially over the collection of objects until we find a match to our search pattern. For collections containing *n* items, the best-case search is when the target value is equal to the first item in the collection, which means, only one comparison is required. In the worst-case scenario, the target value is not found in the collection at all, which means *n* comparisons are required. This means the cost of a linear search is $O(n)$. If you look back at the code examples, you will see $O(n)$ searches in several places:

C#

Here's the linear search algorithm from our C# code but reformatted to use a `for` loop, which better demonstrates the concept of $O(n)$ cost:

```csharp
for (int i = 0; i < _users.Count; i++)
{
    if (_users[i] == u)
    {
        containsUser = true;
        break;
    }
}
```

Java

Here's the linear search algorithm from our Java code but reformatted to use a `for` loop, which better demonstrates the concept of **O**(*n*) cost:

```
for (int i = 0; I < _users.size(); i++)
{
    if (_users[i].equals(u))
    {
        containsUser = true;
        break;
    }
}
```

Objective-C

Here's the linear search algorithm from our Objective-C code but reformatted to use a `for` loop which better demonstrates the concept of **O**(*n*) cost:

```
for (int i = 1; i < [_users count]; i++)
{
    if (((User*)[_users objectAtIndex:i]).userId == u.userId)
    {
        containsUser = YES;
        break;
    }
}
```

Swift

Our Swift code does not include an example of a linear search, but one example could look like this:

```
for i in 1..<_users.count
{
    //Perform comparison
}
```

Primitive arrays

Primitive arrays are simply arrays that only contain primitive types. In C#, Java, and Swift, you declare a primitive array by declaring an array on a primitive type. As a weakly typed language, Objective-C does not support explicitly typed arrays, and therefore does not support explicitly primitive arrays.

C#

```
int[] array = new int[10];
```

Java

```
int[] array = new int[10];
```

Objective-C

```
NSArray *array = [NSArray array];
```

Swift

```
var array: Array = [UInt]()
```

Object arrays

Object arrays are simply arrays that contain only instances of a particular object. In C#, Java, and Swift, you declare an object array by declaring an array on class. As a weakly typed language, Objective-C does not support explicitly typed arrays and, therefore, does not support explicitly object arrays.

C#

```
Vehicle[] cars = new Vehicle[10];
```

Java

```
Vehicle[] cars = new Vehicle[10];
```

Objective-C

```
NSArray *array = [NSArray array];
```

Swift

```
var vehicle: Array = [Vehicle]()
```

Mixed arrays

When working with arrays, you declare the array using one data type, and all of the elements in the array must match that data type. Typically, this constraint is suitable, since the elements are normally closely related to one another or share similar property values. At other times, the elements in your array are not closely related or do not have similar property values. In these circumstances, it is desirable to have the ability to mix-and-match types within the same array. C# and Java share a similar mechanism for accomplishing this–declaring the array as the root class object type. Arrays in Objective-C are already mixed by default due to the language being weakly typed. Swift provides the `AnyObject` type for declaring mixed arrays.

C#

```
Object[] data = new Object[10];
```

Java

```
Object[] data = new Object[10];
```

Objective-C

```
NSArray *data = [NSArray array];
```

Swift

```
var data: Array = [AnyObject]()
```

Working with mixed arrays can seem convenient at the first glance, but be aware that you as the developer take the responsibility for type checking away from the compiler. This won't be a major adjustment for developers with weakly typed languages such as Objective-C, but developers experienced in strongly typed languages will need to be very attentive to this concern.

Multidimensional arrays

A multidimensional array is an array containing one or more additional arrays. The four languages we are working with can each support multidimensional arrays of *1...n* dimensions. However, be aware that multidimensional arrays greater than three levels deep become extremely difficult to manage.

It sometimes helps to conceptualize multidimensional arrays in terms relative to their dimensions. For example, a 2D array might have rows and columns, or *x* and *y* values. Similarly, a 3D array might have *x*, *y*, and *z* values. Let's look at an example of 2D and 3D arrays in each language.

C#

Multidimensional arrays in C# are created with the `[,]` syntax, where each `,` represents one additional dimension within the array. The corresponding `new` initializer must provide the correct number of size arguments to match the definition or the code will not compile:

```
//Initialize
int[,] twoDArray = new int[5, 5];
int[, ,] threeDArray = new int[5, 6, 7];

//Set values
twoDArray[2,5] = 90;
threeDArray[0, 0, 4] = 18;

//Get values
int x2y5 = twoDArray[2,5];
int x0y0z4 = threeDArray[0,0,4];
```

Java

The syntax for creating multidimensional arrays in Java simply involves stringing pairs of `[]` where each pair represents one dimension within the array. The corresponding `new` initializer must provide the correct number of bracketed size arguments to match the definition or the code will not compile:

```
//Initialize
int[][] twoDArray = new int[5][5];
int[][][] threeDArray = new int[5][6][7];

//Set values
twoDArray[2][5] = 90;
threeDArray[0][0][4] = 18;

//Get values
int x2y5 = twoDArray[2][5];
int x0y0z4 = threeDArray[0][0][4];
```

Objective-C

Objective-C does not directly support multidimensional arrays with the `NSArray` class. If a multidimensional array is required in your code, you will need to use `NSMutableArray` or a plain C array, both of which are outside the scope of this chapter.

Swift

Multidimensional arrays in Swift can seem somewhat confusing at first glance, but what you need to realize is that you are creating arrays of arrays. The definition syntax is `[[Int]]` while the initialization syntax is `[[1, 2], [3, 4]]` where the values used at initialization can be any value of the specified type:

```
//Initialize
var twoDArray: [[Int]] = [[1, 2], [3, 4]]
var threeDArray: [[[Int]]] = [[[1, 2, 3], [4, 5, 6], [7, 8, 9]], [[1,
2, 3], [4, 5, 6], [7, 8, 9]], [[1, 2, 3], [4, 5, 6], [7, 8, 9]]]

//Set values
twoDArray[0][1] = 90;
threeDArray[0][0][2] = 18;

//Get values
var x0y1: Int = twoDArray[0][1];
var x0y0z2: Int = threeDArray[0][0][2];
```

Jagged Arrays

Jagged arrays are created when a multidimensional array contains arrays of different sizes. There are rare scenarios when such a design is necessary, but be aware that jagged arrays can be very complex and difficult to manage. C#, Java, and Swift support jagged arrays. Objective-C does not support multidimensional arrays using `NSArray`, and therefore, does not support jagged arrays using it. As with multidimensional arrays, Objective-C can support jagged arrays using either `NSMutableArray` or plain C arrays.

Summary

In this chapter, you learned the basic definition of an array structure, how arrays look in memory, and how each of the four languages we are discussing implement some form of the plain C array structure. Next, we discussed the difference between mutable and immutable arrays. Using examples, we looked at how each of the four languages we are discussing implements arrays and array functionality. In the remainder of the chapter, we examined the linear search algorithm and introduced the big **O** notation, including how this notation is applied to arrays with examples of simple iteration. We discussed the difference between primitive arrays, object arrays, and mixed arrays. Finally, we examined multidimensional arrays and their counterpart, jagged arrays.

As a final note, it is important to know when to use an array. Arrays are great for containing small lists of constant data or data that changes very little to not at all. If you find yourself constantly manipulating the data in your array or constantly adding and removing objects, then you will want to examine alternative data structures such as the List which we will discuss in the following chapter.

3
Lists: Linear Collections

In our last chapter, we introduced the array data structure upon which many of the structures we will examine in this text are based. Although arrays provide good performance for static collections of data, our coding examples proved that they are inflexible and inefficient for many applications–so much so that even something as simple as adding or deleting an element from a collection is an extremely complex and costly operation.

Lists are, in some ways, an evolution of the array. A list can be defined as a finite, ordered series of objects or values called **elements**. An empty list is a list with no elements, while the length of a list is the total number of elements in the collection. The first item in a list is called the **head**, while the last item is called the **tail**. In a list with a length of 1, the head and tail are the same object.

 While arrays are a *concrete* data structure, a list is an abstract concept of a data structure that many languages provide a concrete implementation of. We will examine this distinction in more detail with one of the Java examples later in this chapter.

Ordered lists should not be confused with sorted lists because lists can be either **sorted** or **unsorted**. Ordered simply means that each element has a defined position in the list. Objects in a sorted list have some type of relationship between them, while objects in an unsorted list have no notable relationship. For example, when my wife creates a shopping list, she sits down and carefully organizes the groceries in relation to how she knows the supermarket is arranged. Items on her list are types of groceries and they are arranged according to their relative positions in the supermarket so they have a *spatial relationship*. This is a sorted list. I, on the other hand, create a shopping list by slapping a piece of paper on the fridge and scribbling items on the paper as I notice shelves are empty or containers are missing. Although the items on my list are all types of groceries, they are not arranged in any particular way so they have *no notable relationship* to one another. This is an example of an unsorted list.

In this chapter we will cover the following:

- Definition of a list data structure
- Initializing lists
- Example applications for lists
- List implementations
- Append, insert, and remove operations
- Array-based lists
- Linked lists
- Doubly linked lists
- Searching

List implementations

One of the most common implementations of the list data structure is the *array-based* list. Generally speaking, an array-based list is simply a contiguous list of array positions, each holding a *pointer* to a list element. Since the list is based on an array, its functionality and performance are very similar to that of an array.

As seen in the previous examples, another common implementation is the **linked list**. A linked list is also a sequence of elements, except most implementations refer to the elements as **nodes**. In a linked list, the pointers to the elements are not contained in an array structure, but rather a pointer exists in memory to identify the first node. Then each node contains a link to the subsequent node in the list.

Finally, there is the **doubly linked list**. In a doubly linked list, each node contains a link to both the subsequent node in the list and the previous node in the list. A doubly linked list makes traversing the list bidirectionally a much simpler process. The previous link in the head node and the next link in the tail node are both null. An alternative to this is to have the previous link in the head node point to the tail and the next link in the tail node point to the head, which changes the doubly linked list to a **circular linked list**.

The term doubly linked list is not used very often, but if you work with the LinkedList classes in Java or C#, you are in fact working with a doubly linked list. C# and Java do not provide a **singly linked list** type, and the doubly linked list provides you with the same functionality and more, so you should never need one. However, you could easily implement one of your own if you really wanted to for academic purposes.

Typically, each of the concrete implementations of this structure provides you with convenience methods allowing you to append, insert, and remove elements from the list. Both array-based and link-based lists provide access to the basic append, insert, and remove operations. However, the way in which these operations are implemented and their associated cost vary slightly between the two implementations. Where existing methods for this functionality are not baked in, it is typically a trivial exercise to create that functionality.

 As with other implementations of abstract data structures, when given a choice between using methods we create ourselves and any methods provided by the framework, choose the latter as they will typically be more robust and reliable.

Array-based lists

The append operation in an array-based list costs $O(1)$, as we can always determine the new element's position by simply incrementing the index of the tail position:

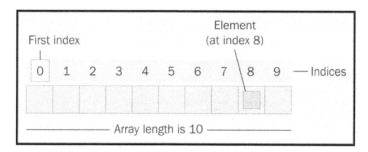

Whenever we insert an element into an array-based list, we need to also manage the position of the existing objects in the array to accommodate the new nodes. Inserting an element into the list at index i requires us to shift all of the elements in positions greater than i one position toward the tail, meaning that we will need to perform $n - i$ operations where there are n elements already in the list. Inserting at the head position is a worst-case operation, costing $O(n)$. Since we always count the cost of the worst case when evaluating an algorithm's efficiency, inserting an element costs $O(n)$.

Removing an element from the list at index i requires us to shift all of the elements in positions greater than i one position toward the head, meaning that we will need to perform $n - i - 1$ operations where there are n elements in the list. Removing from the head position is a worst-case operation, costing **O**(n). Therefore, removing an element costs **O**(n), as depicted in the following diagram:

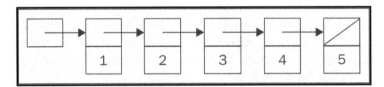

Linked list

As with an array-based list, the append operation costs **O**(*1*). However, the insert and remove operations also cost **O**(*1*). One of the key advantages of the linked list over the array-based list is mutability. Unlike an array, a linked list is a series of discrete objects related to one another by memory pointers, so inserting or removing elements is simply a matter of adding or modifying those pointers. In other words, a linked list is capable of growing and shrinking to accommodate additions to and deletions from the collection in a very efficient manner.

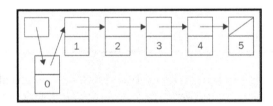

If we wish to insert an element at position i, we need to change the original pointer $i - 1 \rightarrow i$ to point to our new element at i, and insert a new pointer for $i \rightarrow i + 1$. Similarly, removing an element at i requires adjusting the pointer from $i - 1 \rightarrow i$ and making it $i - 1 \rightarrow i + 1$.

Instantiating lists

Like other data structures, lists must be defined and instantiated prior to being used. Each of the four languages that we will examine in this text has varying support for, and unique implementations of, the list data structure. Let's briefly examine how to instantiate a list in each language.

C#

Instantiating lists in C# requires the use of the `new` keyword:

```
//Array backed lists
ArrayList myArrayList = new ArrayList();
List<string> myOtherArrayList = new List<string>();

//Linked lists
LinkedList<string> myLinkedList = new LinkedList<string>();
```

The C# `ArrayList` class originated in .NET 1.0, and it is not used very often anymore. Most developers prefer to use the generic concrete implementation, `List<of T>`, for an array-based list. This is also true for the generic concrete linked list implementation, `LinkedList<of T>`. There is no non-generic linked list data structure in C#.

Java

Like C#, initializing a list in Java requires the use of the `new` keyword:

```
//Array backed lists
List<string> myArrayList = new ArrayList<string>();

//Linked lists
LinkedList<string> myLinkedList = new LinkedList<string>();
```

Java developers will create an array-based list using a concrete implementation of the generic abstract `List<E>` class. This is also true of the concrete linked list implementation, `LinkedList<E>`. There is no non-generic linked list data structure in Java.

Objective-C

The process of creating a list in Objective-C is as follows:

```
//Array backed lists
NSArray *myArrayList = [NSArray array];

//Linked lists
NSMutableArray *myLinkedList = [NSMutableArray array];
```

If you read the chapter on arrays, this example has probably caught your attention. In fact, this is not a mistake. The closest implementation for an array-based list in Objective-C is found in the NSArray class, while the closest implementation of a linked list is found in the NSMutableArray class. That's because NSArray and NSMutableArray are known as **class clusters**. Class clusters provide public APIs that are really abstract classes. When you initialize one of these classes you get back the concrete implementation of a data structure, which is custom tailored for the data you provided. These implementations can even change at runtime if the nature of the data set changes, making array classes extremely flexible. This means that many of the data structures we will discuss in this text will be implemented in Objective-C (and Swift) by only three abstract classes.

Class clusters in Objective-C

Class clusters are a design pattern based on the **Abstract Factory** pattern, which returns a type adhering to a certain interface (C#/Java) or protocol (Objective-C/Swift). They are leveraged heavily in the **Foundation** framework and this is a good thing.

Class clusters group private, concrete subclasses under an abstract superclass or API. This public API is much simpler to work with than working with each subclass directly. NSNumber, NSString, NSArray, and NSDictionary are all examples of class clusters in Foundation.

Swift

Finally, here's how to instantiate a list in Swift:

```
//Lists
var myArray = [string]()
var myOtherArray: Array<string> = [String]()
```

Swift also uses class clusters for many different abstract collections. For lists, we use the Array class, which is both generic and mutable by default. There is a shorthand and an explicit declaration for arrays in Swift. Although more verbose, the explicit definition more clearly demonstrates the generic nature of the API.

Revisiting users logged in to a service

In Chapter 2, *Arrays: Foundational Structures*, we created an app to keep track of users logged into a web service, using an array as the underlying data structure containing the User objects. However, this design can be greatly improved upon by using a list data structure. Let's revisit the users logged into a service problem here, and by replacing the class array with a list, we will see that our original code is both abbreviated and more readable in most cases.

C#

In this example, we have replaced the User[] object with a List<User> object. Much of this refactor is obvious, but three lines of code should be noted. First, in the CanAddUser() method, we have replaced 15 lines of code with 2 lines of code by leveraging the List<T>.Contains() method and condensing our logic loop. Next, in the UserAuthenticated() method, we have leveraged the List<T>.Add() method, which replaced the call to Array.Resize() and the error-prone approach to assigning an object using the subscription operator. Finally, we replaced nearly 20 lines of complex and ugly code using the List<T>.Remove() method. The convenience and power afforded by this wrapper class should be obvious based solely on the abbreviated code:

```
List<User> _users;
public LoggedInUserList()
{
    _users = new List<User>();
}

bool CanAddUser(User user)
{
    if (_users.Contains(user) || _users.Count >= 30)
    {
        return false;
    } else {
        return true;
    }
}

public void UserAuthenticated(User user)
{
    if (this.CanAddUser(user))
    {
        _users.Add(user);
    }
}
```

```
    public void UserLoggedOut(User user)
    {
        _users.Remove(user);
    }
```

Java

In this example, we have replaced the `User[]` object with a `List<User>` object. Much of this refactor is obvious, but three lines of code should be noted. First, in the `CanAddUser()` method, we have replaced 15 lines of code with 2 lines of code by leveraging the `List<E>.contains()` method and condensing our logic loop. Next, in the `UserAuthenticated()` method, we are leveraging the `List<E>.add()` method, which replaced the call to `Array.copyOf()` and the error-prone approach to assigning an object using the subscription operator. Finally, we replaced nearly 20 lines of complex and ugly code using the `List<E>.remove()` method:

```java
List<User> _users;
public LoggedInUserList()
{
    _users = new LinkedList<User>;
}

boolean CanAddUser(User user)
{
    if (_users.contains(user) || _users.size() >= 30)
    {
        return false;
    } else {
        return true;
    }
}

public void UserAuthenticated(User user)
{
    if (this.CanAddUser(user))
    {
        _users.add(user);
    }
}

public void UserLoggedOut(User user)
{
    _users.remove(user);
}
```

The following screenshot demonstrates another benefit of using generic classes when available. As you can see, our code completion, or **Intellisense**, suggests potential completion options including the proper type to be included in the collection. This can save you from having to check back repeatedly to make sure that you are using the correct object and collection, which is both time-consuming and annoying.

```
if (this.CanAddUser(user))
{
    _users.a
}           m    add(User e)
         m  add(int index, User element)
lic voi  m  addAll(Collection<? extends User> c)
         m  addAll(int index, Collection<? extends User> c)
```

Objective-C

In this example, we have replaced the NSArray _users object with an NSMutableArray _users object. In this example, besides some consolidation and code cleanup, there is really only one refactor. In userLoggedOut:, we replaced nearly 20 lines of complex and ugly code using the NSMutableArray removeObject: method instead of checking indices, looping, and merging objects:

```
@interface EDSLoggedInUserList ()
{
    NSMutableArray *_users;
}
-(instancetype)init
{
    if (self = [super init])
    {
        _users = [NSMutableArray array];
    }
    return self;
}

-(BOOL)canAddUser:(EDSUser *)user
{
    if ([_users containsObject:user] || [_users count] >= 30)
    {
        return false;
    } else {
        return true;
    }
}
```

```objc
- (void)userAuthenticated:(EDSUser *)user
{
    if ([self canAddUser:user])
    {
        [_users addObject:user];
    }
}

- (void)userLoggedOut:(EDSUser *)user
{
    [_users removeObject:user];
}
```

Swift

If you look carefully at this code in comparison to the original, you'll see that effectively they are the same! That's because Swift `Arrays` are already mutable and they already support generic types, so our original `LoggedInUserArray` class was already functioning as much like a linked, as Swift is capable of producing output with out-of-the-box code. We could create our own implementation of a linked list in Swift but that would only be necessary in very specific use cases:

```swift
var _users: Array = [User]()
init() { }

func canAddUser(user: User) -> Bool
{
    if (_users.contains(user) || _users.count >= 30)
    {
        return false;
    } else {
        return true;
    }
}

public func userAuthenticated(user: User)
{
    if (self.canAddUser(user))
    {
        _users.append(user)
    }
}

public func userLoggedOut(user: User)
{
    if let index = _users.indexOf(user)
    {
```

```
            _users.removeAtIndex(index)
        }
    }
```

 These refactored examples using some varieties of the list data structure are not only streamlined, they are also more performant than their array counterparts. For both of these reasons, the list structure is proven as the superior choice for this application.

Generics

You may have noticed the `List<T>.Contains()` method in our C# example or the `List<E>.Add()` method in our Java example. These methods are part of classes that have been defined as generic. In computer science, generics allow you to define a class or method without specifying the data type until the class is declared or the method is called. For example, suppose you have a method that adds two number values together. In order to work directly with the individual types, you could create multiple overloads of an `Add()` method:

```
//C#
public int Add(int a, int b)
public double Add(double a, double b)
public float Add(float a, float b)
```

Generics allow you to create a single method that is customized for the type that invokes it, greatly simplifying your code. In this example, `T` can be substituted for whatever type the caller needs:

```
public T Add<T>(T a, T b)
```

Generics are an incredibly powerful tool, which we will discuss in greater detail in `Chapter 12`, *Sorting: Bringing Order Out Of Chaos*.

Case study: bike route

Business problem: A mobile app is to be written for biking enthusiasts who like to travel off-road. One of the key business requirements is the ability to store waypoints in a route. The route has to have a beginning and an end, and it needs to be traversable in both directions. The app also needs the ability to modify the biker's route in real time to allow for detours around hazards, visiting rest areas, or adding points of interest.

Due to the nature of the app and its requirements, the class that represents the route will need several basic pieces of functionality. First, it will require the ability to add, remove, and insert waypoints. Next, it will require the ability to start the route and traverse it to route forward and backward. Finally, the class should be able to easily identify the start and finish lines as well as the currently focused waypoint.

Since the nature of this data is such that all waypoints have a spatial relationship to one another, and the app must traverse from point to point utilizing that relationship, an array would be a poor selection as a data structure. However, since a List inherently provides a mechanism for both defining and traversing relationships between objects in the collection, the developer has chosen to use a linked list structure to build this component.

C#

C# conveniently exposes a linked list structure through the `LinkedList<T>` class and list nodes through the `LinkedListNode<T>` class. Therefore, building this class in C# should be a fairly straightforward procedure. Here's an example of what a simple implementation in C# looks like:

```
LinkedList<Waypoint> route;
LinkedListNode<Waypoint> current;
public WaypointList()
{
    this.route = new LinkedList<Waypoint>();
}
```

First, we declare two properties. The first is the `route` property, which is `LinkedList<Waypoint>`. The next object is the `current` node. We have declared both objects without explicitly defining their scope, so they default to `private`. We want these fields to be private because we only permit the methods in this class to modify their values. Our constructor only instantiates the `route` property because the `current` node will be assigned on an as-needed basis:

```
public void AddWaypoints(List<Waypoint> waypoints)
{
    foreach (Waypoint w in waypoints)
```

```
        {
             this.route.AddLast(w);
        }
    }

    public bool RemoveWaypoint(Waypoint waypoint)
    {
        return this.route.Remove(waypoint);
    }
```

The `AddWaypoints(List<Waypoint>)` method allows us to add *1...n* new waypoints to the existing route. C# does not provide a mechanism for merging `List<T>` with a `LinkedList<T>`, so we must resort to looping through `waypoints` and adding the new nodes individually using `LinkedList<T>.AddLast()`, meaning this operation costs $O(i)$, where *i* is the number of elements in the `waypoints` list.

The `RemoveWaypoint(Waypoint)` method simply calls `LinkedList<T>.Remove()` on the route, passing `waypoint` as a parameter. As this is technically a search operation, it also costs $O(n)$:

```
    public void InsertWaypointsBefore(List<Waypoint> waypoints, Waypoint
  before)
    {
        LinkedListNode<Waypoint> node = this.route.Find(before);
        if (node != null)
        {
            foreach (Waypoint w in waypoints)
            {
                this.route.AddBefore(node, w);
            }
        } else {
                this.AddWaypoints(waypoints);
        }
    }
```

The `InsertWaypointsBefore(List<Waypoint>, Waypoint)` method gives our class the ability to create alternate routes and add intermediate destinations on-the-fly. First, we attempt to locate the `before` node. If we find it, we begin inserting the list of new waypoints sequentially before the `before` node. Otherwise, we immediately call `AddWaypoints(List<Waypoint>)` to append the new list of waypoints onto the route. Although the functionality of this loop may seem quirky, by adding each item sequentially just prior to the `before` node, we shift `before` one node closer to the tail with each operation, ensuring that each new node is inserted in the correct order.

This is the most expensive operation in this class as it is a combination of a search and an insert. This means its operational cost is $O(n+i)$ where n is the number of elements in the existing `route` collection and i is the number of elements in the `waypoints` list:

```
public bool StartRoute()
{
    if (this.route.Count > 1)
    {
        this.current = this.StartingLine();
        return this.MoveToNextWaypoint();
    }
    return false;
}
```

The `StartRoute()` method is used to set our initial current position and denote that it has been deactivated. Since our overall class represents a route, which is by definition a 2-dimensional object at the very least, the `StartRoute()` method immediately validates that `route` has at least two waypoints. If not, we return `false` because the route is not yet ready to be traversed. If we do have two or more waypoints, we set the `current` waypoint to the starting line and move to the next point. The `StartRoute()` method has an $O(1)$ operational cost.

We could have easily duplicated the critical code from the `StartingLine()` method and the `MoveToNextWaypoint()` method locally in `StartRoute()`. Doing so would mean that if we ever wanted to change how we identify the starting line or how we navigate the route, we would need to maintain that code in multiple locations. By following this pattern of code reuse, we minimize the amount of work and number of potential new bugs such a refactor could introduce.

Next we'll look at the methods that alter the object's position.

```
public bool MoveToNextWaypoint()
{
    if (this.current != null)
    {
        this.current.Value.DeactivateWaypoint();
        if (this.current != this.FinishLine())
        {
            this.current = this.current.Next;
            return true;
        }
        return false;
    }
    return false;
```

```
    }

public bool MoveToPreviousWaypoint()
{
    if (this.current != null && this.current != this.StartingLine())
    {
        this.current = this.current.Previous;
        this.current.Value.ReactivateWaypoint();
        return true;
    }
    return false;
}
```

The MoveToNextWayPoint() and MoveToPreviousWaypoint() methods introduce our route traversal functionality. In MoveToNextWaypoint(), we check that the current waypoint is not null, and then we deactivate it. Next, we check whether we are at the finish line, and if not, we set current to the next node in route and return true. The MoveToPreviousWaypoint() method verifies that current is not null and makes sure that we are not at the starting line. If so, we move current to the previous waypoint and reactivate it. If any of our checks in these two methods fail, we return false. Each of these methods has an **O**(*1*) operational cost.

This dual false return seen in MoveToNextWaypoint() may seem like a design flaw, but remember that our class is not responsible for the overall functionality of the app, only the functionality of the route. It is the responsibility of the *caller* to check whether the route is ready to traverse before calling MoveToNextWaypoint(). Our return value is only signaling the success or failure of the operation.

Lastly, we'll look at the methods that indicate position:

```
public LinkedListNode<Waypoint> StartingLine()
{
    return this.route.First;
}

public LinkedListNode<Waypoint> FinishLine()
{
    return this.route.Last;
}

public LinkedListNode<Waypoint> CurrentPosition()
{
    return this.current;
}
```

We add the `StartingLine()` and `FinishLine()` methods to expose the head and tail nodes of the route collection. Finally, we add the `CurrentPosition()` method to expose which node in the route is our next immediate destination. Each of these methods has an O(*1*) operational cost.

Java

Java also exposes a linked list data structure through the `LinkedList<E>` class. However, Java does not provide an implementation of the list node structure. This is because, in Java, you generally do not work with the nodes directly but through a list iterator. The `ListIterator<E>` class provides the necessary functionality to implement a linked list structure in the basic sense. If we needed our own node class, it would be easy to implement one. Here's an example of what a simple implementation of our `WaypointList` class might look like in Java:

```
LinkedList<Waypoint> route;
Waypoint current;
public WaypointList()
{
    this.route = new LinkedList<Waypoint>();
}
```

First, we declare two properties. The first is the `route`, which is an abstract `List<Waypoint>`, and the next object is the `current` node. We have declared both objects without explicitly defining their scope, so they default to `package-private`, which is fine for our case. We want these fields to be private because we only permit the methods in this class to modify their values. Our constructor only instantiates the `route` because the `current` node will be assigned on an as-needed basis:

```
public void AddWaypoints(List<Waypoint> waypoints)
{
    this.route.addAll(waypoints);
}

public boolean RemoveWaypoint(Waypoint waypoint)
{
    return this.route.remove(waypoint);
}
```

The `AddWaypoints(List<Waypoint>)` method allows us to add *1...n* new waypoints to the existing route. We append objects to our list using the `LinkedList<E>.addAll()` method. This operation is quite simple and costs **O**(*1*). The `RemoveWaypoint(Waypoint)` method simply calls `LinkedList<E>.remove()` on the route, passing `waypoint` as a parameter. As this is technically a search operation, it costs **O**(*n*):

```
public void InsertWaypointsBefore(List<Waypoint> waypoints, Waypoint
before)
{
    int index = this.route.indexOf(before);
    if (index >= 0)
    {
        this.route.addAll(index, waypoints);
    } else {
        this.AddWaypoints(waypoints);
    }
}
```

The `InsertWaypointsBefore(List<Waypoint>, Waypoint)` method gives our class the ability to create alternate routes and add intermediate destinations on the fly. First, we attempt to locate the `before` node using `LinkedList<E>.indexOf()`. The `indexOf()` method returns −1 if it cannot find the object, so we confirm that the value is greater than −1; otherwise we immediately call `AddWaypoints(List<Waypoint>)` to append the new list of waypoints onto the route. If the `before` node is valid, we add the list of new waypoints before the `before` node.

This is the most expensive method operation in this class as it is a combination of a search and an insert. This means its operational cost is **O**(*n+i*), where *n* is the number of elements in the existing `route` and *i* is the number of elements in the waypoints list:

```
public boolean StartRoute()
{
    if (this.route.size() > 1)
    {
        this.current = this.StartingLine();
        return this.MoveToNextWaypoint();
    }
    return false;
}
```

The `StartRoute()` method is used to set our initial current position and denote that it has been deactivated. Since our overall class represents a route, which is by definition a 2-dimensional object at the very least, the `StartRoute()` method immediately validates that `route` has at least two waypoints, and if not, we return `false` because `route` is not yet ready to be traversed. If we do have two or more waypoints, we set the `current` waypoint to the starting line and move to the next point. `StartRoute()` has an **O**(1) operational cost:

```
public boolean MoveToNextWaypoint()
{
    if (this.current != null)
    {
        this.current.DeactivateWaypoint();
        if (this.current != this.FinishLine())
        {
            int index = this.route.indexOf(this.current);
            this.current = this.route.listIterator(index).next();
            return true;
        }
        return false;
    }
    return false;
}

public boolean MoveToPreviousWaypoint()
{
    if (this.current != null && this.current != this.StartingLine())
    {
        int index = this.route.indexOf(this.current);
        this.current = this.route.listIterator(index).previous();
        this.current.ReactivateWaypoint();
        return true;
    }
    return false;
}
```

The `MoveToNextWayPoint()` and `MoveToPreviousWaypoint()` methods introduce our route traversal functionality. In the `MoveToNextWaypoint()` method, we check whether the current waypoint is not `null`, and then we deactivate it. Next, we check whether we are not at the finish line, and if not, we set `current` to the next by assigning it to the `listIterator` property and the `next()` method of `route`, and then return `true`. The `MoveToPreviousWaypoint()` method verifies that `current` is not `null` and makes sure that we are not at the starting line. If so, we set `current` to the previous waypoint and reactivate it. If any of our checks in these two methods fail, we return `false`. Due to the need to search for a match for `current`, each of these methods has an **O**(n+1) operational cost:

```
public Waypoint StartingLine()
{
    return this.route.getFirst();
}

public Waypoint FinishLine()
{
    return this.route.getLast();
}

public Waypoint CurrentWaypoint()
{
    return this.current;
}
```

We add the `StartingLine()` and `FinishLine()` methods to expose the head and tail nodes of the route collection. Finally, we add the `CurrentPosition()` method to expose which node in the route is our next immediate destination. Each of these methods has an O(1) operational cost.

Objective-C

Objective-C does not expose any implementation of a linked list out-of-the-box. Although we could create our own implementation, the purpose of this text is to demonstrate the best approach given the tools available. For this scenario, we will once again use the class cluster, `NSMutableArray`. Here's a simple example of how the `EDSWaypointList` class might be implemented in Objective-C:

```
@interface EDSWaypointList()
{
    NSMutableArray *_route;
    EDSWaypoint *_current;
}
-(instancetype)init
{
    if (self = [super init])
    {
        _route = [NSMutableArray array];
    }
    return self;
}
```

First, we declare two `ivar` properties. The first is `_route`, which is an `NSMutableArray` array. The next object is the `_current` node. Again, we have declared these as ivars because we only permit the methods in this class to modify their values. Our initializer only instantiates the `_route` because the `_current` node will be assigned on an as-needed basis:

```
-(void)addWaypoints:(NSArray*)waypoints
{
    [_route addObjectsFromArray:waypoints];
}

-(BOOL)removeWaypoint:(EDSWaypoint*)waypoint
{
    if ([_route containsObject:waypoint])
    {
        [_route removeObject:waypoint];
        return YES;
    }
    return NO;
}
```

The `addWaypoints:` method allows us to add *1...n* new waypoints to the existing route. `NSMutableArray` allows us to merge the new array with the existing route by calling `addObjectsFromArray:`. This operation is quite simple and costs **O(*1*)**.

The `removeWaypoint:` method confirms that `_route` contains `waypoint` using `containsObject:`, then calls `removeObject:`. If we were not concerned with the success or failure of this operation, we could have simply called `removeObject:` and moved on. Note that, since our `_route` object is an array-backed list, it allows for **O(*1*)** search operations. Since we do not know the index of waypoint in advance, the `removeObject:` operation still costs **O(*n*)**:

```
-(void)insertWaypoints:(NSArray*)waypoints
beforeWaypoint:(EDSWaypoint*)before
{
    NSUInteger index = [_route indexOfObject:before];
    if (index == NSNotFound)
    {
        [self addWaypoints:waypoints];
    } else {
        NSRange range = NSMakeRange(index, [waypoints count]);
        NSIndexSet *indexSet =
[NSIndexSetindexSetWithIndexesInRange:range];
        [_route insertObjects:waypoints atIndexes:indexSet];
    }
}
```

The `insertWaypoints:beforeWaypoint:` method gives our class the ability to create alternate routes and add intermediate destinations on the fly. First, we attempt to locate the `before` node using `indexOfObject:`. If we cannot find it, we immediately call `addWaypoints:` to append the new list of waypoints onto the route. Otherwise, we create some ugly code to define an `NSRange` object and an `NSIndexSet` object, and use these with `insertObjects:atIndexes:`. Since this method represents a search and an insert, its operational cost is $O(n+1)$, where n is the number of elements in the existing _route object:

```
-(BOOL) startRoute
{
    if ([_route count] > 1)
    {
        _current = [self startingLine];
        return [self moveToNextWaypoint];
    }
    return NO;
}
```

The `startRoute:` method is used to set our initial current position and denote that it has been deactivated. Since our overall class represents a route, which is by definition a 2-dimensional object at the very least, the `startRoute:` method immediately validates that _route has at least two waypoints; if not we return NO because the route is not yet ready to be traversed. If we do have two or more waypoints, we set the _current waypoint to the starting line and move to the next point. `startRoute:` has an $O(1)$ operational cost.

```
-(BOOL) moveToNextWaypoint
{
    if (_current)
    {
        [_current deactivateWaypoint];
        if (_current != [self finishLine])
        {
            NSUInteger index = [_route indexOfObject:_current];
            _current = [_route objectAtIndex:index+1];
            return YES;
        }
        return NO;
    }
    return NO;
}

-(BOOL) moveToPreviousWaypoint
{
    if (_current && _current != [self startingLine])
    {
        NSUInteger index = [_route indexOfObject:_current];
```

```
        _current = [_route objectAtIndex:index-1];
        [_current reactivateWaypoint];
        return YES;
    }
    return NO;
}
```

In `moveToNextWaypoint:`, we check whether the current waypoint is not `nil`, and then we deactivate it. Next, we verify that we are not at the finish line, and if not, we get the index of `_current` in the list and assign the next highest index object to the property, then return `YES`. The `moveToPreviousWaypoint:` method verifies that `_current` is not `nil`, and makes sure that we are not at the starting line. If so, we set `_current` to the previous waypoint and reactivate it, and then we return `YES`. If any of our checks in these two methods fail, we return `NO`. Due to the need to search for a match for `_current`, each of these methods has an **O**(*n*+1) operational cost:

```
- (EDSWaypoint *) startingLine
{
    return [_route firstObject];
}

- (EDSWaypoint *) finishLine
{
    return [_route lastObject];
}

- (EDSWaypoint *) currentWaypoint
{
    return _current;
}
```

We add the `startingLine:` and `finishLine:` methods to expose the head and tail nodes of the route collection. Finally, we add the `currentPosition:` method to expose which node in the route is our next immediate destination. Each of these methods has an **O**(1) operational cost.

Swift

Similar to Objective-C, Swift does not expose any implementation of a linked list data structure. Therefore, we will use the Swift `Array` class to create our data structure. Here's a simple example of how this class might be implemented using Swift:

```
var _route: Array = [Waypoint]()
var _current: Waypoint?
init() { }
```

First, we declare two properties. The first is _route, which is an array. The next object is the _current node, which is a Waypoint object, flagged as optional. Again, we have declared these as private because we only permit the methods in this class to modify their values. Our initializer does not need to instantiate either object because the declaration instantiates _route, and _current is flagged as optional and will only be assigned on an as-needed basis:

```
public func addWaypoints(waypoints: Array<Waypoint>)
{
    _route.appendContentsOf(waypoints)
}

public func removeWaypoint(waypoint: Waypoint) -> Bool
{
    if let index = _route.indexOf(waypoint)
    {
        _route.removeAtIndex(index)
        return true
    }
    return false
}
```

The addWaypoints(Array<Waypoint>) method allows us to add *1...n* new waypoints to the existing route. Array allows us to merge the new array with the existing route by calling appendContentsOf(Array). This operation is quite simple and costs **O**(1).

The removeWaypoint(Waypoint) method confirms that _route contains waypoint and gets its index in one operation by calling if .. indexOf(). If we do not retrieve an index, we return false, otherwise we call removeAtIndex() and return true. Note that, since our _route object is an array-backed list, the removeAtIndex() operation only costs **O**(1):

```
public func insertWaypoints(waypoints: Array<Waypoint>, before:
Waypoint)
{
    if let index = _route.indexOf(before)
    {
        _route.insertContentsOf(waypoints, at:index)
    } else {
        addWaypoints(waypoints)
    }
}
```

The `insertWaypoints(Array<Waypoint>, Waypoint)` method first attempts to locate the `before` node using `if..indexOf()`. If we cannot find it, we immediately call `addWaypoints()` to append the new list of waypoints onto the route. Otherwise, we call `insertContentOf()`. Since this method represents a search and an insert, its operational cost is **O**(*n*+1), where *n* is the number of elements in the existing `_route`:

```
public func startRoute() -> Bool
{
    if _route.count > 1
    {
        _current = startingLine()
        return moveToNextWaypoint()
    }
    return false
}
```

The `startRoute:` object is used to set our initial current position and denote that it has been deactivated. If we have two or more waypoints, we set the `_current` waypoint to the starting line and move to the next point. The `startRoute()` object has an **O**(1) operational cost:

```
public func moveToNextWaypoint() -> Bool
{
    if (_current != nil)
    {
        _current!.DeactivateWaypoint()
        if _current != self.finishLine()
        {
            let index = _route.indexOf(_current!)
            _current = _route[index!+1]
            return true
        }
        return false;
    }
    return false
}

public func moveToPreviousWaypoint() -> Bool
{
    if (_current != nil && _current != self.startingLine())
    {
        let index = _route.indexOf(_current!)
        _current = _route[index!-1]
        _current!.ReactivateWaypoint()
        return true
```

```
        }
    return false
}
```

In `moveToNextWaypoint()`, we verify that the current waypoint is not `nil`, and then we deactivate it. Next, we confirm that we are not at the finish line; and if not, we get the index of `_current` in the list, and assign the next highest index object to `_current`, and then we return `true`. The `moveToPreviousWaypoint()` method verifies that `_current` is not `nil` and makes sure that we are not at the starting line. If so, we set `_current` to the previous waypoint, reactivate it, and return `YES`. If any of our checks in these two methods fail, we return `NO`. Due to the need to search for a match for `_current`, each of these methods has an **O**(n+1) operational cost:

```
public func startingLine() -> Waypoint
{
    return _route.first!
}

public func finishLine() -> Waypoint
{
    return _route.last!
}

public func currentWaypoint() -> Waypoint
{
    return _current!;
}
```

We add the `startingLine()` and `finishLine()` methods to expose the head and tail nodes of the route collection. Finally, we add the `currentPosition()` method to expose which node in the route is our next immediate destination. Each of these methods has an **O**(1) operational cost.

Doubly linked list

A doubly linked list has the added overhead of n additional pointers where n is the length of the list. This additional pointer provides for simple reverse-traversal of the list. The added overhead is somewhat negligible and can typically be ignored except in very special cases. The append, insert, and remove operations still only cost **O**(1).

Searching

Array backed lists provides a $O(1)$ operational cost for searches if the index of the object is known in advance. Otherwise, all searches in lists cost $O(n)$ for unsorted lists and $O(\log n)$ for sorted lists where a binary search pattern is applied. Binary search algorithms will be discussed in much greater detail in `Chapter 13`, *Searching: Finding What You Need*.

A few pointers

Many languages view memory as a series of successive cells, each a certain number of bytes in size and each with a unique address. Pointers are memory management tools, which are really objects that reference, or point to, a memory cell's address. By utilizing pointers, a program can store objects in memory that are themselves larger than a single memory block. Some languages use the * operator to denote the assignment of a pointer. If you use Objective-C, or if you have worked with C/C++, you will already be very familiar with this operator. C#, Java, and Swift developers won't have had too much experience with this operator, but you should be familiarize yourself with how pointers work anyway, and here's why:

When an object in memory no longer has a pointer referencing its memory address, it should be de-allocated or removed from memory. Removing unused objects to prevent them from filling up memory is known as **memory management**. In some older languages, managing memory pointers is a tedious and often bug-prone task for the uninitiated. Most modern languages spare us from this drudgery through the use of some form of memory management device. C#, Java, and Swift use what's known as **Garbage Collection** (**GC**), while modern Objective-C provides **Automatic Reference Counting** (**ARC**) for automatic memory management.

Although these tools are great, you should not rely too completely on GC or ARC to manage your memory. GC and ARC are not perfect to start with, but both can be thwarted by a poor implementation. What will separate programmers from engineers is the ability to diagnose and repair memory management issues. Understanding pointers and their use will better equip you to catch what GC or ARC can very often miss.

A deeper discussion on pointers is beyond the scope of this book, but you should definitely take the time to research and familiarize yourself with this topic. Better still, spend some time writing code in a language that utilizes manual memory management like C or C++. Your career will thank you.

Summary

In this chapter, you learned the basic definition of the list structure, including the difference between sorted and unsorted list and array-backed versus linked lists. We discussed how to initialize lists or pseudo lists in each of the four languages we utilize in this text. We revisited the logged-in users class to see if we could improve its performance using lists instead of arrays and learned about interesting differences between the four languages including their use of generics and class clusters in the process. Next, we created a class to represent a route for biking enthusiasts, taking advantage of the properties of linked lists to manipulate and dynamically alter our collection of waypoints on the fly.

In our advanced topics section, we examined different implementations of list structures in more detail, including array-based lists, (singly) linked lists, and doubly linked lists. Finally, for each implementation, we evaluated the performance of basic operations including appending, inserting, removing, and searching nodes.

4
Stacks: LIFO Collections

A **stack** is an abstract data structure that serves as a collection of objects that are inserted and removed based on a **last-in first-out** (**LIFO**) principle. Accordingly, the two operations that most clearly define a stack structure are **push**, which adds objects to the collection, and **pop**, which removes objects from the collection. Other common operations include peek, clear, count, empty and full, all of which will be examined in the Advanced topics section later in this chapter.

Stacks can be either array-based or linked list-based. And, similar to linked lists, stacks can be either sorted or unsorted. Considering the structure of a linked list, a linked list-based stack will be more efficient for sorting operations than an array-based stack.

A stack data structure is well suited for any application that requires the ability to add and remove objects only from the tail of a list. A good example of this is backtracking along a specified path or series of operations. If the application allows for adding or removing data from any point within the collection, then a linked list would be a better choice than the data structures we have already examined.

In this chapter we will cover:

- Definition of a Stack data structure
- Initializing stacks
- Case study: motion planning algorithm
- Stack implementations
- Common stack operations
- Array-based stacks
- List-based stacks
- Searching

Initializing stacks

Each language provides varying levels of support for the stack data structure. The following are some examples of initializing the collection, adding an object to the collection, and then removing the top object from the collection.

C#

C# provides a concrete implementation of the stack data structure through the `Stack<T>` generic class.

```
Stack<MyObject> aStack = new Stack<MyObject>();
aStack.Push(anObject);
aStack.Pop();
```

Java

Java provides a concrete implementation of the stack data structure through the `Stack<T>` generic class.

```
Stack<MyObject> aStack = new Stack<MyObject>();
aStack.push(anObject);
aStack.pop();
```

Objective-C

Objective-C does not provide a concrete implementation of the stack data structure, but one can be easily creating using the class cluster `NSMutableArray`. Be aware that this will create an array-based implementation of the stack, which is generally less efficient than a linked list-based implementation.

```
NSMutableArray<MyObject *> *aStack = [NSMutableArray array];
[aStack addObject:anObject];
[aStack removeLastObject];
```

UINavigationController

It's not entirely accurate to state that Objective-C does not provide a stack data structure. Any amount of iOS programming in Objective-C will immediately expose a developer to an implementation of the stack data structure through use of the `UINavigationController` class.

The `UINavigationController` class manages the navigation stack, which is an array-based stack of view controllers. The class exposes several methods corresponding to the basic stack operations. These include `pushViewController:animated:` (*push*), `popViewControllerAnimated:` (*pop*), `popToRootViewControllerAnimated:` (*clear*…sort of), and `topViewController:` (*peek*). The navigation stack is never *empty* unless it is a *nil* object, and it can only be considered *full* when your app adds so many view controllers that the device runs out of system resources.

Since this is an array-based implementation, you can get the *count* of the stack by simply examining `count` on the collection itself. However, this is not a collection class you can use for just any purpose in your application. If you need a stack for more general circumstances, you are going to need to build one of your own.

Swift

Like Objective-C, Swift does not provide a concrete implementation of the stack data structure, but the Array class does expose some stack-like operations. The following example demonstrates the `popLast()` method, which removes and returns the last object in the array:

```
var aStack: Array [MyObject] ();
aStack.append(anObject)
aStack.popLast()
```

Stack operations

Not all implementations of stack data structures expose the same operational methods. However, the more common operations should be available or made available as needed by the developer. Each of these operations, whether they are part of an array-based implementation or a linked list-based one, have an operational cost of **O**(*1*).

- **push**: The push operation adds a new object onto the stack by either appending to the collection, if it is array-based, or adding a new node to the collection if it is linked list-based.
- **pop**: The pop operation is the opposite of push. In most implementations, the pop operation both removes and returns the top object off the stack to the caller.
- **peek**: The peek operation returns the top object off the stack to the caller, but does not remove the object from the collection.
- **clear**: The clear operation removes all objects from the stack, effectively resetting the collection to the empty state.
- **count**: The count operation, sometimes referred to as size or length, returns the total number of objects in the collection.
- **empty**: The empty operation typically returns a Boolean value denoting whether the collection has any objects.
- **full**: The full operation typically returns a Boolean value denoting whether the collection is at capacity or if there is still room to add more objects.

Case study: motion planning algorithm

Business problem: An industrial engineer programs a robotic manufacturing device to insert bolts in sequential receptacles on a widget, then attach and tighten nuts onto each bolt. The robot carriers a different tool for each operation, and can switch between them automatically on command. However, the process of switching between tools adds considerable time to the overall workflow, especially when the tool is switched back and forth over each bolt. This has been identified as a source of inefficiency, and the engineer wants to improve the speed of the process, reducing the overall time required to complete each unit.

In order to eliminate the latency introduced by switching between tools repeatedly, the engineer decides to program the robot to install all of the bolts first, and then switch tools before returning and installing all of the nuts. To further improve performance, he does not want the robot to reset to it's original starting position, but instead he wants it to retrace it's own steps while installing the nuts. By removing the reset before installing the nuts, his workflow eliminates two additional traversals across the widget. To accomplish his goals, the engineer needs to store the commands used to move the robot across the widget while inserting the bolts, and then play them back in reverse order.

Due to the nature of the data and the application, the class that represents the commands will need several basic pieces of functionality. First, it requires some mechanism for adding and removing commands as part of normal operation, as well as the ability to reset the system when the workflow encounters an error. In the case of a reset, the class must be able to report the count of commands currently waiting to be executed in order to account for inventory loss. Finally, the class should be able to easily report when the command list is at capacity or when the commands have all been completed.

C#

As we have seen in the prior implementation examples, C# conveniently exposes a stack data structure through the `Stack<T>` class. There follows an example of what a simple implementation in C# might look like:

```
public Stack<Command> _commandStack { get; private set; }
int _capacity;
public CommandStack(int commandCapacity)
{
    this._commandStack = new Stack<Command>(commandCapacity);
    this._capacity = commandCapacity;
}
```

Our class declares two fields. The first is _commandStack, which represents our stack data structure and the core of this class. The field is publicly visible but can only be modified by the methods within our class. The second field is _capacity. This field maintains our caller-defined maximum number of commands in the collection. Finally, the constructor initializes _commandStack and assigns commandCapacity to _capacity.

```
public bool IsFull()
{
    return this._commandStack.Count >= this._capacity;
}

public bool IsEmpty()
{
    return this._commandStack.Count == 0;
```

```
    }
```

Our first order of business is to establish some validation for our collection. The first validation method, `IsFull()`, checks if our stack has reached it's capacity. Since our business rules state that the robot must backtrack through all of its commands before it can proceed to a new widget, we will always track the number of commands that are being added into our collection. If for whatever reason we find that we have exceeded the pre-defined capacity for `_commandStack`, something has gone wrong during the previous backtracking operation and must be addressed. Therefore, we check that `_commandStack.Count` is greater than or equal to `_capacity` and return the value. `IsEmpty()` is the next validation method. This method must be called prior to any operations that could attempt to read from our stack by *peeking* at the collection. Both of these operations have an **O**(*1*) cost.

```
public bool PerformCommand(Command command)
{
    if (!this.IsFull())
    {
        this._commandStack.Push(command);
        return true;
    }
    return false;
}
```

The `PerformCommand(Command)` method provides the *push* functionality of our class. It accepts a single parameter of type `Command`, then checks if `_commandStack` is full. If it is full, the `PerformCmmand()` method returns `false`. Otherwise, we add `command` to our collection by calling the `Stack<T>.Push()` method. Then the method returns `true` to the caller. This operation has an **O**(*1*) cost.

```
public bool PerformCommands(List<Command> commands)
{
    bool inserted = true;
    foreach (Command c in commands)
    {
        inserted = this.PerformCommand(c);
    }
    return inserted;
}
```

In case the caller has a script of commands that can be executed successively, our class includes the `PerformCommands(List<Command>)` class. The `PerformCommands()` method accepts a list of commands, and inserts them sequentially into our collection by calling `PerformCommand()`. This operation has an **O**(*n*) cost, where *n* is the number of elements in `commands`.

```
public Command UndoCommand()
{
    return this._commandStack.Pop();
}
```

The `UndoCommand()` method provides the *pop* functionality of our class. It takes no parameters, but pops the last `Command` from our stack by calling `Stack<T>.Pop()`. The `Pop()` method removes the last `Command` from our `_commandStack` collection and returns it. If `_commandStack` is empty, `Pop()` returns a `null` object. This behavior actually works to our advantage, at least within the scope of this block of code. Since the `UndoCommand()` method is designed to return an instance of `Command`, we would be forced to return `null` anyway if `_commandStack` were empty. Therefore, it would be a waste of time to first check `IsEmpty()` before calling `Pop()`. This operation has an **O(*1*)** cost.

```
public void Reset()
{
    this._commandStack.Clear();
}

public int TotalCommands()
{
    return this._commandStack.Count;
}
```

The final pair of methods of our `CommandStack` class, `Reset()` and `TotalCommands()`, provide the *clear* functionality and the *count* functionality, respectively.

Java

As seen in the prior implementation examples, Java also exposes a stack data structure through the `Stack<E>` class, which is an extension of `Vector<E>` including five methods that allow it to operate as a class. However, the Java documentation for `Stack<E>` recommends that you should use `Deque<E>` in favor of `Stack<E>`. However, since we will be evaluating `Queue<E>` and `Deque<E>` in `Chapter` 5, *Queues: FIFO Collections*, we will use the `Stack<E>` class here. Here's an example of what a simple implementation in Java might look like:

```
private Stack<Command> _commandStack;
public Stack<Command> GetCommandStack()
{
    return this._commandStack;
}

int _capacity;
```

```
public CommandStack(int commandCapacity)
{
    this._commandStack = new Stack<Command>();
    this._capacity = commandCapacity;
}
```

Our class declares three fields. The first is _commandStack, which represents our stack data structure and the core of this class. The field is private, but we also declare a publicly visible getter called GetCommandStack(). This is necessary because only methods within our class should be able to modify the collection. The second field is _capacity. This field maintains our caller-defined maximum number of commands in the collection. Finally, the constructor initializes _commandStack and assigns commandCapacity to _capacity.

```
public boolean isFull()
{
    return this._commandStack.size() >= this._capacity;
}

public boolean isEmpty()
{
    return this._commandStack.empty();
}
```

Again, we need to establish some validation for our collection at the outset. The first validation method, isFull(), checks if our stack has reached it's capacity. Since our business rules state that the robot must backtrack through all of it's commands before it can proceed to a new widget, we will track the number of commands that are being added into our collection. If for whatever reason we find that we have exceeded the pre-defined capacity for _commandStack, something has gone wrong during the previous backtracking operation and must be addressed. Therefore, we check that _commandStack.size() is greater than or equal to _capacity and return the value. isEmpty() is the next validation method. This method must be called prior to any operations that could attempt to read from our stack by *peeking* at the collection. Both of these operations have an **O**(*1*) cost.

```
public boolean performCommand(Command command)
{
    if (!this.IsFull())
    {
        this._commandStack.push(command);
        return true;
    }
    return false;
}
```

The performCommand(Command) method provides the *push* functionality of our class. It accepts a single parameter of type Command, then checks if _commandStack is full. If it is full, performCmmand() returns false. Otherwise, we add command to our collection by calling the Stack<t>.push() method. Then the method returns true to the caller. This operation has an **O**(*1*) cost.

```
public boolean performCommands(List<Command> commands)
{
    boolean inserted = true;
    for (Command c : commands)
    {
        inserted = this.performCommand(c);
    }
    return inserted;
}
```

In case the caller has a script of commands that can be executed successively then our class includes the performCommands(List<Command>) method as well.
The performCommands() method accepts a list of commands, and inserts them sequentially into our collection by calling performCommand(). This operation has an **O**(*n*) cost, where *n* is the number of elements in commands.

```
public Command undoCommand()
{
    return this._commandStack.pop();
}
```

The undoCommand() method provides the *pop* functionality of our class. It takes no parameters, but pops the last Command from our stack by calling Stack<E>.pop(). The pop() method removes the last Command from our _commandStack collection and returns it. If _commandStack is empty, pop() returns a null object. As with the C# example, this behavior works to our advantage within the scope of this block of code. Since the undoCommand() method is designed to return an instance of Command, we would be forced to return null anyway if _commandStack were empty. Therefore, it would be a waste of time to first check isEmpty() before calling pop(). This operation has an **O**(*1*) cost.

```
public void reset()
{
    this._commandStack.removeAllElements();
}

public int totalCommands()
{
    return this._commandStack.size();
}
```

The final two methods of our `CommandStack` class, `Reset()` and `TotalCommands()`, provide the *clear* and *count* functionalities respectively.

Objective-C

As we have seen before (and probably will again before this text is through), Objective-C does not expose an explicit concrete implementation of the stack data structure, but instead provides the `NSMutableArray` class cluster for this purpose. Some could argue that this is a weakness in Objective-C, citing that by not providing methods for every conceivable operation that a developer could need is inconvenient. On the other hand, one could argue that Objective-C is much more powerful in its simplicity, providing the developer with a streamlined API and the basic components necessary to build whichever data structure he may require. I will leave you to come to your own conclusion on the matter. Meanwhile, here's an example of what a simple implementation in Objective-C might look like:

```objc
@interface EDSCommandStack()
{
    NSMutableArray<EDSCommand*> *_commandStack;
    NSInteger _capacity;
}

-(instancetype)initWithCommandCapacity:(NSInteger)commandCapacity
{
    if (self = [super init])
    {
        _commandStack = [NSMutableArray array];
        _capacity = capacity;
    }
    return self;
}
```

Our class declares two **ivar** properties. The first is _commandStack, which represents our stack data structure and the core of this class. The property is private, but we also declare a publicly visible accessor called `commandStack`. This is necessary because only methods within our class should be able to modify the collection. The second property is _capacity. This property maintains our caller defined maximum number of commands in the collection. Finally, the constructor initializes _commandStack and assigns commandCapacity to _capacity.

```objc
-(BOOL)isFull
{
    return [_commandStack count] >= _capacity;
}

-(BOOL)isEmpty
```

```
{
    return [_commandStack count] == 0;
}
```

Again, we need to establish some validation for our collection at the outset. The first validation method, isFull:, checks if our stack has reached it's capacity. Since our business rules state that the robot must backtrack through all of it's commands before it can proceed to a new widget, we will track the number of commands that are being added into our collection. If for whatever reason we find that we have exceeded the pre-defined capacity for _commandStack, something has gone wrong during the previous backtracking operation and must be addressed. Therefore, we check that [_commandStack count] is greater than or equal to _capacity and return the value. isEmpty: is the next validation method. Both of these operations have an **O**(*1*) cost.

 Since Objective-C is quite forgiving about passing around nil objects, you may not even consider isEmpty: to be a validation method but more of a property in its own right. However, consider that, if this method were declared as a property, we would need to declare it as readonly, in addition to including the method in our implementation file. Otherwise, Objective-C would dynamically generate the ivar _isEmpty on our behalf, and callers could modify the value directly. For the sake of simplicity and clarity, in this case it's better to just declare the value as a method.

```
-(BOOL)performCommand:(EDSCommand*)command
{
    if (![self isFull])
    {
        [_commandStack addObject:command];
        return YES;
    }
    return NO;
}
```

The performCommand: method provides the *push* functionality of our class. It accepts a single parameter of type Command, then checks if _commandStack is full. If it is full, performCmmand: returns NO. Otherwise, we add command to our collection by calling the addObject: method. Then the method returns YES to the caller. This operation has an **O**(*1*) cost.

```
-(BOOL)performCommands:(NSArray<EDSCommand*> *)commands
{
    bool inserted = true;
    for (EDSCommand *c in commands) {
        inserted =  [self performCommand:c];
```

```
        }
        return inserted;
    }
```

In case the caller has a script of commands that can be executed successively, our class includes the `performCommands:` class. `performCommands:` accepts an array of `EDSCommand` objects, and inserts them sequentially into our collection by calling `performCommand:`. This operation has an **O**(n) cost, where *n* is the number of elements in `commands`.

```
    - (EDSCommand*) undoCommand
    {
        EDSCommand *c = [_commandStack lastObject];
        [_commandStack removeLastObject];
        return c;
    }
```

The `undoCommand:` method provides the *pop* functionality of our class. Since Objective-C does not provide a concrete implementation of the stack structure, our class needs to be somewhat creative here. This method grabs the top object from the stack by calling `lastObject`, then it removes the command from the collection by calling `removeLastObject`. Finally, it returns the `Command` object `c` to the caller. This series of calls effectively mimics the *pop* functionality found in the concrete stack implementations of C# and Java. Although the method has to jump through a hoop or two to get the job done, we are always working with the last object in the array so this operation still has an **O**(*1*) cost.

```
    - (void) reset
    {
        [_commandStack removeAllObjects];
    }

    - (NSInteger) totalCommands
    {
        return [_commandStack count];
    }
```

Once again, the final pair of methods of our `CommandStack` class, `reset()` and `totalCommands()`, provide the *clear* functionality and the *count* functionality, respectively. Objective-C rules!

Swift

Like Objective-C, Swift does not expose a concrete implementation of the stack data structure, but we can use the mutable, generic `Array` class for this purpose. Here's an example of what a simple implementation in Swift might look like:

```
public fileprivate(set) var _commandStack: Array = [Command]()
public fileprivate(set) var _capacity: Int;

public init (commandCapacity: Int)
{
    _capacity = commandCapacity;
}
```

Our class declares two properties. The first is _commandStack, which represents our stack data structure and is again the core of this class. The property is publicly visible but can only be modified by the methods within our class. The second property is _capacity. This field maintains our caller defined maximum number of commands in the collection. Finally, the constructor initializes _commandStack and assigns commandCapacity to _capacity.

```
public func IsFull() -> Bool
{
    return _commandStack.count >= _capacity
}

public func IsEmpty() -> Bool
{
    return _commandStack.count == 0;
}
```

As with the examples in other languages, we include two validation methods called IsFull() and IsEmpty(). The IsFull() method checks if our stack has reached it's capacity. Since our business rules state that the robot must backtrack through all of it's commands before it can proceed to a new widget, we will track the number of commands that are being added into our collection. If for whatever reason we find that we have exceeded the pre-defined capacity for _commandStack, something has gone wrong with the previous backtracking operation and must be addressed. Therefore, we check that _commandStack.count is greater than or equal to _capacity and return the value. IsEmpty() must be called prior to any operations that could attempt to read from our stack by *peeking* at the collection. Both of these operations have an **O(1)** cost.

```
public func PerformCommand(_command: Command) -> Bool
{
    if (!IsFull())
    {
```

```
                _commandStack.append(command)
                return true;
        }
        return false;
}
```

The `PerformCommand(Command)` method provides the *push* functionality of our class. It accepts a single parameter of type `Command`, then checks if `_commandStack` is full. If it is full, the `PerformCmmand()` method returns `false`. Otherwise, we add `command` to our collection by calling the `Array.append()` method. Then the method returns `true` to the caller. This operation has an **O(*1*)** cost.

```
public func PerformCommands(_commands: [Command]) -> Bool
{
    var inserted: Bool = true;
    for c in commands
    {
        inserted = PerformCommand(c);
    }
    return inserted;
}
```

In case the caller has a script of commands that can be executed successively our class includes the `PerformCommands(List<Command>)` class. `PerformCommands()` accepts a list of commands, and inserts them sequentially into our collection by calling the `PerformCommand()` method. This operation has an **O(*n*)** cost, where *n* is the number of elements in `commands`.

```
public func UndoCommand() -> Command
{
    return _commandStack.popLast()!
}
```

The `UndoCommand()` method provides the *pop* functionality of our class. It takes no parameters, but pops the last `Command` from our stack by calling `Array.popLast()!` with the forced unwrapping operator to access the value *wrapped* inside the `return`, assuming the object is not `nil`. The `popLast()` method removes the top `Command` from our `_commandStack` collection and returns it. If `_commandStack` is empty, `popLast()` returns `nil`. As seen in Java and Objective-C, this behavior works to our advantage within the scope of this block of code. Since the `UndoCommand()` method is designed to return an instance of `Command`, we would be forced to return `nil` anyway if `_commandStack` were empty. Therefore, it would be a waste of time to first check `IsEmpty()` before calling `popLast()`. This operation has an **O(*1*)** cost.

```
public func Reset()
```

```
{
    _commandStack.removeAll()
}

public func TotalCommands() -> Int
{
    return _commandStack.count;
}
```

The final pair of methods of our `CommandStack` class, `Reset()` and `TotalCommands()`, provide the *clear* and *count* functionalities, respectively.

 The **nil coalescing operator**, or **null coalescing operator** as it is termed in other languages, is shorthand for the more verbose ternary operator and the explicit `if...else` statement. Languages such as C# and Swift designate `??` for this operator. Swift goes a step further by including the `!`, or unwrapping operator, for cases where a return value is optional, or potentially nil. The `??` operator in Swift is necessary for defining a default value when unwrapping an **optional** type.

Advanced topics – stack implementations

Now that we have seen how stacks are used in common practice, lets examine the different types of stack implementation you may encounter. The two most common implementations are the array-based stack and the linked list-based stack. We will examine each of these here.

Array-based stack

An array-based stack utilizes a mutable array to represent the collection. In this implementation, the 0 position in the array represents the *bottom* of the stack. Therefore, `array[0]` is the first object pushed onto the stack and the last one popped off. Array-based structures are not practical for a sorted stack as any reorganizing of the structure would require significantly more operational cost than that of a list-based stack. The Tower of Hanoi puzzle is the quintessential example of sorting am array-based stack, with an operational cost of $O(2^n)$, where n is the number of plates on the starting tower. The Tower of Hanoi puzzle will be examined in more detail in `Chapter 12`, *Sorting: Bringing Order Out Of Chaos*.

Linked list-based stack

The linked list-based stack utilizes a pointer to the *bottom* object on the stack, and subsequent pointers as each new object is linked from the last object in the list. Popping an object from the top of the stack simply involves removing the last object from the collection. For applications requiring sorted data, a linked list stack is far more efficient.

Summary

In this chapter we learned the basic definition of the Stack data structure, including how to initialize concrete implementations of the structure in each of the four languages we are discussing. Next, we discussed the most common operations associated with the stack data structure and their operational cost. We examined a case study using stacks to track commands passed to a robotic manufacturing device. These examples demonstrated how C# and Java provide concrete implementations of a stack whereas Objective-C and Swift do not. Finally, we examined the two most common types of stacks, the array-based and the linked-list-based, and showed how the array-based stack is not well suited for a sorted stack.

5

Queues: FIFO Collections

A **queue** is an abstract data structure that serves as a linear collection of objects that are inserted and removed based on the **first-in first-out** (**FIFO**) principle. The two most notable operations of a queue are **enqueue**, which adds objects to the tail or back of the collection, and **dequeue**, which removes objects from the head or front of the collection. The following figure demonstrates the queue data structure as well as these two basic operations. Other common operations include **peek**, **empty**, and **full**, all of which will be examined later in this chapter:

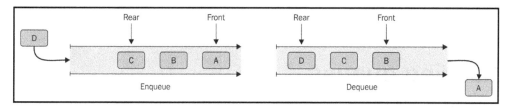

Queues are very similar to stacks and they share some of the same functionality. Even two of their primary operations are very similar, just implemented on opposite principles. Like a stack, a queue can be either array-based or linked list-based, and the linked list based version is more efficient in most cases. However, unlike a stack, which can be sorted or unsorted, a queue is not intended to be sorted at all and sorting a queue whenever an object is added to the collection results in a terrible $O(n.log(n))$ operational cost. One alternative version of the queue, called a **priority queue**, is based on a **heap** data structure. The priority queue does support a type of sorting, but it is still expensive and not generally used outside special applications.

Overall, a queue data structure is well suited for any application that requires the ability to prioritize operations on a *first-come first-served* basis. If you are having trouble visualizing a queue structure, just think of any time you had to stand in line. In primary school, we waited for the drinking fountain; in supermarkets, we wait for the cashier; in the deli, we wait for *our number*; in various government offices, we wait (and wait) for the next available teller. In fact, we have all been queuing since the day we were born... unless you are a twin in which case you started just a little sooner than most of us.

In this chapter, we will cover the following topics:

- Definition of a queue data structure
- Initializing queues
- Case study – customer service
- Queue implementations
- Common queue operations
- Array-based queues
- List-based queues
- Heap-based queues
- Double-ended queues
- Priority queues

Initializing queues

Each language provides varying levels of support for the queue data structure. Here are some examples of initializing the collection, adding an object to the back of the collection, and then removing the head object from the head of the collection.

C#

C# provides a concrete implementation of the queue data structure through the `Queue<T>` generic class:

```
Queue<MyObject> aQueue = new Queue<MyObject>();
aQueue.Enqueue(anObject);
aQueue.Dequeue();
```

Java

Java provides the abstract `Queue<E>` interface, and several concrete implementations of the queue data structure use this interface. Queue is also extended to the `Deque<E>` interface that represents a **double-ended queue**. The `ArrayDeque<E>` class is one concrete implementation of the `Deque<E>` interface:

```
ArrayDeque<MyObject> aQueue = new ArrayDeque<MyObject>();
aQueue.addLast(anObject);
aQueue.getFirst();
```

Objective-C

Objective-C does not provide a concrete implementation of the queue data structure, but one can be easily created using the `NSMutableArray` class cluster. Be aware that this will create an array-based implementation of the queue, which is *generally* less efficient than a linked list-based implementation:

```
NSMutableArray<MyObject *> *aStack = [NSMutableArray array];
[aStack addObject:anObject];
[aStack removeObjectAtIndex:0];
```

I was curious about the measurable difference in efficiency between a stack and a queue implemented with `NSMutableArray`, so I performed a series of simple tests. In these tests, I began by instantiating an `NSMutableArray` object with 1,000,000 `EDSUser` objects. In the first test, I treated the array as a stack and sequentially *popped* each item from the tail of the array by calling the `removeLastObject` object. In the second test, I treated the array as a queue and sequentially *dequeued* each user from the head of the array by calling `removeObjectAtIndex:0`. Using a `for` loop, I performed each series of tests 1,000 times, then averaged the time it took to remove all of the objects through each iteration. I was expecting the queue structure to operate on-par, or slightly less efficiently than, the stack structure, so I was surprised by these results:

Average stack time: 0.202993
Average queue time: 0.184913

As you can see, the queue structure actually performed slightly *better* than the stack structure, clocking in at about 18 milliseconds faster on average. Of course, results will vary between environments and 18 milliseconds is hardly worth noting, but following these tests, I feel confident in saying that the NSMutableArray class is suitably efficient to function as a queue structure. If you would like to run the test yourself, execute the static methods stackTest and queueTest in EDSCollectionTests found in the Objective-C code files for this text.

Swift

Like Objective-C, Swift does not provide a concrete implementation of the queue data structure, but the Array class can be used to implement the structure. The following example demonstrates the append() and popLast() methods:

```
var aStack: Array [MyObject]();
aStack.append(anObject)
aStack.popLast()
```

Queue operations

Not all implementations of queue data structures expose the same operational methods. However, the more common operations should be available or made available as needed by the developer:

- **enqueue**: The enqueue operation adds a new object into the back of the queue by either appending to the collection, if it is array-based, or adding a new node to the collection if it is linked list-based.
- **dequeue**: The dequeue operation is the opposite of enqueue. In most implementations, the dequeue operation both removes and returns the first object from the array or list to the caller.
- **peek**: The peek operation returns the first object from the array or list to the caller, but does not remove the object from the collection.
- **count**: The count operation returns the total number of objects or nodes currently in the collection.
- **empty**: The empty operation typically returns a boolean value denoting whether the collection has any objects.

- **full**: The full operation typically returns a boolean value denoting whether the collection is at capacity or if there is still room to add more objects. Not all implementations allow the caller to define the capacity, but this detail can be easily added using the queue count.

Case study: customer service

Business problem: A small software firm wants to break into a new market with a mobile app for tracking customer service requests at **Department of Motor Vehicles (DMV)** service locations. The app will allow users to *take a number* with their mobile device as they pass into a **geofence** representing the service area. This will allow customers to immediately move to the next available window or to take a seat and wait comfortably for an associate to assist them. One primary business requirement states that service will be delivered to customers on a first-come, first-served basis. In addition to the business requirements, the team wants to implement the core functionality with a generic design so that they can expand to new markets without the need to modify the underlying business logic.

The developer in charge of creating the core functionality decides that the class that keeps track of each customer's position in line should be bundled with the web service. This class will require some mechanism for adding and removing customers as part of normal operation, as well as the ability to clear all of the customers from the waiting list when the office closes for the day. As customers will typically like to know how long they can expect to wait before speaking with an associate; the class must also be able to report the number of customers currently waiting to be seen in total as well as those in front of the current customer. In the event that the customer's mobile device crosses the geofence again, they have effectively left the service area and forfeited their place in line. Therefore, although removing an object from the middle of a queue is not a queue-like operation, the class should also be able to cancel a customer's position from the line when they leave before speaking with an associate. Finally, the class should be able to report when the customer list is empty and when it has reached the occupancy limit of the location.

C#

As seen in the implementation examples, C# has queue support in the Queue<T> class. This class is generic, and it includes all of the basic operations that we need to implement the CustomerQueue class. Here's an example of what a simple implementation using C# might look like:

```
Queue<Customer> _custQueue;
int _cap;
```

```
public CustomerQueue(int capacity)
{
    _custQueue = new Queue<Customer>();
    _cap = capacity;
}
```

Our class declares two fields. The first is _custQueue, which represents our queue data structure and the core of this class. The field is private, so only methods within our class can modify it. The second field is _cap and it maintains our caller-defined maximum number of customers in the collection. Finally, the constructor initializes _custQueue and assigns capacity to _cap:

```
private bool CanCheckinCustomer()
{
    return this._custQueue.Count < this._cap;
}
```

The CanCheckinCustomer() method adds simple validation to CustomerQueue by confirming that _custQueue.Count is less than the defined capacity and returning the result:

```
public void CustomerCheckin(Customer c)
{
    if (this.CanCheckinCustomer())
    {
        this._custQueue.Enqueue(c);
    }
}
```

The first of the two basic queue operations, *enqueue*, is wrapped in the CustomerCheckin(Customer) method. This method validates that a new Customer object can be added and then calls Enqueue(T) to add c to the _custQueue collection. This operation has an **O(*1*)** cost:

```
public Customer CustomerConsultation()
{
    return this._custQueue.Peek();
}
```

In order to maintain an accurate number of customers currently waiting in line, we don't want to dequeue a customer until an associate has attended to their needs or inquiry. Therefore, when a customer has reached the head of the queue, the CustomerConsultation() method calls Peek(). This returns the next Customer object in _custQueue but does not remove that object from the collection. Effectively, this method provides the necessary data for a Now Serving: message or something equivalent. This operation has an **O(1)** cost:

```
public void CustomerCheckout()
{
    this._custQueue.Dequeue();
}
```

Once an associate has completed a transaction with their current customer, the customer's place in the queue can be cleared. The CustomerCheckout() method calls the Dequeue() method, which removes the Customer object from the front position of _custQueue. This operation has an **O(1)** cost:

```
public void ClearCustomers()
{
    this._custQueue.Clear();
}
```

When it's time to close the doors our class needs a way to clear out stragglers. The ClearCustomers() method provides the *clear* functionality, so our class can reset the collection to an empty state:

```
public void CustomerCancel(Customer c)
{
    Queue<Customer> tempQueue = new Queue<Customer>();
    foreach (Customer cust in this._custQueue)
    {
        if (cust.Equals(c))
        {
            continue;
        }
        tempQueue.Enqueue(c);
    }
    this._custQueue = tempQueue;
}
```

The `CustomerCancel(Customer)` method introduces the non-queue operation to remove the `Customer` objects from the `_custQueue` collection. As `Queue<T>` provides no interface for this operation, we need to improvise. This method first creates a temporary queue collection, `tempQueue`, then loops through every `Customer` object in `_custQueue`. If `cust` is not equal to `c`, it is added to `tempQueue`. When our `for` loop has finished, only those customers who are still in line will have been added to `tempQueue`. Finally, `tempQueue` is assigned to `_custQueue`. This operation has an **O**(n) cost, but this is acceptable as the method should not be called often as part of normal operations:

```
public int CustomerPosition(Customer c)
{
    if (this._custQueue.Contains(c))
    {
        int i = 0;
        foreach (Customer cust in this._custQueue)
        {
            if (cust.Equals(c))
            {
                return i;
            }
            i++;
        }
    }
    return -1;
}
```

In order to estimate a customer's current wait time with any sort of accuracy, it is necessary to know their position in the queue and `CustomerPosition(Customer)` gives our class that functionality. Again, `Queue<T>` does not provide the functionality, so we need to write our own. The `CustomerPosition(Customer)` method checks whether `_custQueue` contains the `Customer` we are looking for. If the collection does not contain `Customer c`, the method returns `-1`. Otherwise, it loops through the entire collection until `c` is located. The `Customer c` object located at the back of the queue is the worst case for both the `Queue<T>.Contains(T)` method and the `foreach` loop, each representing an **O**(n) cost. Since these operations are nested, this method carries an overall cost of **O**($2n$):

```
public int CustomersInLine()
{
    return this._custQueue.Count;
}

public bool IsLineEmpty()
{
    return this._custQueue.Count == 0;
}
```

```
public bool IsLineFull()
{
    return this._custQueue.Count == this.cap;
}
```

The final three methods, `CustomersInLine()`, `IsLineEmpty()`, and `IsLineFull()`, introduce the *count*, *empty*, and *full* functionality for our class. Each of these operations has an **O**(*1*) cost.

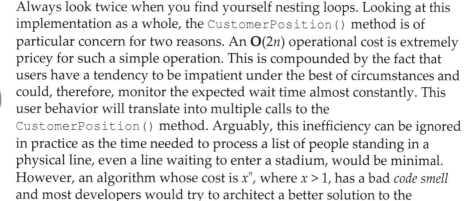

Nested Loops

Always look twice when you find yourself nesting loops. Looking at this implementation as a whole, the `CustomerPosition()` method is of particular concern for two reasons. An **O**(*2n*) operational cost is extremely pricey for such a simple operation. This is compounded by the fact that users have a tendency to be impatient under the best of circumstances and could, therefore, monitor the expected wait time almost constantly. This user behavior will translate into multiple calls to the `CustomerPosition()` method. Arguably, this inefficiency can be ignored in practice as the time needed to process a list of people standing in a physical line, even a line waiting to enter a stadium, would be minimal. However, an algorithm whose cost is x^n, where $x > 1$, has a bad *code smell* and most developers would try to architect a better solution to the problem before releasing this one into the wild.

Java

As discussed in the implementation examples, Java supports several concrete implementations of lists that could be used for a queue class, but the most appropriate versions conform to the double-ended queue `Dequeue<E>` interface. One concrete implementation is the `ArrayQueue<E>` class. Here's an example of what a simple implementation using Java's `ArrayQueue<E>` class might look like:

```
ArrayQueue<Customer> _custQueue;
int _cap;

public CustomerQueue(int capacity)
{
    _custQueue = new ArrayDeque<Customer>();
    _cap = capacity;
}
```

Our class declares two fields. The first is _custQueue, which represents our queue data structure and the core of this class. The field is private, so only methods within our class can modify it. The second field is _cap, which maintains our caller-defined maximum number of customers in the collection. Finally, the constructor initializes _custQueue and assigns capacity to _cap:

```
private boolean canCheckinCustomer()
{
    return this._custQueue.size() < this._cap;
}
```

The canCheckinCustomer() method adds simple validation to CustomerQueue by confirming that _custQueue.size() is less than the defined capacity and returning the result:

```
public void customerCheckin(Customer c)
{
    if (this.canCheckinCustomer())
    {
        this._custQueue.addLast(c);
    }
}
```

The first of the two basic queue operations, *enqueue*, is wrapped in the customerCheckin(Customer) method. This method confirms that we can add a new Customer to the queue then calls AddLast(E) to add c to the _custQueue collection. This operation has an **O***(1)* cost:

```
public Customer customerConsultation()
{
    return this._custQueue.peek();
}
```

In order to maintain an accurate number of customers currently waiting in line, we don't want to dequeue a customer until an associate has attended to their needs or inquiry. Therefore, when a customer has reached the head of the queue the customerConsultation() method calls peek(). This returns the next Customer in _custQueue, but it does not remove that object from the collection. This operation has an **O***(1)* cost:

```
public void customerCheckout()
{
    this._custQueue.removeFirst();
}
```

Once an associate has completed a transaction with their current customer, the customer's place in the queue can be cleared. The `customerCheckout()` method calls `Dequeue()`, which removes the `Customer` object from the front position of `_custQueue`. This operation has an **O(1)** cost:

```
public void clearCustomers()
{
    this._custQueue.clear();
}
```

The `ClearCustomers()` method provides the *clear* functionality, so our class can reset the collection to an empty state:

```
public void customerCancel(Customer c)
{
    this._custQueue.remove(c);
}
```

The `customerCancel(Customer)` method introduces the non-queue operation to remove `Customer` objects from the `_custQueue` collection. As `ArrayQueue<E>` provides the `remove(E)` method to remove any objects matching E from the queue, `customerCancel(Customer)` simply calls that method. This operation has an **O(n)** cost, but this is acceptable as the method should not be called often during normal operations:

```
public int customerPosition(Customer c)
{
    if (this._custQueue.contains(c))
    {
        int i = 0;
        for (Customer cust : this._custQueue)
        {
            if (cust.equals(c))
            {
                return i;
            }
            i++;
        }
    }

    return -1;
}
```

In order to estimate a customer's current wait time with any sort of accuracy, it is necessary to know their position in the queue. The `customerPosition(Customer)` method gives our class a position functionality. The `ArrayQueue<E>` interface does not provide this functionality, so we need to write our own. `CustomerPosition(Customer)` checks whether `_custQueue` contains the `Customer` we are looking for. If the collection does not contain `Customer c`, the method returns −1. Otherwise, it loops through the entire collection until `c` is located. The `Customer c` object located at the back of the queue is the worst case for both the `Queue<T>.Contains(T)` method and the `foreach` loop, each representing an **O(n)** cost. Since these operations are nested, this method carries an overall cost of **O(2n)**:

```
public int customersInLine()
{
    return this._custQueue.size();
}

public boolean isLineEmpty()
{
    return this._custQueue.size() == 0;
}

public boolean isLineFull()
{
    return this._custQueue.size() == this._cap;
}
```

The final three methods, `customersInLine()`, `isLineEmpty()`, and `isLineFull()`, introduce the *count, empty,* and *full* functionality for our class. Each of these operations have an **O(1)** cost.

Objective-C

As discussed earlier, Objective-C does not provide a concrete implementation of a queue data structure, but one can be mimicked easily using the `NSMutableArray` class cluster. Here's what a simple example of that implementation might look like:

```
NSMutableArray *_custQueue;
int _cap;

-(instancetype)initWithCapacity:(int)capacity
{
    if (self = [super init])
    {
        _custQueue = [NSMutableArray array];
        _cap = capacity;
```

```
    }
    return self;
}
```

Our class declares two **ivar** properties. The first is an `NSMutableArray` object named `_custQueue`, which represents our queue data structure and the core of this class. The second field is `_cap`. This field maintains our caller-defined maximum number of customers in the collection. Both of these are ivars, so only methods in our class can modify their values. Finally, the constructor initializes `_custQueue` and assigns `capacity` to `_cap`:

```
- (BOOL) canCheckinCustomer
{
    return [_custQueue count] < _cap;
}
```

The `canCheckinCustomer:` adds simple validation to `CustomerQueue` by confirming that `[_custQueue count]` is less than the defined capacity and returning the result:

```
- (void) checkInCustomer: (EDSCustomer*)c
{
    if ([self canCheckinCustomer])
    {
        [_custQueue addObject:c];
    }
}
```

The first of the two basic queue operations, *enqueue,* is wrapped in the `checkInCustomer:` method. This method confirms that we can add a new `Customer` to the queue and then calls `addObject:` method to add c to the `_custQueue` collection. This operation has an **O**(*1*) cost:

```
- (EDSCustomer*) customerConsultation
{
    return [_custQueue firstObject];
}
```

In order to maintain an accurate number of customers currently waiting in line, we don't want to *dequeue* a customer until an associate has attended to their needs or inquiry. Therefore, when a customer has reached the head of the queue, the `customerConsultation:` method returns `firstObject`. This returns the next `Customer` in `_custQueue`, but it does not remove that object from the collection. This operation has an **O**(*1*) cost:

```
- (void) checkoutCustomer
{
    [_custQueue removeObjectAtIndex:0];
```

```
    }
```

Once an associate has completed a transaction with their current customer, the customer's place in the queue can be cleared. The `checkoutCustomer:` method calls `removeObjectAtIndex:0`, which removes the `Customer` object from the front position of `_custQueue`. This operation has an **O**(*1*) cost:

```
- (void) clearCustomers
{
    [_custQueue removeAllObjects];
}
```

The `clearCustomers:` method provides the *clear* functionality, so our class can reset the collection to an empty state:

```
- (void) cancelCustomer: (EDSCustomer*) c
{
    NSUInteger index = [self positionOfCustomer:c];
    if (index != -1)
    {
        [_custQueue removeObjectAtIndex:index];
    }
}
```

The `cancelCustomer:` method introduces the non-queue operation to remove the `Customer` objects from the `_custQueue` collection. As `NSMutableArray` provides the `removeObjectAtIndex:` property, `cancelCustomer:` simply calls that method. This operation has an **O**(*n+1*) cost, but this is acceptable as the method should not be called often during normal operations:

```
- (NSUInteger) positionOfCustomer: (EDSCustomer*) c
{
    return [_custQueue indexOfObject:c];
}
```

In order to estimate a customer's current wait time with any sort of accuracy, it is necessary to know their position in the queue. The `positionOfCustomer:` property gives our class a position functionality by simply returning `indexOfObject:`. This operation has an **O**(*n*) cost:

```
- (NSUInteger) customersInLine
{
    return [_custQueue count];
}

- (BOOL) isLineEmpty
```

```
    {
        return [_custQueue count] == 0;
    }

    -(BOOL)isLineFull
    {
        return [_custQueue count] == _cap;
    }
```

The final three methods, `customersInLine()`, `isLineEmpty()`, and `isLineFull()`, introduce the *count*, *empty*, and *full* functionality for our class. Each of these operations has an **O**(*1*) cost.

Swift

As discussed earlier, Swift does not provide a concrete implementation of a queue data structure, but one can be mimicked easily using the `Array` class. Here's what a simple example of that implementation might look like:

```
    var _custQueue: Array = [Customer]()
    var _cap: Int;

    public init(capacity: Int)
    {
        _cap = capacity;
    }
```

Our class declares two properties. The first is an `Array` of `Customer` named `_custQueue`, which represents our queue data structure and the core of this class. The second field is `_cap`. This field maintains our caller-defined maximum number of customers in the collection. Both of these are private, so only methods in our class can modify their values. Finally, the constructor initializes `_custQueue` and assigns `capacity` to `_cap`:

```
    public func canCheckinCustomer() -> Bool
    {
        return _custQueue.count < _cap
    }
```

The `canCheckinCustomer()` method adds simple validation to `CustomerQueue` by confirming that `_custQueue.count` is less than the defined capacity and returning the result:

```
    public func checkInCustomer(c: Customer)
    {
        if canCheckinCustomer()
        {
```

```
            _custQueue.append
      }
  }
```

The first of the two basic queue operations, *enqueue*, is wrapped in the
`checkInCustomer()` method. This method confirms that we can add a new `Customer` to
the queue and then calls `append()` to add `c` to the `_custQueue` collection. This operation
has an **O**(1) cost:

```
  public func customerConsultation() -> Customer
  {
      return _custQueue.first!
  }
```

When a customer has reached the head of the queue, the `customerConsultation()`
method calls `first!`. This returns the next `Customer` in `_custQueue`, but does not remove
that object from the collection. This operation has an **O**(*1*) cost:

```
  public func checkoutCustomer()
  {
      _custQueue.removeFirst()
  }
```

Once an associate has completed a transaction with their current customer, the customer's
place in the queue can be cleared. The `checkoutCustomer()` method calls `removeFirst`,
which removes the `Customer` object from the front position of `_custQueue`. This operation
has an **O**(*1*) cost:

```
  public func clearCustomers()
  {
      _custQueue.removeAll()
  }
```

The `clearCustomers()` method provides the *clear* functionality, so our class can reset the
collection to an empty state:

```
  public func cancelCustomer(c: Customer)
  {
      if let index = _custQueue.index(of: c)
      {
          _custQueue.removeAtIndex(at: index)
      }
  }
```

The `cancelCustomer(Customer)` method introduces the non-queue operation to remove `Customer` objects from the `_custQueue` collection. As `Array` does not provide a simple remove type method, we need to improvise once again. Our code first sets the conditional `var index` using `indexOf()`. If `index` has a value, the method passes `index` to `removeAtIndex()`. This operation has an **O**(*n*+1) cost.

 In the Swift implementation, we are not calling the instance method `positionOfCustomer()`. This is because the `let ... =` notation is an initializer for a **conditional binding,** and `positionOfCustomer()` returns `Int`, which is not an optional value. Since both `positionOfCustomer()` and this method use the same `indexOf()` method call, there is no difference in the operational cost.

The code for this is shown as follows:

```
public func positionOfCustomer(c: Customer) -> Int
{
    return _custQueue.index(of:c)!
}
```

In order to estimate a customer's current wait time with any sort of accuracy, it is necessary to know their position in the queue. The `positionOfCustomer()` method gives our class position functionality by simply returning `indexOf()`. This operation has an **O**(*n*) cost:

```
public func customersInLine() -> Int
{
    return _custQueue.count
}

public func isLineEmpty() -> Bool
{
    return _custQueue.count == 0
}

public func isLineFull() -> Bool
{
    return _custQueue.count == _cap
}
```

The final three methods, `customersInLine()`, `isLineEmpty()`, and `isLineFull()`, introduce the *count, empty,* and *full* functionality for our class. Each of these operations has an **O**(*1*) cost. Overall, the Swift queue implementation is very similar to its counterparts in C#, Java, and Objective-C even though the Swift language is considerably different from the others.

Advanced topics

Queue data structures can be built on several different underlying data structures. Each foundation provides different advantages, and the type that is chosen typically depends on the application's needs. The three most common implementations are array based, linked list based, and heap-based.

Queue data structures are also found in two additional variations, including the double-ended queue and the priority queue. Again, each variation offers advantages and disadvantages and the type that is chosen will largely depend on the needs of your application.

Array-based queues

Array-based queues utilize a mutable array to represent the queue. Both of the examples in Objective-C and Swift take this form. In this implementation, the [0] position of the array represents the head or front of the queue. Although, generally speaking, queues are strictly FIFO collections and developers should not attempt to sort them, array-based queues are particularly difficult and costly to sort. If your application absolutely requires a sorted collection, you should consider using some other data structure entirely, such as a list.

Linked list-based queues

The **linked list-based queues** utilize a pointer to the front of the queue, and subsequent pointers as each new object is appended onto the collection. Dequeing an object from the front of the line simply involves moving the head pointer from the object at node 0 to the object at node 1. If your collection of objects must be a sorted queue, prefer a link-based queue to an array-based one.

Heap-based queues

A **heap-based queue** is a queue created with a **heap** collection as it's backer. Heaps are themselves specialized **tree-based data structures** where the objects are naturally sorted in ascending (**min heap**) or descending (**max heap**) order based on some value or property native to the object.

Heaps should not be confused with the heap, or the pool of dynamically allocated memory, of a computer system. We will discuss the concept of heaps in greater detail in `Chapter 10`, *Heaps: Ordered Trees*. Methods for sorting heap data structures will be discussed extensively in `Chapter 12`, *Sorting: Bringing Order Out Of Chaos*.

Double-ended queues

A **double-ended queue** is a collection where objects can be added to or removed from either the front or the back. The `ArrayQueue<E>` interface is Java's concrete implementation of the `Queue<E>` interface and is an example of a double-ended queue.

Priority queues

A **priority queue** sorts objects in the collection based on some value or **priority**. Due to the natural hierarchical structure of a heap, priority queues are most often implemented as a heap-based queue. In this design, objects with a higher priority naturally sort closest to the front of the line so that, each time an object is dequeued, it is always the one with the highest priority. In the case where two or more objects share a priority, the object that has been in the queue longest will be dequeued first.

Summary

In this chapter, you learned the basic definition of the queue data structure, including how to initialize concrete implementations of the structure in each of the four languages we are discussing. Next, we discussed the most common operations associated with the queue data structure and their operational cost. We examined an example application using queues to track customers waiting in a *first-come, first-served* line. These examples demonstrated how C# and Java provided concrete implementations of a queue, whereas Objective-C and Swift do not. Following this, we examined the three most common types of queue implementations, including array-based, linked-list based, and heap-based queues. Finally, we looked at double-ended and priority variations of the queue data structure.

6
Dictionaries: Keyed Collections

A **dictionary** is an abstract data structure that can be described as a collection of keys and associated values, where each key only appears once within the collection. This associated relationship between the keys and values is why dictionaries are sometimes referred to as **associative arrays**. Dictionaries are also known as **maps**, or more specifically, **hash maps** for **hash table**-based dictionaries and **tree maps** for **search tree**-based dictionaries. The four most common functions associated with a dictionary are **add**, **update**, **get**, and **remove**. Other common operations include **contains**, **count**, **reassign**, and **set**. Each of these operations will be examined in detail later in this chapter.

The mapped, or associative, nature of dictionaries allows for extremely efficient insert, search, and update operations. By specifying the key when creating, editing, or getting a value, most operations in a well-designed dictionary have a minimal $O(1)$ cost. Perhaps, it's because of this efficiency that dictionaries are one of the most common data structures you will encounter in your day-to-day development experience.

You might be wondering why something described as a collection of associated keys and values should be referred to as a dictionary. This name is an analogy with a physical dictionary, where each word (key) has an associated definition (value). If this is still a little too abstract, consider a valet service. When you pull up a car to an event, you step out of your car and someone hands you a little ticket before driving away with your vehicle. This ticket represents your car, and only your car. There are no other tickets with the same identifier as the one you are now holding. Therefore, there is only one-way to get your car back is presenting this specific ticket to the valet service. Once you do so, someone rolls up with your vehicle, you hand them a tip, and then you drive away.

This process is a concrete example of the dictionary data structure. Each ticket represents a *key*, while each vehicle represents a *value* of some type. Each key is unique and uniquely identifies one specific value. When your code calls for a value, the valet service is the *collection* that uses the key to locate and return the value you are looking for. Tipping your development machine is optional.

In this chapter, we will cover the following topics:

- Definition of a dictionary data structure
- Initializing dictionaries
- Hash tables
- Common dictionary operations
- Case study – arcade ticket totals
- Hash table based dictionaries
- Search tree based dictionaries

Initializing dictionaries

Dictionaries are so commonplace that it's no wonder that each of the languages we are examining supports them with concrete implementations. Here are some examples of initializing a dictionary, adding a few key/value pairs to the collection, and then removing one of those pairs from the collection.

C#

C# provides a concrete implementation of the dictionary data structure through the `Dictionary<TKey, TValue>` class. Since this class is generic, the caller may define the types used for both the keys and values. Here is an example:

```
Dictionary<string, int> dict = new Dictionary<string, int>();
```

This example initializes a new dictionary where the keys will be `string` types, and the values will be `int` types:

```
dict.Add("green", 1);
dict.Add("yellow", 2);
dict.Add("red", 3);
dict.Add("blue", 4);
dict.Remove("blue");
Console.WriteLine("{0}", dict["red"]);

// Output: 3
```

Java

Java provides a `Dictionary<K, V>` class, but it has been recently deprecated in favor of any class that implements the `Map<K, V>` interface. Here, we'll look at an example of the `HashMap<K, V>` class. This class extends `AbstractMap<K, V>` and implements the `Map<K, V>` interface:

```
HashMap<String, String> dict = new HashMap<String, String>();
dict.put("green", "1");
dict.put("yellow", "2");
dict.put("red", "3");
dict.put("blue", "4");
dict.remove("blue");
System.out.println(dict.get("red"));

// Output: 3
```

This class is called `HashMap` because it is a concrete, hash table based implementation of a map. It is interesting to note that Java will not permit primitives to be used as either the keys or the values in a `HashMap` class, so in our preceding example, we are substituting String types for our values.

Hash tables

Since one of Java's dictionary implementations is called a **hash map**, this seems like a good time to introduce **hash tables**, which are sometimes referred to as hash maps. Hash tables use a **hash function** to map data to indexed positions in an array. Technically, a hash function is any function that can be used to plot data of a random size to data of a static size.

In well-designed hash tables, the search, insert, and delete functions have an **O**(1) cost, as the complexity is independent of the number of elements the collection contains. In many situations, hash tables are much more efficient in comparison to arrays, lists, or other lookup data structures. This is the reason they are so frequently used to build dictionaries. This is also the reason they are commonly used in database indexing, caches, and as the foundation of the **set** data structure. We will discuss sets in more detail in `Chapter 7`, *Sets: No Duplicates*.

In truth, hash tables are a data structure unto themselves, although they are most commonly used to create associative arrays. So, why then are we not examining the hash table data structure in more depth? In most languages, a dictionary is preferred over a hash table for similar applications. This is because dictionaries are **generically typed**, while hash tables rely on the language's root object type to assign values internally, such as C#'s object type. While hash tables permit virtually any object to be used as a key or value, a generically typed dictionary will limit the caller to assigning only objects of the declared types as the key or value of an element. This approach is both type-safe as well as more efficient because values do not need to be **boxed** and **unboxed** (cast) every time a value is updated or retrieved.

That being said, do not make the mistake of assuming that a dictionary is simply a hash table by another name. It is true that a hash table roughly corresponds to some variation of Dictionary<object, object>, but it is a different class with different functionality and methods.

Objective-C

Objective-C provides immutable as well as mutable dictionary classes, NSDictionary and NSMutableDictionary, respectively. Since we'll be working with a mutable dictionary in our example later, let's just examine NSDictionary here. NSDictionary can be initialized with a literal array of *1...n* key/value pairs using the @{K : V, K : V} syntax. There are also two common initializer methods. The first is dictionaryWithObjectsAndKeys:, which accepts an array of object/key pairs terminated by nil. The second is dictionaryWithObjects:forKeys:, which accepts an array of objects and a second array of keys. Similar to Java's HashMap, Objective-C's NSDictionary and NSMutableDictionary class clusters do not permit scalar data to be used as keys or values:

```
NSDictionary *dict = [NSDictionary dictionaryWithObjectsAndKeys:
[NSNumber numberWithInt:1], @"green",
[NSNumber numberWithInt:2], @"yellow",
[NSNumber numberwithInt:3], @"red", nil];

NSArray *colors = @[@"green", @"yellow", @"red"];
NSArray *positions = @[[NSNumber numberWithInt:1],
                       [NSNumber numberWithInt:2],
                       [NSNumber numberWithInt:3]];

dict = [NSDictionary dictionaryWithObjects:positions forKeys:colors];
NSLog(@"%li", (long)[(NSNumber*)[_points valueForKey:@"red"]
```

```
        integerValue]);

        // Output: 3
```

You might notice that the `dictionaryWithObjects:forKeys:` approach is more verbose, making it slightly more readable. However, you must take extra care to ensure that your keys and values are correctly mapped to one another.

Swift

Dictionaries in Swift are created using the `Dictionary` class. Swift dictionaries are mutable when initialized as variables using `var`, but can also be created as immutable by initializing them as constants using `let`. Keys used in the dictionary can be either integers or strings. The `Dictionary` class can also accept values of any type, including those types normally considered primitives in other languages, since these are actually named types in Swift and are defined in the Swift standard library using structures. In either case, both your key and value types must be declared when the collection is initialized, and these cannot be changed later. Since we'll be working with a variable, or mutable, dictionary later, we'll initialize a constant immutable collection here:

```
        let dict:[String: Int] = ["green":1, "yellow":2, "red":3]
        print(dict[red])

        // Output: 3
```

 We will examine **structures** in more detail later in `Chapter 8`, *Structs: Complex Types*.

Dictionary operations

Not all concrete implementations of the dictionary data structures expose the same operational methods. However, the more common operations should be available or made available as needed by the developer. Here are some operations:

- **add**: The add operation, sometimes referred to as an insert, introduces a new key/value pair into the collection. Add operations have an **O(***1***)** cost.
- **get**: The get operation, sometimes called a **lookup**, returns the value mapped to a given key. If no value is found for the given key, some dictionaries will raise an *exception*. By specifying the key, get operations have an **O(***1***)** cost.

- **update**: The update operation allows the caller to modify a value that is already a part of the collection. Not all dictionary implementations provide a defined update method, but rather support updating a value via *reference*. This means the object can be modified directly once it has been pulled from the dictionary using a get operation. By specifying the key, update operations have an $O(1)$ cost.
- **remove**: The remove, or *delete*, operation will remove a key/value pair from the collection given a valid key. Most dictionaries will gracefully ignore a specified key that does not exist. By specifying the key, remove operations have an $O(1)$ cost.
- **contains**: The contains operation returns a Boolean value, identifying whether a given key can be found in the collection. Contains operations must iterate through the collection of keys in the dictionary to search for a match. Therefore, this operation has a worst-case cost of $O(n)$.
- **count**: Count, sometimes referred to as *size*, can be either a method or simply a property of the collection that returns the number of key/value elements within the dictionary. Count is typically a simple property on the collection and, therefore, has an $O(1)$ cost.
- **reassign**: A reassign operation allows for assigning a new value to an existing key. This operation is somewhat less common in many implementations as the update operation serves as the reassign operation. By specifying the key, reassign operations have an $O(1)$ cost.
- **set**: The set operation is sometimes seen as a single replacement for both add and reassign operations. Set will either insert a new key/value pair if the key does not already exist, or it will reassign the value to the specified key. There is no need to support set, add, and reassign operations within the same implementation. As with add and update, set operations have an $O(1)$ cost.

Case study: arcade ticket totals

Business problem: an arcade manager wants to cut costs by eliminating physical tickets from her games. Tickets are very costly and wasteful, since they must be thrown away or recycled once a customer has redeemed them. She has decided to introduce an electronic point system that allows customers to earn points rather than tickets, and store the points digitally. Once she has the hardware in place to support the changeover, she needs a mobile app that allows her and her customers to efficiently track their current point totals.

This app has several key requirements. First, it should store data for the customer based solely on the name they provide during check-in. Second, it must keep a running total of all points earned, lost, and redeemed. Third, it must be capable of showing the customer's points and the total number of customers in the arcade at any given time. Finally, it should allow for the removal of individual customer records or all customer records at once. Based on these requirements, the developer decides that a dictionary will be the most efficient way to track all customer points, so the core class's functionality will be based on that data structure.

C#

C# provides the generic collection `Dictionary<TKey, TValue>`. This class provides all of the basic operations we would expect to see in a concrete dictionary implementation, with the added benefit of generic type casting:

```
Dictionary<string, int> _points;
public PointsDictionary()
{
    _points = new Dictionary<string, int>();
}
```

Using `Dictionary<TKey, TValue>`, we create one private field for our class called `_points`. Our constructor instantiates this field, giving us the underlying data structure to build our `PointsDictionary` class on:

```
//Update - private
private int UpdateCustomerPoints(string customerName, int points)
{
    if (this.CustomerExists(customerName))
    {
        _points[customerName] = _points[customerName] += points;
        return _points[customerName];
    }
    return 0;
}
```

The `UpdateCustomerPoints(string customerName, int points)` method provides the core *update* functionality for our class. This method first confirms that the key exists in our collection. If the key does not exist, the method immediately returns 0. Otherwise, we use subscript notation to both get the key and update the key's value. Using subscript notation once again, we finally return the updated value to the caller.

We keep this method private, choosing to create several additional update methods that are more fitting to our business requirements. These public methods, discussed later, will expose the update functionality to the caller:

```
//Add
public void RegisterCustomer(string customerName)
{
    this.RegisterCustomer(customerName, 0);
}

public void RegisterCustomer(string customerName, int previousBalance)
{
    _points.Add(customerName, previousBalance);
}
```

The two `RegisterCustomer()` methods provide the *add* functionality to our class. In both cases, we require a customer name to act as the key. If a returning customer checks in with a previous balance, we want to acknowledge it so that our class overloads the method. Ultimately, the overloaded method calls `Dictionary<TKey, TValue>.Add(T)` to insert a new record into the collection:

```
//Get
public int GetCustomerPoints(string customerName)
{
    int points;
    _points.TryGetValue(customerName, out points);

    return points;
}
```

Our *get* functionality is introduced by the `GetCustomerPoints(string customerName)` method. In this method, we use `TryGetValue()` to safely confirm that the `customerName` key exists and to get the value at the same time. If the key does not exist, the app handles the issue gracefully and does not assign any value to `points`. The method then returns whatever value is currently set in `points`:

```
//Update - public
public int AddCustomerPoints(string customerName, int points)
{
    return this.UpdateCustomerPoints(customerName, points);
}

public int RemoveCustomerPoints(string customerName, int points)
{
    return this.UpdateCustomerPoints(customerName, -points);
}
```

```
public int RedeemCustomerPoints(string customerName, int points)
{
    //Perform any accounting actions
    return this.UpdateCustomerPoints(customerName, -points);
}
```

Next, we come to the public update methods, AddCustomerPoints(string customerName, int points), RemoveCustomerPoints(string customerName, int points), and RedeemCustomerPoints(string customerName, int points). Each of these methods calls the private UpdateCustomerPoints(string customerName, int points) method, but first it negates points in the case of the latter two:

```
//Remove
public int CustomerCheckout(string customerName)
{
    int points = this.GetCustomerPoints(customerName);
    _points.Remove(customerName);
    return points;
}
```

The CustomerCheckout(string customerName) method introduces the collection's *remove* functionality. The method first records the final value for the customer key, and then calls Dictionary<TKey, TValue>.Remove(T) to delete the customer's key from the collection. Finally, it returns the customer's last point value to the caller:

```
//Contains
public bool CustomerExists(string customerName)
{
    return _points.ContainsKey(customerName);
}
```

The Dictionary<TKey, TValue> interface conveniently provides the ContainsKey() method, which the CustomerExists(string customerName) method uses to introduce our class' *contains* functionality:

```
//Count
public int CustomersOnPremises()
{
    return _points.Count;
}
```

Using the `Count` field on the `Dictionary<TKey, TValue>` class, `CustomersOnPremises()` provides the *count* functionality:

```
public void ClosingTime()
{
    //Perform any accounting actions
    _points.Clear();
}
```

Finally, as per our business requirements, we need a way to remove all of the objects from the collection. The `ClosingTime()` method uses the `Dictionary<TKey, TValue>.Clear()` method to accomplish this task.

Java

As mentioned previously, Java supplies a `Dictionary` class, but it has been deprecated in favor of any class that implements `Map<K, V>` interface. The `HashMap<K, V>` implements the interface and provides a dictionary based on a hash table. As with the previous C# example, the `HashMap<K, V>` class exposes all the basic operations we would expect to see in a concrete implementation of a dictionary:

```
HashMap<String, Integer> _points;
public PointsDictionary()
{
    _points = new HashMap<>();
}
```

An instance of `HashMap<K, V>` becomes the core of our Java `PointsDictionary` class. Again, we name the private field _points, while our constructor instantiates the collection. You may note that we are not explicitly declaring types when we instantiate the _points collection. In Java, it is not necessary to explicitly declare types at instantiation when we have already defined the key and value types at declaration. You can declare the types if you really want to, but this will generate a warning in the compiler:

```
private Integer UpdateCustomerPoints(String customerName, int points)
{
    if (this.CustomerExists(customerName))
    {
        _points.put(customerName, _points.get(customerName) + points);
        return _points.get(customerName);
    }
    return 0;
}
```

The `UpdateCustomerPoints(string customerName, int points)` method provides the core *update* functionality for our class. This method first confirms that the key exists in our collection. If the key does not exist, the method immediately returns 0. Otherwise, we use `put()` and `get()` to update the key's value. Using `get()` once again, we finally return the updated value to the caller:

```
//Add
public void RegisterCustomer(String customerName)
{
    this.RegisterCustomer(customerName, 0);
}

public void RegisterCustomer(String customerName, int previousBalance)
{
    _points.put(customerName, previousBalance);
}
```

The two `RegisterCustomer()` methods provide the *add* functionality to our class. In both cases, we require a customer name to act as the key. If a returning customer is checking in with a previous balance, we want to acknowledge it so that our class overloads the method. Ultimately, the overloaded method calls `HashMap<K, V>.put(E)` to insert a new record into the collection:

```
//Get
public Integer GetCustomerPoints(String customerName)
{
    return _points.get(customerName) == null ? 0 :
_points.get(customerName);
}
```

Our *get* functionality is introduced by the `GetCustomerPoints(string customerName)` method. In this method, we use the `get()` method, checking that the return value is not null, to safely confirm that the `customerName` key exists. Using a ternary operator, we return 0 if it does not or the value if it does:

```
//Update
public Integer AddCustomerPoints(String customerName, int points)
{
    return this.UpdateCustomerPoints(customerName, points);
}

public Integer RemoveCustomerPoints(String customerName, int points)
{
    return this.UpdateCustomerPoints(customerName, -points);
}
```

```
public Integer RedeemCustomerPoints(String customerName, int points)
{
    //Perform any accounting actions
    return this.UpdateCustomerPoints(customerName, -points);
}
```

Next, we come to the public update methods, AddCustomerPoints(String customerName, int points), RemoveCustomerPoints(String customerName, int points), and RedeemCustomerPoints(String customerName, int points). Each of these methods calls the private UpdateCustomerPoints(String customerName, int points) method, but first it negates points in the case of the latter two:

```
//Remove
public Integer CustomerCheckout(String customerName)
{
    Integer points = this.GetCustomerPoints(customerName);
    _points.remove(customerName);
    return points;
}
```

The CustomerCheckout(String customerName) method introduces the collection's *remove* functionality. The method first records the final value for the customer key and then calls HashMap<K, V>.remove(E) to delete the customer's key from the collection. Finally, it returns the customer's last point value to the caller:

```
//Contains
public boolean CustomerExists(String customerName)
{
    return _points.containsKey(customerName);
}
```

The HashMap<K, V> method conveniently provides the containsKey() method, which the CustomerExists(String customerName) method uses to introduce our class' *contains* functionality:

```
//Count
public int CustomersOnPremises()
{
    return _points.size();
}
```

Using the size() field on the HashMap<K, V> class, CustomersOnPremises() provides the *count* functionality:

```
//Clear
public void ClosingTime()
```

```
    {
        //Perform accounting actions
        _points.clear();
    }
```

Finally, per our business requirements, we need a way to remove all of the objects from the collection. The `ClosingTime()` method uses the `HashMap<K, V>.clear()` method to accomplish this task.

Objective-C

For our Objective-C example, we will use the `NSMutableDictionary` class cluster to represent our collection. The `NSMutableDictionary` class cluster does not expose all of the basic operations we would expect to see in a concrete implementation of a dictionary, but those that are not readily available are very simple to replicate. It is important to note that Objective-C does not allow scalar values to be added to instances of the `NSDictionary` or `NSMutableDictionary` collections. Therefore, since we are trying to store integers for our values, we will have to place each of the `NSInteger` scalars in `NSNumber` wrappers before they can be added to the collection. Unfortunately, this adds some overhead to our implementation as all of these values must be boxed and unboxed as they are inserted or retrieved from the collection:

```
@interface EDSPointsDictionary ()
{
    NSMutableDictionary<NSString*, NSNumber*> *_points;
}

@implementation EDSPointsDictionary

-(instancetype)init
{
    if (self = [super init])
    {
        _points = [NSMutableDictionary dictionary];
    }
    return self;
}
```

Using the class cluster `NSMutableDictionary`, we create an ivar for our class called `_points`. Our initializer instantiates this dictionary, giving us the underlying data structure to build our `PointsDictionary` class on:

```
-(NSInteger)updatePoints:(NSInteger)points
    forCustomer:(NSString*)customerName
{
    if ([self customerExists:customerName])
```

```
        {
            NSInteger exPoints = [[_points objectForKey:customerName]
integerValue];
            exPoints += points;
            [_points setValue:[NSNumber numberWithInteger:exPoints]
forKey:customerName];
            return [[_points objectForKey:customerName] integerValue];
        }
        return 0;
    }
```

The `updatePoints:forCustomer:` method provides the core *update* functionality for our class. This method first confirms that the key exists in our collection by calling our `customerExists:` method. If the key does not exist, the method immediately returns 0. Otherwise, the method uses `objectForKey:` to get the stored `NSNumber` object. From this, we immediately extract the `NSInteger` value by calling `integerValue` on the object. Next, the value is adjusted and updated in the dictionary using `setValue:forKey:`. Using `objectForKey:` once again, we finally return the updated value to the caller:

```
//Add
-(void)registerCustomer:(NSString*)customerName
{
    [self registerCustomer:customerName withPreviousBalance:0];
}

-(void)registerCustomer:(NSString*)customerName
    withPreviousBalance:(NSInteger)previousBalance
{
    NSNumber *points = [NSNumber numberWithInteger:previousBalance];
    [_points setObject:points forKey:customerName];
}
```

The `registerCustomer:` methods provide the *add* functionality to our class. In both cases, we require a customer name to act as the key. If a returning customer is checking in with a previous balance, we want to acknowledge it so that our class overloads the method in `registerCustomer:withPreviousBalance:`. Ultimately, the overloaded method is calls `setObject:forKey:` to insert a new key/value pair into the dictionary:

```
//Get
-(NSInteger)getCustomerPoints:(NSString*)customerName
{
    NSNumber *rawsPoints = [_points objectForKey:customerName];
    return rawsPoints ? [rawsPoints integerValue] : 0;
}
```

Our *get* functionality is introduced by the `getCustomerPoints:` method. In this method, we use `objectForKey:` to get the `NSNumber` object for the passed key and assign it to `rawPoints`. Next, the method checks that `rawPoints` is not `nil` and returns `integerValue` of `rawPoints` if it is available, or 0 otherwise:

```
//Update
-(NSInteger)addPoints:(NSInteger)points
    toCustomer:(NSString*)customerName
{
    return [self updatePoints:points forCustomer:customerName];
}

-(NSInteger)removePoints:(NSInteger)points
    fromCustomer:(NSString*)customerName
{
    return [self updatePoints:-points forCustomer:customerName];
}

-(NSInteger)redeemPoints:(NSInteger)points
    forCustomer:(NSString*)customerName
{
    //Perform any accounting actions
    return [self updatePoints:-points forCustomer:customerName];
}
```

Next, we come to the public update methods, `addPoints:toCustomer:`, `removePoints:fromCustomer:` and `redeemPoints:forCustomer:`. Each of these methods calls the private `updatePoints:forCustomer:` method, but first, it negates `points` in the case of the latter two:

```
-(NSInteger)customerCheckout:(NSString*)customerName
{
    NSInteger points = [[_points objectForKey:customerName]
integerValue];
    [_points removeObjectForKey:customerName];
    return points;
}
```

The `customerCheckout:`, method introduces the collection's *remove* functionality. The method first records the final value for the customer key, and then calls `removeObjectForKey:` to delete the customer's key from the collection. Finally, it returns the customer's last point value to the caller:

```
//Contains
-(bool)customerExists:(NSString*)customerName
{
```

```
      return [_points objectForKey:customerName];
}
```

The `NSMutableDictionary` class cluster does not provide a mechanism for determining whether a key exists in the collection. A simple workaround is to just call `objectForKey:`; and if the returned value is `nil`, the key does not exist, and `nil` evaluates to `NO`. Based on this principle, therefore, our `customerExists:` method simply returns `objectForKey:`, allowing the return value to be evaluated as a `BOOL`:

```
//Count
-(NSInteger)customersOnPremises
{
    return [_points count];
}
```

Using the `count` property on the `NSDictionary` class, `customersOnPremises` provides the *count* functionality:

```
//Clear
-(void)closingTime
{
    [_points removeAllObjects];
}
```

Finally, as per our business requirements, we need a way to remove all of the objects from the collection. The `closingTime` method uses the `removeAllObjects` method to accomplish this task.

Swift

Swift provides the `Dictionary` class which, like Objective-C's `NSMutableDictionary`, does not expose all of the operations we would expect to see in a concrete implementation of a dictionary data structure. Again, these missing functions are simple to replicate. It is worth noting the difference between the Swift dictionary's value type and its Objective-C counterpart. Since primitives in Swift are wrapped in `struct`s, we have no problem adding `Int` objects to our collection:

```
var _points = Dictionary<String, Int>()
```

Using the `Dictionary` class, we create a private property for our class called `_points`. Since our property is declared and instantiated simultaneously and there is no other custom code requiring instantiation, we can exclude the explicit public initializer and rely on the default initializer:

```
public func updatePointsForCustomer(points: Int, customerName: String)
-> Int
    {
        if customerExists(customerName)
        {
            _points[customerName] = _points[customerName]! + points
            return _points[customerName]!
        }
        return 0
    }
```

The `updatePointsForCustomer()` method provides the core *update* functionality for our class. This method first confirms that the key exists in our collection by calling our `customerExists()` method. If the key does not exist, the method immediately returns 0. Otherwise, the method uses subscript notation to get the stored value. Next, the value is adjusted and updated in the dictionary, again using subscript notation. Finally, we return the updated value to the caller:

```
//Add
public func registerCustomer(customerName: String)
    {
        registerCustomerWithPreviousBalance(customerName, previousBalance:
0)
    }

public func registerCustomerWithPreviousBalance(customerName: String,
previousBalance: Int)
    {
        _points[customerName] = previousBalance;
    }
```

The `registerCustomer()` methods provide the *add* functionality to our class. In both cases, we require a customer name to act as the key. If a returning customer checks in with a previous balance, we want to acknowledge it so that our class overloads the method in `registerCustomerWithPreviousBalance()`. Ultimately, the overloaded method uses subscript notation to insert a new key/value pair into the dictionary:

```
//Get
public func getCustomerPoints(customerName: String) -> Int
    {
        let rawsPoints = _points[customerName]
```

```
        return rawsPoints != nil ? rawsPoints! : 0;
    }
```

Our *get* functionality is introduced by the `getCustomerPoints()` method. In this method, we use subscript notation to get the value for our key, but then we confirm the return value is not `nil` before returning the value. If the value is not `nil`, our method returns the value; otherwise, it returns 0:

```
    //Update
    public func addPointsToCustomer(points: Int, customerName: String) ->
Int
    {
        return updatePointsForCustomer(points, customerName: customerName)
    }

    public func removePointsFromCustomer(points: Int, customerName: String)
-> Int
    {
        return updatePointsForCustomer(-points, customerName: customerName)
    }

    public func redeemPointsForCustomer(points: Int, customerName: String)
-> Int
    {
        //Perform any accounting actions
        return updatePointsForCustomer(-points, customerName: customerName)
    }
```

Next, we come to the public update methods, `addPointsToCustomer()`, `removePointsFromCustomer()`, and `redeemPointsForCustomer()`. Each of these methods calls the private `updatePointsForCustomer()` method, but first, it negates `points` in the case of the latter two:

```
    public func customerCheckout(customerName: String) -> Int
    {
        let points = _points[customerName]
        _points.removeValueForKey(customerName)
        return points!;
    }
```

The `customerCheckout()` method introduces the collection's *remove* functionality. The method first records the final value for the customer key, and then calls `removeObjectForKey:` to delete the customer's key from the collection. Finally, it returns the customer's last point value to the caller:

```
    //Contains
```

```
public func customerExists(customerName: String) -> Bool
{
    return _points[customerName] != nil
}
```

Similar to `NSMutableDictionary`, `Dictionary` does not provide a mechanism for determining whether a key exists in the collection. Luckily, our workaround from Objective-C works just fine in Swift as well. Our method uses subscript notation, and if the returned value is `nil`, the key does not exist, and `nil` evaluates to `false`. Based on this principle, therefore, our `customerExists()` method simply returns `_points[cusrtomerName]`, allowing the return value to be evaluated as `Bool`:

```
//Count
public func customersOnPremises() -> Int
{
    return _points.count
}
```

Using the `count` property on the `Dictionary` class, `customersOnPremises()` provides the *count* functionality:

```
//Clear
public func closingTime()
{
    _points.removeAll()
}
```

Finally, per our business requirements we need a way to remove all of the objects from the collection. The `closingTime()` method uses the `Dictionary.removeAll()` method to accomplish this task.

Advanced topics

Now that we have examined how dictionaries are used in common applications, we should take some time to examine how dictionaries are implemented under the hood. The majority of dictionaries come in two distinct flavors: hash table based and search tree based. Although the mechanics of the two approaches are similar, and they typically share many of the same methods and functionality, the inner workings and ideal applications for each type are very different.

Hash table based dictionaries

The most common implementation of a dictionary is the **hash table based** associative array. When properly implemented, the hash table approach is extremely efficient and allows for O(1) complexity searches, inserts, and deletes. In each of the languages we are examining, the basic dictionary classes are based on hash tables by default. The general concept of a hash table based dictionary is that mapping for a specified key is stored at an index of an array, where the index is obtained by applying a hash function to the key. Callers then examine the same index of the array for the specified key and use the binding that is stored there to retrieve the value of the element.

Hash table based dictionaries have one drawback, the hash function has the potential to create **collisions**, or it can sometimes attempt to map two keys to the same index. Therefore, hash table based implementations must have a mechanism in place to resolve these conflicts. Many **collision resolution strategies** exist, but the details of these are beyond the scope of this text.

Search tree based dictionaries

A less common implementation of a dictionary is the **search tree based** associative array. Dictionaries based on search trees are well suited to sorting keys and values by some criteria or property of the value, plus they can be built to work more efficiently with custom key or value types. Another advantage of a search tree based implementation is the addition of operations beyond the basic functions described earlier, such as the ability to find a mapping whose key is similar to a specified key. These advantages come at a price, however, in that, the basic operations in search tree based implementations have a higher cost, while the collections themselves are more restrictive on the types of data they can work with. Sorting operations relating to search tree based dictionaries will be discussed in more detail in Chapter 12, *Sorting: Bringing Order Out Of Chaos*.

Summary

In this chapter, you learned the basic definition of the dictionary, or associative array, data structure. You learned how to initialize dictionaries, and we examined the hash table data structure upon which most concrete dictionary implementations are based. We discussed the various common operations found in dictionaries, including their operational costs. Following this, we examined a case study where dictionaries would be very beneficial. Finally, we looked at two varying implementations of dictionaries, including the hash table based dictionary and the search tree based dictionary.

7
Sets: No Duplicates

Within the confines of computer science, **sets** are typically used as a simple collection of objects that contain no duplicates. In the broader realm of mathematics in general, however, a set is an abstract data structure that can be described as a collection of distinct objects or values stored in no particular order. For the purpose of this discussion, we will choose to view a set as the computer implementation of a mathematically finite set.

When working with problems to which the mathematical concepts of set theory can be applied, set data structures provide a powerful group of tools for combining and examining relationships between collections of similar objects. However, even outside set theory and mathematics, the set data structure provides functionality that can be useful in everyday applications. For example, since a set naturally eliminates duplicates, any application that requires maintaining or editing a collection of unique elements would benefit from storing objects in a set data structure. Similarly, if you need to eliminate duplicates from an existing collection, most implementations of the set data structure will allow you to create a new set from a collection of arrays; and in doing so, you will filter out duplicates automatically. Overall, sets are a relatively simple data structure, which provide tremendous functionality and power in analyzing collections of data.

In this chapter, we will cover the following:

- Definition of the set data structure
- Set theory
- Initializing sets
- Common set operations
- Revisiting the users logged in to a service problem
- Case study – music playlists

- Hash table-based sets
- Tree-based sets
- Array-based sets

Set theory

The concept of a set is relatively simple, but in practice a concrete implementation can be somewhat difficult to understand due to its mathematical origins. Therefore, in order to fully appreciate the set data structure, it becomes necessary to examine some of the characteristics and functions of **set theory** upon which the set data structure is built. Set theory is a branch of mathematics that studies collections, or *sets*, of objects. Although set theory is a major area of research in mathematics with many interrelated sub-fields, we really only need to examine five functions for combining and relating sets to one another to understand the set data structure:

- **Union**: A union is one of the fundamental methods of combining and relating sets to one another. A union of a series of *n* sets is the set of only those distinct elements contained in those sets. This means that, if you combine sets *A* and *B*, the resulting set will only contain unique elements from set *A* and *B*. If an element exists in both *A* and *B*, it will only appear once in our result set. We use the notation $A \cup B$ to denote the *union* of sets *A* and *B*. The following Venn diagram represents the union of two sets:

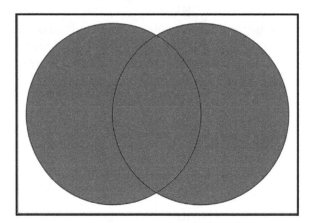

- **Intersection**: An intersection is the second fundamental method of combining and relating sets to one another. An intersection of a collection of n sets is the set of elements that exist in each of the sets being evaluated. So if we examine sets A and B for an intersection, our resulting set will only include those elements that exist in both A and B. Any elements that are unique to A or B will be discarded. We use the notation $A \cap B$ to denote the *intersection* of set A with set B. The following Venn diagram represents the intersection of two sets:

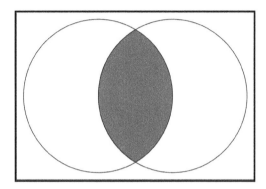

- **Difference**: The difference operation is the opposite of the intersection operation. The difference of a collection of n sets is the set of elements that are unique to each set being evaluated. If we examine sets A and B for a difference, our resulting set will only include those elements that exist in either A or B. Any elements that are part of the intersection of A and B will be discarded. We use the notation $A \triangle B$ to denote the *difference* between sets A and B. The following Venn diagram represents the difference of two sets:

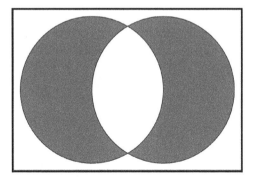

- **Compliment**: The compliment, or the **relative compliment**, of *A* in *B* is the set of elements that are found in *B* but not found in *A*. If we examine sets *A* and *B* for a compliment, only those elements that are unique to *B* will be included in our result set. Any elements that are unique to *A* or are part of the intersection of *A* and *B* will be discarded. We use the notation $B \setminus A$ to denote the relative compliment of set *A* with respect to set *B*. The following Venn diagram represents the compliment of two sets:

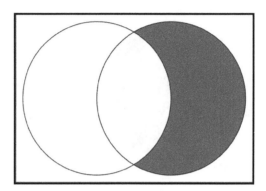

- **Subset**: The subset is the final fundamental method of combining and relating sets to one another. The subset operation determines if set *A* is a subset of set *B*, or rather if set *B* is a **superset** of set *A*. This relationship of one set being a subset of another is called an **inclusion**, or a **containment** when considering one set is a superset of another set. In the next figure, we can say that *A* is the subset of *B* or *B* is the superset of *A*. We use the notation $A \subset B$ to denote that set *A* is an inclusion of set *B*, or $B \supset A$ to denote that set *B* is the containment of set *A*.

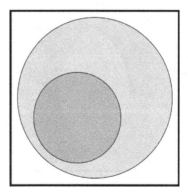

Initializing sets

Sets are not terribly commonplace in development, but each of the languages we are examining supports data structures with some form of concrete implementations. Here are some examples of initializing a set, adding a few values to the collection including one duplicate, and printing the set's count to the console after each step.

C#

C# provides a concrete implementation of the set data structure through the `HashSet<T>` class. Since this class is generic, the caller may define the type used for elements. For example, the following example initializes a new set where the elements will be `string` types:

```
HashSet<string, int> mySet = new HashSet<string>();
mySet.Add("green");
Console.WriteLine("{0}", mySet.Count);
mySet.Add("yellow");
Console.WriteLine("{0}", mySet.Count);
mySet.Add("red");
Console.WriteLine("{0}", mySet.Count);
mySet.Add("red");
Console.WriteLine("{0}", mySet.Count);
mySet.Add("blue");
Console.WriteLine("{0}", mySet.Count);
/* Output:
1
2
3
3 since "red" already exists in the collection
4
*/
```

Java

Java provides a `HashSet<E>` class as well as other classes that implement the `Set<E>` interface. In this chapter, we'll look at an example of the `HashSet<E>` class only:

```
HashSet<String> mySet = new HashSet< >();
mySet.add("green");
System.out.println(mySet.size());
mySet.add("yellow");
System.out.println(mySet.size());
mySet.add("red");
System.out.println(mySet.size());
mySet.add("red");
```

```
System.out.println(mySet.size());
mySet.add("blue");
System.out.println(mySet.size());

/* Output:
1
2
3
3 since "red" already exists in the collection
4
*/
```

Objective-C

Objective-C provides immutable as well as mutable set classes, NSSet and NSMutableSet. In this chapter, we will only be examining the mutable version in detail:

```
NSMutableSet *mySet = [NSMutableSet set];
[mySet addObject:@"green"];
NSLog(@"%li", (long)[mySet count]);
[mySet addObject:@"yellow"];
NSLog(@"%li", (long)[mySet count]);
[mySet addObject:@"red"];
NSLog(@"%li", (long)[mySet count]);
[mySet addObject:@"red"];
NSLog(@"%li", (long)[mySet count]);
[mySet addObject:@"blue"];
NSLog(@"%li", (long)[mySet count]);

/* Output:
1
2
3
3 since "red" already exists in the collection
4
*/
```

Swift

Sets in Swift are created using the Set class. Swift sets are mutable when initialized as **variables** using var, but they can also be created as immutable by initializing them as **constants** using let. In this chapter, we will only be examining the mutable version in detail:

```
let mySet: Set<String> = Set<String>()
mySet.insert(@"green")
print(mySet.count)
```

```
mySet.insert(@"yellow")
print(mySet.count)
mySet.insert(@"red")
print(mySet.count)
mySet.insert(@"red")
print(mySet.count)
mySet.insert(@"blue")
print(mySet.count)

/* Output:
1
2
3
3 since "red" already exists in the collection
4
*/
```

Set operations

Not all concrete implementations of the set data structures expose the same operational methods. However, the more common operations should be available or can be made available as needed by the developer. As you examine these operations, note how the language is similar to the language of set theory operations discussed earlier. You will find that most of the set data structure functionality will closely mirror that of set theory in general:

- **add**: The add operation, sometimes referred to as an insert, introduces a new object into the collection if that object does not already exist in the collection. This functionality, which prevents duplicate objects from being added to the collection, is one of the core advantages of using a set over many other data structures. Most implementations of the set data structure will return a Boolean value denoting whether or not the element could be added to the collection. Add operations have an **O**(n) cost.
- **remove**: The remove, or delete, operation allows the caller to remove a value or object from the collection if it exists. Most implementations of the set data structure return a Boolean value denoting whether or not the remove operation was successful. Remove operations have an **O**(n) cost.

- **capacity**: The capacity operation returns the maximum number of values the set can hold. This is not an operation that developers will naturally see in the four languages we are discussing as each of the mutable sets found in these languages can dynamically resize on demand. However, some implementations do permit the set to be limited in size as part of its definition. Capacity has an **O**(1) operational cost.

- **union**: The union operation returns a new set containing the unique elements of two or more sets. Therefore, this operation has a worst-case cost of **O**(*n+m*), where *n* is the size of the first set and *m* is the size of the second set.

- **intersection**: The intersection operation returns only those elements that are shared between two or more sets. This means that, if you supply the method with two sets, you will only get back those elements that already exist in both sets. Intersection carries an **O**(*n*m*), where *n* is the size of the first set and *m* is the size of the second set. Interestingly, if you attempt to perform an intersection on a series of three or more sets, the cost becomes *(n-1)* * **O**(*L*), where *n* is the number of *sets* involved in the operation and *L* is the size of the largest set in the series. Obviously, this cost is quite high and using this operation on multiple sets simultaneously could get out of hand very quickly.

- **difference**: The difference operation is the opposite of the intersection operation, returning only those elements that are unique to each set. This operation has an operational cost of **O**(*m*), where *m* is the length of the shorter of the two sets being evaluated.

- **subset**: The subset operation returns a Boolean value determining whether set *A* is a subset of set *B*. For set *A* to be considered a subset of set *B*, every element within set *A* must also be included in set *B*. If only a portion of the elements of set *A* are contained in set *B*, then sets *A* and *B* share an intersection, but *A* is not a subset of *B*. This operation has an operational cost of **O**(*m*), where *m* is the length of set *A*.

- **count**: The count, or size, operation represents the *cardinality* of a particular set, which is really just the set theory way of saying the number of elements in the set. Count is typically a simple property on the collection and, therefore, has an **O**(*1*) cost.

- **isEmpty**: The isEmpty operation returns a Boolean value representing whether the set contains any elements at all. Some implementations provide a corresponding `isFull` operation, but only for those instances where the set capacity can be limited to a specific value. Both `isEmpty` and `isFull` have an **O**(*1*) cost.

Example: revisiting users logged in to a service

Let's revisit the users logged into a service problem from `Chapter 2`, *Arrays: Foundational Collection*, one more time and examine how the code will be changed if we had chosen a set as the underlying data structure rather than an array or list.

C#

In this example, we have replaced the `List<User>` object with a `HashSet<User>` object. The majority of our code is unchanged, but you should note the exclusion of the `CanAddUser(User)` method. Originally, this method validated the *authenticated user* action by ensuring that the collection had room for another object and then ensuring that the object to be added was not already included in the collection. A set data structure eliminates the need for the second step as it intrinsically prevents duplicate objects from being added. Since the only validation our class now requires is a capacity check, we can handle that inline with the `UserAuthenticated(User)` functionality. As an added bonus, we can now easily report whether or not the user was successfully added, as `HashSet<T>.Add(T)` returns `true` for success, and `false` when the object already exists in the set:

```csharp
public class LoggedInUserSet
{
    HashSet<User> _users;

    public LoggedInUserSet()
    {
        _users = new HashSet<User>();
    }

    public bool UserAuthenticated(User user)
    {
        if (_users.Count < 30)
        {
            return _users.Add(user);
        }
        return false;
    }

    public void UserLoggedOut(User user)
    {
        _users.Remove(user);
    }
}
```

Java

Changes in our Java example almost mirror those of our C# example. Again, we have replaced the `List<User>` object with a `HashSet<User>` object. The majority of our code is unchanged, except for the exclusion of the `canAddUser(User)` method. In Java, the `HashSet<E>` class implements the `Set<E>` interface and is based on a set data structure, which eliminates the need for checking whether an object exists in the collection before adding it. Since the only validation our class now requires is a capacity check, we can handle that inline with the `userAuthenticated(User)` functionality. Again, we can now easily report whether or not the user was successfully added, as `HashSet<E>.add(E)` returns `true` for success, and `false` when the object already exists in the set:

```
HashSet<User> _users;

public LoggedInUserSet()
{
    _users = new HashSet<User>();
}

public boolean userAuthenticated(User user)
{
    if (_users.size() < 30)
    {
        return _users.add(user);
    }
    return false;
}

public void userLoggedOut(User user)
{
    _users.remove(user);
}
```

Objective-C

Changes to our Objective-C example yield some interesting results. Although we are exchanging the `NSMutableArray` collection for an `NSMutableSet` collection, the majority of our code remains the same, including the fact that we are not going to return a `BOOL` representing the success or failure of our `addObject:` operation. This is because `addObject:` does not return a value; if we were to include it in `userAuthenticated:`, we would have to resort to calling the `containsObject:` method prior to calling `addObject:` on our set collection. Since the entire point of this exercise is to use a set to eliminate the need to check for duplicates before adding new objects, to re-introduce this functionality would defeat the purpose and potentially put us in a more costly position than if we simply stuck with an array or list.

This is not to say that there are no valid applications that could benefit from a set as well as a report on the success or failure of an `addObject:` operation; this is just not one of those cases:

```
@interface EDSLoggedInUserSet ()
{
    NSMutableSet *_users;
}
@end

@implementation EDSLoggedInUserSet
-(instancetype) init
{
    if (self = [super init])
    {
        _users = [NSMutableSet set];
    }
    return self;
}

-(void) userAuthenticated: (EDSUser *)user
{
    if ([_users count] < 30)
    {
        [_users addObject:user];
    }
}

-(void) userLoggedOut: (EDSUser *)user
{
    [_users removeObject:user];
}
```

Swift

The outcome of our Swift example is almost exactly like that of our Objective-C example. Again, we are replacing our array with a set, but sets in Swift function much like they do in Objective-C. Therefore, our final code is more abbreviated but does not immediately provide the same functionality as our C# and Java implementations:

```
var _users: Set<User> = Set<User>()

public func userAuthenticated(user: User)
{
    if (_users.count < 30)
    {
        _users.insert(user)
```

```
        }
    }

    public func userLoggedOut(user: User)
    {
        if let index = _users.indexOf(user)
        {
            _users.removeAtIndex(index)
        }
    }
```

We would need a contract

If you look carefully at each of the three solutions to the logged in user business problem, you will probably notice they all share common public methods. In our array implementation, list implementation, and set implementation, we have two public methods named `UserAuthenticated()` and `UserLoggedOut()`, or some variation of these names depending on the language. This would not be an issue if we were to just choose one implementation that best suits our needs and move on. However, what if there were justifiable reasons to keep each one of these classes in our solution to efficiently work within specific environmental conditions?

In actuality, it is very common to see multiple classes that share the same public-facing methods but have uniquely implemented functionality under the hood. If we were to simply create three (or more) separate implementations that are completely independent of one another, our application would have a resulting *code smell*. That's because, whenever we want to use a specific implementation, we will need to call for it by name, which requires some advance knowledge of which classes and implementations are available. Plus, although our code might work just fine, it will be fragile, inextensible, and more difficult to maintain in the long term.

A better solution would involve defining a contract that each class implements. In C# or Java, we would define an interface, while in Objective-C and Swift, we would define a protocol. The difference between these two patterns is mostly semantics, as they will both provide our caller with the names of the methods, what the methods expect, and what the methods will return. What is important is that by doing this, we greatly simplify and harden our implementation of both the functionality and the calling class structures.

Case-study: music playlists

Business problem: A music streaming service wants to provide their users with a better streaming experience. Currently, user playlists are a simple collection of songs dumped into a bucket that provides no means of filtering or ordering the collection. The content management team has heard the complaints of their users and has tasked the engineering team with building a better playlist.

This new playlist tool will have several key requirements. The more basic requirements include the ability to add and remove songs from the list, the ability to differentiate between an empty list and a list with elements, as well the ability to report on the total count of elements in the list. For those customers who are not interested in paying for the premium service, the lists will be limited to a 100 songs so our playlist tool must also have the ability to set a capacity and easily identify when the capacity has been met.

Additionally, many premium users are known to have thousands of songs in their playlist, as well as multiple themed playlists for everything from riding their bike to doing the laundry. For these users the playlist tool must include some advanced analysis and editing features. First, there must be a way to easily consolidate playlists and, since we don't want to have songs that exist in both playlists to appear twice, this consolidation must prevent duplicates. Next, the playlist should be able to easily identify songs that are duplicated between two lists as well as identify songs that are unique to specific lists. Finally, some users will want to know more information about their collection of playlists, such as whether one playlist exists as part of another playlist. Based on these requirements, the developer decides that a set will be the most efficient way to represent the playlists, so the core class's functionality will be based on that data structure.

C#

C# provides the generic collection `HashSet<T>`. This class provides all of the basic operations we would expect to see in a concrete set implementation with the added benefit of generic type casting:

```
HashSet<Song> _songs;
public Int16 capacity { get; private set; }
public bool premiumUser { get; private set; }
public bool isEmpty
{
    get
    {
        return _songs.Count == 0;
    }
}

public bool isFull
```

```
        {
            get
            {
                if (this.premiumUser)
                {
                    return false;
                }
                else
                {
                    return _songs.Count == this.capacity;
                }
            }
        }

    public PlaylistSet(bool premiumUser, Int16 capacity)
    {
        _songs = new HashSet<Song>();
        this.premiumUser = premiumUser;
        this.capacity = capacity;
    }
```

Using the `HashSet<T>` interface, we create one private field for our class called `_songs`. Our constructor instantiates this field, giving us the underlying data structure to build our `PlaylistSet` class on. We also create four public fields: `capacity`, `premiumUser`, `isEmpty`, and `isFull`. The `capacity` field stores the maximum numbers of songs non-premium users can store in their playlist, while `premiumUser` denotes whether this list belongs to a premium account or not. The `isEmpty` and `isFull` fields allow our class to easily implement the two operations of the same name. The `isEmpty` field simply returns whether or not the count of the set is 0. The `isFull` field first checks whether this list belongs to a premium account. If `true`, the collection is never full as we allow premium users to store unlimited songs in their playlists. If this list does not belong to a premium account, our getter ensures that the current count of `_songs` has not exceeded the capacity and returns that comparison:

```
    public bool AddSong(Song song)
    {
        if (!this.isFull)
        {
            return _songs.Add(song);
        }
        return false;
    }
```

The AddSong(Song song) method provides the *add* functionality to our class. This method first confirms that the collection is not full. If this is so, the method returns false as we cannot add any more songs to the list. Otherwise, the method returns the result of HashSet<T>.Add(T) which returns true if song is added, meaning the song was not already in the list.

```
public bool RemoveSong(Song song)
{
    return _songs.Remove(song);
}
```

The RemoveSong(Song song) method provides *remove* functionality to our class. This method simply returns the result of HashSet<T>.Remove(T), which will return true if the song exists in the list; otherwise, it will return false:

```
public void MergeWithPlaylist(HashSet<Song> playlist)
{
    _songs.UnionWith(playlist);
}
```

The MergeWithPlaylist(HashSet<Song> playlist) method provides the *union* functionality for our class. Luckily, HashSet<T> exposes the union functionality with the Union(HashSet<T>) method, so our method simply calls it. In this case, Union() will merge the playlist parameter with our existing _songs list:

```
public HashSet<Song> FindSharedSongsInPlaylist(HashSet<Song> playlist)
{
    HashSet<Song> songsCopy = new HashSet<Song>(_songs);
    songsCopy.IntersectWith(playlist);
    return songsCopy;
}
```

Next, the FindSharedSongsInPlaylist(HashSet<Song> playlist) method provides the *intersection* functionality to our class. Again, HashSet<T> conveniently provides the IntersectWith(HashSet<T>) method, which our method takes advantage of. Note that this method does not modify our list in-place, but rather returns the actual intersection of our list and the playlist parameter. We do this because it would not be very useful to simply eliminate songs that are unique to one list or the other. This method will instead be used for informational purposes by other functions within the overall application.

Since we are not modifying the existing list but only returning information about the intersection, our method first makes a copy of the _songs set using the overloaded HashSet<T> object. Then, our method modifies the copied list and returns the result of the intersection operation:

```
public HashSet<Song> FindUniqueSongs(HashSet<Song> playlist)
{
    HashSet<Song> songsCopy = new HashSet<Song>(_songs);
    songsCopy.ExceptWith(playlist);
    return songsCopy;
}
```

The FindUniqueSongs(HashSet<Song> playlist) method provides the *difference* functionality to our class and works under a methodology that is very similar to the previous method. Again, this method does not modify our existing set in place but returns the results of the ExceptWith() operation on the copied set and the playlist parameter:

```
public bool IsSubset(HashSet<Song> playlist)
{
    return _songs.IsSubsetOf(playlist);
}

public bool IsSuperset(HashSet<Song> playlist)
{
    return _songs.IsSupersetOf(playlist);
}
```

The IsSubset(HashSet<Song> playlist) and IsSuperset(HashSet<Song> playlist) methods provide the functionalities implied by their names. These methods utilize the HashSet<T>.IsSubSetOf(HashSet<T>) and HashSet<T>.IsSuperSetOf(HashSet<T>) methods, respectively and return a Boolean value representing the result of those comparisons:

```
public int TotalSongs()
{
    return _songs.Count;
}
```

Finally, the TotalSongs() method returns the number of elements found in the _songs set, providing *count* functionality to our collection.

Java

Java provides the generic collection `HashSet<E>` that implements the `Set<E>` interface. This class provides all of the basic operations we would expect to see in a concrete set implementation with the added benefit of generic type casting:

```java
private HashSet<Song> _songs;
public int capacity;
public boolean premiumUser;
public boolean isEmpty()
{
    return _songs.size() == 0;
}

public boolean isFull()
{
    if (this.premiumUser)
    {
        return false;
    }
    else {
        return _songs.size() == this.capacity;
    }
}

public PlaylistSet(boolean premiumUser, int capacity)
{
    _songs = new HashSet<>();
    this.premiumUser = premiumUser;
    this.capacity = capacity;
}
```

Using `HashSet<E>`, we create one private field for our class called _songs. Our constructor instantiates this field, giving us the underlying data structure to build our `PlaylistSet` class on. We also create two public fields and two public accessors: `capacity`, `premiumUser`, `isEmpty()`, and `isFull()`. The `capacity` field stores the maximum numbers of songs non-premium users can store in their playlist, while `premiumUser` denotes whether this list belongs to a premium account or not. The `isEmpty()` and `isFull()` accessors allow our class to easily implement the two operations of the same name. These two accessors function exactly as their C# field counterparts. The `isEmpty()` method simply returns whether or not the count of the set is 0. The `isFull()` method first checks whether this list belongs to a premium account.

If `true`, the collection is never full as we allow premium users to store unlimited songs in their playlists. If this list does not belong to a premium account, our getter ensures that the current count of _songs has not exceeded `capacity` and returns that comparison:

```
public boolean addSong(Song song)
{
    if (!this.isFull())
    {
        return _songs.add(song);
    }
    return false;
}
```

The `addSong(Song song)` method provides *add* functionality to our class. This method first confirms that the collection is not full. If so, the method returns `false` as we cannot add any more songs to the list. Otherwise, the method returns the result of `HashSet<E>.add(E)`, which will return `true` if the song is added, and that too only if the song is not already in this playlist:

```
public boolean removeSong(Song song)
{
    return _songs.remove(song);
}
```

The `removeSong(Song song)` method provides the *remove* functionality to our class. This method simply returns the result of `HashSet<E>.remove(E)`, which will return `true` if the song exists in the set; otherwise, it will return `false`.

```
public void mergeWithPlaylist(HashSet<Song> playlist)
{
    _songs.addAll(playlist);
}
```

The `mergeWithPlaylist(HashSet<Song> playlist)` method provides *union* functionality for our class, and this is where our class begins to truly diverge from our previous C# example. `HashSet<E>` exposes the *union* functionality we're looking for, but only by calling the `HashSet<E>.addAll(HashSet<E>)` method. This method accepts a set of `Song` objects as a parameter and attempts to add each one to our _songs collection. If the `Song` element being added already exists in the _songs set, that element will be discarded, leaving us with only unique `Song` objects from both lists or a union of the two sets:

```
public HashSet<Song> findSharedSongsInPlaylist(HashSet<Song> playlist)
{
    HashSet<Song> songsCopy = new HashSet<>(_songs);
    songsCopy.retainAll(playlist);
```

```
        return songsCopy;
    }
```

Next, the `findSharedSongsInplaylist(HashSet<Song> playlist)` method provides the *intersection* functionality to our class. Again, `HashSet<E>` exposes intersection functionality, but not directly. Our method uses the `HashSet<E>.retainAll(HashSet<E>)` method, which retains all of the elements in the `_songs` set, that also exist in the `playlist` parameter, or intersection of the two collections. As in our C# example, we are not modifying the `_songs` set in place but rather returning the intersection between a copy of `_songs` and the `playlist` parameter:

```
public HashSet<Song> findUniqueSongs(HashSet<Song> playlist)
{
    HashSet<Song> songsCopy = new HashSet<>(_songs);
    songsCopy.removeAll(playlist);
    return songsCopy;
}
```

The `findUniqueSongs(HashSet<Song> playlist)` method provides the *difference* functionality to our class. Once again, `HashSet<E>` exposes the difference functionality, but through the `removeAll(HashSet<E>)` method. The `removeAll()` method removes all of the `_songs` elements that are also contained in the playlist parameter or the difference between the two collections. Again, this method does not modify our existing set in place but returns the results of the `removeAll()` method, or difference operation, on the `_songs` copy and the `playlist` parameter:

```
public boolean isSubset(HashSet<Song> playlist)
{
    return _songs.containsAll(playlist);
}

public boolean isSuperset(HashSet<Song> playlist)
{
    return playlist.containsAll(_songs);
}
```

The `isSubset(HashSet<Song> playlist)` and `isSuperset(HashSet<Song> playlist)` methods provide the functionality of the same names. These methods both utilize the `HashSet<E>.containsAll(HashSet<E>)` method and return a Boolean value representing the result of those comparisons. Our methods simply swap the source set and the parameter to obtain the desired comparison since `HashSet<E>` does not provide a specific comparator for each function:

```
public int totalSongs()
{
```

```
        return _songs.size();
    }
```

Finally, the `totalSongs()` method returns the number of elements found in the `_songs` set using the collection's `size()` method, providing the *count* functionality to our collection.

Objective-C

Objective-C provides the `NSSet` and `NSMutableSet` class clusters as the concrete implementations of the set data structure. These class clusters provide most of the functionality we would expect to see in a set data structure, and the explicit functions that are missing are very simple to implement, which makes the Objective-C implementation fairly straightforward:

```objc
@interface EDSPlaylistSet ()
{
    NSMutableSet<EDSSong*>* _songs;
    NSInteger _capacity;
    BOOL _premiumUser;
    BOOL _isEmpty;
    BOOL _isFull;
}
@end

@implementation EDSPlaylistSet

-(instancetype)playlistSetWithPremiumUser:(BOOL)isPremiumUser
andCapacity:(NSInteger)capacity
{
    if (self == [super init])
    {
        _songs = [NSMutableSet set];
        _premiumUser = isPremiumUser;
        _capacity = capacity;
    }
    return self;
}

-(BOOL)isEmpty
{
    return [_songs count] == 0;
}

-(BOOL)isFull
{
    if (_premiumUser)
    {
```

```
            return NO;
    }
    else
    {
        return [_songs count] == _capacity;
    }
}
```

Using NSMutableSet, we create one private ivar for our class called _songs. Our initializer instantiates this field, giving us the underlying data structure to build our EDSPlaylistSet class on. We also create four public properties: capacity, premiumUser, isEmpty, and isFull in our header file, backed by private ivars of the same name. The capacity property stores the maximum numbers of songs non-premium users can store in their playlist, while premiumUser denotes if this list belongs to a premium account or not. The isEmpty and isFull properties allow our class to easily implement the two operations of the same name. The isEmpty property simply returns whether or not the count of the set is 0, while the isFull property first checks whether this list belongs to a premium account. If true, the collection is never full as we allow premium users to store unlimited songs in their playlists. If this list does not belong to a premium account, our method ensures that the current count of _songs has not exceeded the capacity and returns that comparison:

```
-(BOOL) addSong:(EDSSong*) song
{
    if (!_isFull && ![_songs containsObject:song])
    {
        [_songs addObject:song];
        return YES;
    }
    return NO;
}
```

The addSong: method provides *add* functionality to our class. This method first confirms that the collection is not full and then confirms that the object is actually contained in the _songs collection. If the collection does not pass both tests, the method returns NO, as we cannot add any more songs to the list or the song already exists in the collection. Otherwise, the method calls addObject: and returns YES:

```
-(BOOL) removeSong:(EDSSong*) song
{
    if ([_songs containsObject:song])
    {
        [_songs removeObject:song];
        return YES;
    }
    else
```

```
        {
            return NO;
        }
    }
```

The `removeSong:` method provides *remove* functionality to our class. This method confirms that the song exists in the collection, then removes the song using `removeObject:`, and finally returns `YES`. If the song does not exist in the collection, the method returns `NO`:

```
- (void)mergeWithPlaylist:(NSMutableSet<EDSSong*>*)playlist
{
    [_songs unionSet:playlist];
}
```

The `mergeWithPlaylist:` method provides *union* functionality for our class. Luckily, `NSSet` exposes the union functionality with the `unionSet:` method, so our method simply calls it. In this case, `unionSet:` will merge the `playlist` parameter with our existing `_songs` list:

```
- (NSMutableSet<EDSSong*>*)findSharedSongsInPlaylist:
  (NSMutableSet<EDSSong*>*)playlist
{
    NSMutableSet *songsCopy = [NSMutableSet setWithSet:_songs];
    [songsCopy intersectSet:playlist];
    return songsCopy;
}
```

Next, the `findSharedSongsInplaylist:` method provides *intersection* functionality to our class. Again, `NSSet` exposes the intersection functionality through the `intersectSet:` method. As in our C# example, we are not modifying the `_songs` set in place but rather returning the intersection between a copy of `_songs` and the `playlist` parameter:

```
- (NSMutableSet<EDSSong*>*)findUniqueSongs:(NSMutableSet<EDSSong*>*)playlist
{
    NSMutableSet *songsCopy = [NSMutableSet setWithSet:_songs];
    [songsCopy minusSet:playlist];
    return songsCopy;
}
```

The `findUniqueSongs:` method provides the *difference* functionality to our class. Once again, `NSSet` exposes the difference functionality through the `minusSet:` method. And again, this method does not modify our existing set in place but returns the results of the `minusSet:`, or difference, operation on the `_songs` copy and the `playlist` parameter:

```
- (BOOL) isSubset: (NSMutableSet<EDSSong*>*) playlist
{
    return [_songs isSubsetOfSet:playlist];
}

- (BOOL) isSuperset: (NSMutableSet<EDSSong*>*) playlist
{
    return;
}
```

The `isSubset:` and `isSuperset:` methods provide the functionalities by their names. These methods utilize the `isSubsetOfSet:` method on `NSSet` in much the same way that our Java example utilizes the `containsAll(HashSet<E>)` method of the `Set<E>` interface:

```
- (NSInteger) totalSongs
{
    return [_songs count];
}
```

Finally, the `totalSongs` method returns the number of elements found in the `_songs` set, providing *count* functionality to our collection.

Swift

Swift provides the `Set` class as a concrete implementation of the set data structure. This class provides all of the functionality we would expect to see in a set data structure, even more so than its Objective-C counterpart, which makes the Swift implementation very clean:

```
var _songs: Set<Song> = Set<Song>()
public private(set) var _capacity: Int
public private(set) var _premiumUser: Bool
public private(set) var _isEmpty: Bool
public private(set) var _isFull: Bool

public init (capacity: Int, premiumUser: Bool)
{
    _capacity = capacity
    _premiumUser = premiumUser
    _isEmpty = true
    _isFull = false
```

```
    }
    public func premiumUser() -> Bool
    {
        return _premiumUser
    }

    public func isEmpty() -> Bool
    {
        return _songs.count == 0
    }

    public func isFull() -> Bool
    {
        if (_premiumUser)
        {
            return false
        }
        else
        {
            return _songs.count == _capacity
        }
    }
```

Using Set, we create one private ivar for our class called _songs and initialize it inline with its declaration, giving us the underlying data structure to build our PlaylistSet class on. We also create four public fields, _capacity, _premiumUser, _isEmpty, and _isFull, as well as public accessors for the last three. The capacity field stores the maximum number of songs non-premium users can store in their playlist while premiumUser denotes whether this list belongs to a premium account or not. The isEmpty and isFull fields allow our class to easily implement the two operations of the same name. The isEmpty() field simply returns whether or not the count of the set is 0. The isFull() field first checks if this list belongs to a premium account. If true, the collection is never full as we allow premium users to store unlimited songs in their playlists. If this list does not belong to a premium account, our getter ensures that the current count of _songs has not exceeded capacity and returns that comparison:

```
    public func addSong(song: Song) -> Bool
    {
        if (!_isFull && !_songs.contains(song))
        {
            _songs.insert(song)
            return true
        }
        return false
    }
```

The addSong(song: Song) method provides *add* functionality to our class. This method first confirms that the collection is not full and then confirms that the object is actually contained in the _songs collection. If the collection does not pass both tests, the method returns false, as we cannot add any more songs to the list or the song already exists in the collection. Otherwise, the method calls insert() and returns true:

```
public func removeSong(song: Song) -> Bool
{
    if (_songs.contains(song))
    {
        _songs.remove(song)
        return true
    }
    else
    {
        return false
    }
}
```

The removeSong(song: Song) method provides *remove* functionality to our class. This method confirms that the song exists in the collection, then removes the song using remove(), and finally returns true. If the song does not exist in the collection, the method returns false:

```
public func mergeWithPlaylist(playlist: Set<Song>)
{
    _songs.unionInPlace(playlist)
}
```

The mergeWithPlaylist(playlist: Set<Song>) method provides the *union* functionality for our class. Luckily, Set exposes the union functionality with the unionInPlace() method, so our method simply calls it. In this case, unionInPlace() will merge the playlist parameter with our existing _songs list:

```
public func findSharedSongsInPlaylist(playlist: Set<Song>) -> Set<Song>
{
    return _songs.intersect(playlist)
}
```

Next, the `findSharedSongsInplaylist(playlist: Set<Song>)` method provides *intersection* functionality to our class. The `Set` class exposes the intersection functionality using the `intersect()` method. The `intersect()` method does not modify `_songs`, but only returns the results of the intersection between `_songs` and the `playlist` parameter, so we simply return the results of this method call:

```
public func findUniqueSongs(playlist: Set<Song>) -> Set<Song>
{
    return _songs.subtract(playlist)
}
```

The `findUniqueSongs(playlist: Set<Song>)` method provides *difference* functionality to our class. Once again, `Set` exposes the difference functionality using the `subtract()` method. The `subtract()` method does not modify `_songs`, but only returns the results of the difference between `_songs` and the `playlist` parameter, so we simply return the results of this method call:

```
public func isSubset(playlist: Set<Song>) -> Bool
{
    return _songs.isSubsetOf(playlist)
}

public func isSuperset(playlist: Set<Song>) -> Bool
{
    return _songs.isSupersetOf(playlist)
}
```

The `isSubset(playlist: Set<Song>)` and `isSuperset(playlist: Set<Song>)` methods provide the functionalities by their names. These methods utilize the `isSubSetOf()` and `isSuperSetOf()` methods, respectively, and return a Boolean value representing the result of those comparisons:

```
public func totalSongs() -> Int
{
    return _songs.count;
}
```

Finally, the `totalSongs()` method returns the number of elements found in the `_songs` set, providing *count* functionality to our collection.

Advanced topics

Now that we have examined how sets are used in common applications, we should take some time to examine how they are implemented under the hood. The majority of sets come in three varieties: hash table-based sets, tree-based sets, and array-based sets.

Hash table-based sets

Hash table-based sets are typically used for unordered collections of data. As such, the majority of sets you will encounter for non-specialized applications will be hash table-based. Hash table-based sets share similar operational costs with dictionaries. For example, search, insert, and delete operations all have an operational cost of $O(n)$.

Tree-based sets

Tree-based sets are typically based on binary search trees, but they sometimes can be based on other structures. Due to their design, the binary search tree allows for very efficient search functions on average, as each node that is examined can allow for branches of the tree to be discarded from the remaining search pattern. Although the worst case scenario for searching a binary search tree has an $O(n)$ operational cost, in practice this is rarely required.

Array-based sets

Arrays can be used to implement subsets of sets, making union, intersection, and difference operations much more efficient in properly organized array-based sets.

Summary

In this chapter, you learned the basic definition of the set data structure. In order to fully appreciate the functionality of the structure, we briefly examined the most basic principles of set theory upon which the set data structure is based. Following this, we looked at the most common operations of sets and how they relate to the set theory functions. We then looked at how to implement a set in each of the four languages we're studying in this text. Next, we revisited the users logged into a service problem one more time to see if we could improve upon its implementation at all using a set data structure as opposed to an array or list. Following this, we examined a case study where sets would be beneficial. Finally, we looked at the varying implementations of sets, including hash table-based sets, tree-based sets, and array-based sets.

8
Structs: Complex Types

A **struct** is a collection of data variables or values that are grouped together under a single memory block, whereas a data structure is typically some sort of collection of objects that are related to one another in some way. Therefore, a struct, also known as a structure, is less of a data structure and more of a complex data type. This definition sounds pretty simple, but appearances are deceiving in this case. The topic of structs is a complex one, and each of the languages we are examining has unique qualities in how structs are supported, if they are supported at all.

In this chapter, we will cover the following:

- Definition of the struct data structure
- Creating structs
- Common applications of structs
- Examples of structs in each language
- Enums

The essentials

Due to varying support from language to language, we're will take a different approach in this chapter. Instead of examining structs as a whole and then examining a case study, we will examine structs and case studies simultaneously for each language. This will give us the opportunity to examine the nuances of structs in each language within the proper context.

C#

In C#, a struct is defined as a value type that encapsulates small groups of related fields, which sounds very similar to the underlying C language implementation. However, C# structs are in fact quite different from those found in C, and they more closely resemble a regular class than a struct from that language. For instance, a C# struct can have methods, fields, properties, constants, indexers, operator methods, nested types, and events as well as defined constructors (but not default constructors, which are defined automatically). Structs can also implement one or more interfaces, all of which make the C# variety much more flexible than C.

However, it would be a mistake to think of structs as lightweight classes. C# structs do not support inheritance, meaning they cannot inherit from classes or other structs, nor can they be used as a base for other structures or classes. Structure members cannot be declared as abstract, protected, or virtual. Unlike classes, structs can be instantiated without using the new keyword, although doing so prevents the resulting object from being used until every field has been assigned. Finally, and perhaps most importantly, structs are value types while classes are reference types.

This final point cannot be overemphasized because it represents the key advantage to choosing a struct in place of a class. Structs are collections of values and, therefore, do not store references to objects such as arrays, for instance. Therefore, when you are passing a struct off to a method, it is passed by value rather than reference. Additionally, according to the MSDN documentation, being a value type means that structs do not require allocation to the heap memory and, therefore, do not carry the overhead that a class does in terms of memory and processing requirements.

What does this mean and why is this beneficial? When you create a new class by using the new operator, the object that is returned will be allocated on the heap. When you instantiate a struct, on the other hand, it gets created directly on the stack and that nets a performance gain because the stack provides much faster memory access than the heap. As long as you don't overload the stack and cause a stack overflow, using structs strategically can be a great way to improve performance in your application.

Now you might be saying to yourself, *Why do we even have classes if structs are so awesome?* For starters, the applications for structs in C# are very limited. According to Microsoft, you should only consider using a struct instead of a class if the instances of the type will be small and short-lived or they are typically embedded in other objects. Furthermore, you should not define a struct unless it meets at least three of the following criteria:

- The struct will logically represent a single value similar to a primitive type such as an integer, double, and so on
- Each instance of the struct will be smaller than 16 bytes
- The data in the struct will be immutable once it has been instantiated
- The struct will not need to be boxed and unboxed repeatedly

Those are some pretty strict requirements! The outlook gets slightly worse when you consider what you can actually do with structs. Here's a hint–not much. Let's examine struct capabilities in comparison to a class:

- You can set and access individual components–classes can do that too.
- You can pass structs to functions–yes, you can do that with a class.
- You can assign the contents of one struct to another using the assignment (=) operator–nothing special here.
- You can return a struct from a function, which actually creates a copy of the struct so now you have two on the stack. Classes? Check. However, classes are superior in this regard because, when a function returns an instance of a class, the object gets passed by reference so there is no need to create an additional copy.
- Structs *cannot* test for equality using the equality (==) operator, because structs may contain other bits of data. Classes can compare using the equality operator, however. In fact, if you want the same functionality in a struct you have to compare fields component, by component which is tedious.

If someone were to score this match-up, I think the result would look something like *structs: 4, classes: 5 (maybe 6)*. So obviously, classes are more flexible in terms of functionality and convenience, which is why higher-level languages with their roots in C typically provide mechanisms to implement these more complex objects.

That is not to say that structs do not have their value. Although their usefulness falls into very niche scenarios, there are times when a struct is the right tool for the job.

Creating structs in C#

Creating a struct in C# is a fairly simple process. Our only two requirements are `using System` and declaring our object using the `struct` keyword. Here's an example:

```
using System;
public struct MyStruct
{
    private int xval;
    public int X
    {
        get
        {
            return xval;
        }
        set
        {
            if (value < 100)
                xval = value;
        }
    }

    public void WriteXToConsole()
    {
        Console.WriteLine("The x value is: {0}", xval);
    }
}

//Usage
MyStruct ms1 = new MyStruct();
MyStruct ms2 = MyStruct();

ms.X = 9;
ms.WriteXToConsole();

//Output
//The x value is: 9
```

As you can see from the preceding example, our struct is declared with a private backing field, a public accessor and one instance method named `WriteXToConsole()`, all perfectly legitimate characteristics of a struct in C#. Note the two instances of `MyStruct`. The first is instantiated using the `new` keyword, while the second is not. Again, both of these operations are perfectly valid in C#, although the latter requires you to populate all of the member properties before you can use the object in any way. If you were to change the `struct` keyword in our definition to class, the second initializer would not compile.

Next, we'll examine an example from Chapter 3, *Lists: Linear Collections*. In that chapter's case study, we built a data structure that stores a list of Waypoint objects. Here's what the Waypoint class looks like in C#:

```
public class Waypoint
{
    public readonly Int32 lat;
    public readonly Int32 lon;
    public Boolean active { get; private set; }

    public Waypoint(Int32 latitude, Int32 longitude)
    {
        this.lat = latitude;
        this.lon = longitude;
        this.active = true;
    }

    public void DeactivateWaypoint()
    {
        this.active = false;
    }

    public void ReactivateWaypoint()
    {
        this.active = true;
    }
}
```

As you can see, this class is pretty simple. It is so simple that it begs the question as to whether or not such a simple collection of values is worthy of the overhead and resources afforded to a class, especially when you consider that our list could contain hundreds of these Waypoint objects. Can we improve performance by converting the class to a struct without requiring significant refactoring to support this change? First, we need to determine whether it is recommended or even possible to do so, and we can make that decision by examining our struct criteria rules.

Rule 1: The struct will logically represent a single value

In this case, our class has three fields, namely `lat`, `lon`, and `active`. Three is definitely not singular, but since the rule is that a struct must *logically represent* a single value, our plan to convert the class to a struct is still valid. This is because the `Waypoint` object represents a *single* location in 2-dimensional space, and we require at least two values to represent a 2D coordinate, so there is no violation there. Also, the active property denotes a state of the waypoint, so this is characteristically acceptable as well. Before you cry foul on this interpretation, allow me to point out that even Microsoft plays fast and loose with this rule. For instance, `System.Drawing.Rectangle` is defined as a structure, and that type stores *four* integers representing both the size and location of a rectangle. Size and location are two properties of one object, and that is considered acceptable, so I believe `Waypoint` is fine here.

Rule 2: Each instance of the struct must be under 16 bytes

Our `Waypoint` class is easily within the margin of safety for this rule. Referring to Chapter 1, *Data Types: Foundational Structures*, the `Int32` structures are 4 bytes in length and Boolean primitives are only 1 byte in length. This means that a single instance of `Waypoint` will weigh in at a grand total of only nine bytes, leaving us seven bytes to spare.

Rule 3: The data must be immutable

The reason that structs should, ideally, be immutable has to do with their status as value types. As mentioned previously, whenever a value type is passed around, you end up with a copy of that value rather than a reference to the original value itself. This means that when you change a value within the struct, you are only changing that struct and none of the others that happen to be hanging around in the stack.

This requirement may represent a problem for us and it is not a trivial one. In our application, we have chosen to store the active state of the `Waypoint` value on the object itself, and this field is definitely not immutable. We could move the property out of the `Waypoint` class somehow, but doing so would require much more refactoring than if we simply left it alone. Since we want to avoid a significant refactor for the time being, we will leave the field alone and count this rule as a strike against our plan. Our only recourse is to examine our usage of the `Waypoint` objects in our code to ensure that we never create a situation where an instance of `Waypoint` is passed in such a way that we lose focus on the correct instance. Technically speaking, so long as `Waypoint` passes the next requirement, we are still in business.

Rule 4: The struct will not require repeated boxing

Since the `Waypoint` object is used as-is once it has been instantiated, each instance will rarely, if ever, be boxed or unboxed. Therefore, our class passes this test and qualifies for conversion to a struct.

Conversion

The next question is, *Can the Waypoint class be converted to a struct?* There are three points of concern in our class that may need to be addressed. First, we have that mutable `active` field to deal with. In its current form, this field is not very struct-like since it really should be immutable. Since we really have no recourse at this stage, we will have to deal with it in another manner. Predominantly, this means we will need to very strictly monitor our usage of `Waypoint` objects to ensure that we are not working on copies of a struct when we believe we are working with the original struct. Although this may become tedious, it is not unreasonable. Our next concern is the defined constructor, but since this is not without a parameter or a default constructor, everything is fine here and we can move on. Finally, our class has two public methods named `DeactivateWaypoint()` and `ReactivateWaypoint()`. Since C# also allows for public methods in a struct, these two are fine where they are as well. In fact, the only thing we really need to do to convert this class to a struct is to change the `class` keyword to a `struct` keyword! Here's our resulting code:

```
public struct Waypoint
{
    public readonly Int32 lat;
    public readonly Int32 lon;
    public Boolean active { get; private set; }

    public Waypoint(Int32 latitude, Int32 longitude)
    {
```

```
            this.lat = latitude;
            this.lon = longitude;
            this.active = true;
        }

        public void DeactivateWaypoint()
        {
            this.active = false;
        }

        public void ReactivateWaypoint()
        {
            this.active = true;
        }
    };
```

Lastly, we need to know if this change will represent any improvement in our app as a whole. Without extensive testing and analysis of the app at runtime, it is impossible to say for sure, but odds are this modification will net a positive impact on the overall performance of our off-road biking application without introducing any further refactoring requirements.

Java

This is going to be a short discussion, since Java does not support structs. Apparently, the authors of Java decided that, when the language finally crawled out of the C programming swamp, it would not be lugging around these non-object-oriented structures. Therefore, our only recourse in Java is to create a class with public properties that will mimic the behavior of a struct, but without any of the performance benefits.

Objective-C

Objective-C does not support structs directly; however, you can implement and use simple C structs in your code. C structs are similar to their C# counterpart, in that they allow you to frame several primitive values into a single more complex value type. However, C structs do not permit the addition of methods or initializers nor any other cool object-oriented programming features that C# structs enjoy. Additionally, C structs cannot contain any objects that inherit from NSObject, as these are classes and not value types.

That being said, structs are actually found very frequently in Objective-C applications. One of the most common applications for structs is in the definition of **enumerations**, or **enums**. Enums are lists of constants representing integer values whose purpose is to create higher levels of abstraction in your code so that developers can focus on what the values symbolize without worrying about how they are implemented in the background. We will examine enums in more detail later in this chapter.

Creating structs in Objective-C

Another common source of structs in Objective-C can be found in the **Core Graphics framework**, which contains four useful structures. We'll examine these structures in detail in order to demonstrate how structures are defined in Objective-C:

- `CGPoint`: This structure contains a simple two-point coordinate system consisting of two `CGFloat` values. Here's what the `CGPoint` struct definition looks like:

  ```
  struct CGPoint {
      CGFloat x;
      CGFloat y;
  };
  typedef struct CGPoint CGPoint;
  ```

- `CGSize`: This structure is simply a container for a width and height, consisting of two `CGFloat` values. Here's what the `CGSize` struct definition looks like:

  ```
  struct CGSize {
      CGFloat width;
      CGFloat height;
  };
  typedef struct CGSize CGSize;
  ```

- `CGRect`: This is a structure that defines both the location and size of a rectangle, consisting of one `CGPoint` value and one `CGSize` value. Here's what the `CGRect` struct definition looks like:

  ```
  struct CGRect {
      CGPoint origin;
      CGSize size;
  };
  typedef struct CGRect CGRect;
  ```

- `CGVector`: This is a structure that simply contains a 2-dimensional vector, consisting of two `CGFloat` values. Here's what the `CGVector` struct definition looks like:

```
struct CGVector {
    CGFloat dx;
    CGFloat dy;
};
typedef struct CGVector CGVector;
```

You should note the `typedef` and `struct` keywords following each of these struct definitions. This line is included for our convenience as programmers. Whenever we need to call on these structs, if the struct were not decorated with the `typedef` keyword, we would always need to precede calls to our struct with the `struct` keyword, like so:

```
struct CGRect rect;
```

Obviously, this would rapidly get tiresome. By applying a `typedef` to the struct name, we allow our callers to simply apply the struct name without the `struct` keyword, like so:

```
CGRect rect;
```

This makes our code easier to write, but also makes it more concise and more readable in the long run.

Now we will take a look at the `EDSWaypoint` class from Chapter 3, *Lists: Linear Collections*, and determine whether we can convert that class to a C struct. Here's the original code:

```
@interface EDSWaypoint ()
{
    NSInteger _lat;
    NSInteger _lon;
    BOOL _active;
}

@end

@implementation EDSWaypoint

- (instancetype)initWithLatitude:(NSInteger)latitude
andLongitude:(NSInteger)longitude
{
    if (self = [super init])
    {
        _lat = latitude;
        _lon = longitude;
        _active = YES;
```

```
        }
        return self;
    }

    - (BOOL) active
    {
        return _active;
    }


    - (void) reactivateWaypoint
    {
        _active = YES;
    }

    - (void) deactivateWaypoint
    {
        _active = NO;
    }

    @end
```

Right away in the interface, we see a few problems with converting this class to a struct. Both the _lat and _lon ivars are NSInteger classes, which means they are invalid for use inside a struct and they will have to go or be changed to a value type. How about the initWithLatitude:andLongitude: initializer? Nope, you cannot define initializers in C structs either. So, now we need to deal with the reactivateWaypoint and deactivateWaypoint methods. Surely these simple properties and methods can pass muster for acceptance into a struct? No, they cannot. Everything here needs to go.

Therefore, the only real question that remains is what should we do with the _active value and the associated – (BOOL) active property. As it turns out, the BOOL type is perfectly acceptable to use within a structure, so we can actually leave the property where it is. However, _active does represent a mutable property within the EDSWaypoint struct and that is frowned upon, right? It may be frowned upon, but structs are not immutable in C. Here's an example using the Core Graphics struct, CGPoint:

```
CGPoint p = CGPointMake(9.0, 5.2);
p.x = 9.8;
p.y = 5.5;
```

If you were to duplicate this code in your app, the compiler would not issue an error or even a warning because `CGPoint` is not immutable and the properties are not read only. Therefore, we can leave the `_active` value in our final struct definition. Unfortunately, the same cannot be said for the `- (BOOL) active` property? Property accessors such as this are forbidden in C structs so this needs to be removed, and that represents a significant change to how our application handles the active state of our `Waypoint` objects. So if we want to convert this class to a structure, we will be left with the following:

```
struct EDSWaypoint {
    int lat;
    int lon;
    BOOL active;
};
typedef struct EDSWaypoint EDSWaypoint;
```

Strictly speaking, the `typedef` declaration is not required but it's bad enough that we will have to refactor our entire `EDSWaypointList` class to support these changes. Let's not add insult to injury by making our poor developers type eight extra characters every time they want to access one of these types.

Swift

As in other languages, structs in Swift are value types that encapsulate small groups of related properties. Similar to structs in C#, Swift structs resemble a regular class more than a C struct and share all of the following abilities with classes:

- Ability to define properties to store values
- Ability to contain methods that define extended functionality
- Ability to define subscripts to provide access to values using subscript notation
- Ability to define custom initializers
- Swift structs can be extended to provide additional functionality beyond their initialized state
- Finally, Swift structs can be defined to conform to protocols that provide customary functionality

Note, however, that Swift structs do not support inheritance, meaning that they cannot inherit from classes or other structs, nor can they be used as a base for other structures or classes. Also, they do not support type casting to enable the compiler to check and interpret the type of an instance at runtime. These structs cannot be explicitly deinitialized like classes to free up their resources, nor do structs support automatic reference counting for memory management. These last two points are related to the fact that structs in Swift, as in other languages, are value types and not classes or reference types.

This final point in relation to Swift bears repeating. Structs are collections of values and, therefore, do not store references to objects like other collections such as arrays or dictionaries, for instance. Therefore, when you are passing a struct as a parameter to or from a method, it is passed by value and not by reference.

So when should you choose to use a struct over a class in Swift? Apple's documentation provides some general rules of thumb to help you make the decision. You should use struct when:

- Your object's primary purpose is to gather a few simple data values
- You anticipate that the object you create will be copied rather than referenced when you assign or send an instance of that object
- Any properties in your object are value types, not classes, and you also expect that their values will be copied rather than referenced
- Your object has no need to inherit properties or behavior from an existing object or type

You will notice that this list is not quite as restrictive as the same list in C#, but it does represent an excellent common-sense approach to deciding whether or not the value added from using a struct outweighs the limited functionality in your object.

Creating structs in Swift

If you have worked with Swift for more than five minutes, odds are you have already worked with some of the built-in structs such as `Int`, `String`, `Array`, `Dictionary`, and many others that are defined in the Swift framework. Here's a quick demonstration on how to define your own struct using Swift:

```
Public struct MyColor {
    var red = 0
    var green = 0
    var blue = 0
    var alpha = 0.0
}
```

The preceding example defines a new structure called `MyColor`, which describes an RGBA-based color definition. This structure has four properties called `red`, `green`, `blue`, and `alpha`. Although these properties have all been defined as mutable variables using `var`, stored properties in Swift can also be defined as immutable using `let`. The first three properties in our struct are inferred to be the `Int` types by setting their default values to `0`, while the remaining property is inferred to be `Double` type by setting its default value to `0.0`. Since we have not defined any custom initializers for our method yet, we could initialize an instance of this object as follows:

```
var color = MyColor()
color.red = 139
color.green = 0
color.blue = 139
color.alpha = .5
```

The preceding code initializes our struct and sets the values to represent something similar to dark magenta with a 50% alpha. This demonstration is fine, but the initialization is somewhat verbose for many developers' taste. What if we want to create a new object in one line? In that case, we need to modify our struct to include a custom initializer, as follows:

```
public struct MyColor {
    var red = 0
    var green = 0
    var blue = 0
    var alpha = 0.0
    public init(R: Int, G: Int, B: Int, A: Double)
    {
        red = R
        green = G
        blue = B
        alpha = A
    }
}

var color = MyColor(R: 139, G:0, B:139, A:0.5)
```

Taking advantage of Swift allowing structs to define custom initializers, we have created an `init` method that accepts RGBA values and assigns them to the properties of our object, greatly simplifying our object creation.

Now we will take a look at the `Waypoint` class from Chapter 3, *Lists: Linear Collections*, and determine whether we can convert that class to a structure. Here's the original code:

```
public class Waypoint : Equatable
{
    var lat: Int
```

```
        var long: Int
        public private(set) var active: Bool
        public init(latitude: Int, longitude: Int) {
            lat = latitude
            long = longitude
            active = true
        }
        public func DeactivateWaypoint()
        {
            active = false;
        }
        public func ReactivateWaypoint()
        {
            active = true;
        }
    }
    public func == (lhs: Waypoint, rhs: Waypoint) -> Bool {
        return (lhs.lat == rhs.lat && lhs.long == rhs.long)
    }
```

Now this is an interesting class object. We will tackle the elephant in the room first: the `Equatable` interface and the public function named == declared *outside* the class structure. Our class is required to implement the `Equatable` interface because several of the methods in `WaypointList` compare two `Waypoint` objects for equality. Without the interface and the associated == method implementation, this would not be possible and our code would not compile. Luckily, Swift structs are permitted to implement interfaces such as `Equatable`, so this really is not an issue and we can move on.

We have already discussed and demonstrated that Swift structs can define custom initializers, so our public `init` method is fine as it is. The `Waypoint` class also has two methods called `DeactivateWaypoint()` and `ActivateWaypoint()`. Since structs are intended to be immutable, the final change we need for our class to become a struct is the addition of the `mutating` keyword to each of these methods to denote that each one modifies, or mutates, one or more of the values in the instance. Here's the final version of our `Waypoint` class:

```
    public struct Waypoint : Equatable
    {
        var lat: Int
        var long: Int
        public private(set) var active: Bool
        public init(latitude: Int, longitude: Int) {
            lat = latitude
            long = longitude
            active = true
        }
```

```
        public mutating func DeactivateWaypoint()
        {
            active = false;
        }
        public mutating func ReactivateWaypoint()
        {
            active = true;
        }
    }

    public func == (lhs: Waypoint, rhs: Waypoint) -> Bool {
        return (lhs.lat == rhs.lat && lhs.long == rhs.long)
    }
```

The addition of the `mutating` keyword to our instance methods will allow us to redefine `Waypoint` as a struct, but it will also introduce a new limitation to our implementation. Consider the following example:

```
    let point = Waypoint(latitude: 5, longitude: 10)
    point.DeactivateWaypoint()
```

This code will fail to compile with the error `Immutable value of type 'Waypoint' has only mutating members named DeactivateWaypoint`. Wait. What now? By including the `mutating` keyword, we are also explicitly declaring that this struct is a mutable type. It's fine to declare this type as immutable, unless you try to call one of the mutating methods at which point the code will fail to compile. Whereas before this change we could declare any instance of `Waypoint` as either mutable using `var` or immutable using `let`, as we saw fit, we are now restricted to only declaring mutable instances of this object if we intend to utilize the `mutating` methods.

Enums

As discussed earlier, enums increase the level of abstraction in your application and allow the developer to focus on the meaning of the values rather than being concerned with how the values are stored in memory. This is because an `enum` type allows you to label specific integer numeric values with meaningful or easy to remember names.

Case study: the Metro line

Business problem: You work with an engineering team tasked with writing an application that keeps track of commuter trains along the Metro. One of the key business requirements is the ability to easily identify which station a train is currently located at or en route to. Each train station has a unique name, but the database tracks the stations by their ID values, such as 1100, 1200, 1300, and so on. Rather than track stations by name, which is both tedious and prone to change over time, your app will utilize the station IDs. However, the reason stations are labeled with names instead of IDs in the first place is to make it easier for commuters to identify them. This is also true for programmers, who would have a difficult time keeping the IDs of dozens or perhaps hundreds of stations in mind while writing code.

You decide to utilize the enum data structure to meet the needs of both your application and your developers. Your enum will provide a map between easy-to-remember station names and the station IDs they are associated with, so your application can utilize the IDs based on the station names while your programmers will use the names.

C#

To avoid confusion where multiple train lines overlap at larger stations, we do not simply want to create an enum with all of the stations in the entire Metro line. Instead, we will create enums based on each line in the Metro. Here's the Silver Line defined as a C# enum:

```
public enum SilverLine
{
    Wiehle_Reston_East = 1000,
    Spring_Hill = 1100,
    Greensboro = 1200,
    Tysons_Corner = 1300,
    McClean = 1400,
    East_Falls_Church = 2000,
    Ballston_MU = 2100,
    Virginia_Sq_GMU = 2200,
    Clarendon = 2300,
    Courthouse = 2400,
    Rosslyn = 3000,
    Foggy_Bottom_GWU = 3100,
    Farragut_West = 3200,
    McPherson_Sq = 3300,
    Metro_Center = 4000,
    Federal_Triangle = 4100,
    Smithsonian = 4200,
    LEnfant_Plaza = 5000,
    Federal_Center_SW = 5100,
    Capital_South = 5200,
    Eastern_Market = 5300,
```

```
        Potomac_Ave = 5400,
        Stadium_Armory = 6000,
        Benning_Road = 6100,
        Capital_Heights = 6200,
        Addison_Road = 6300,
        Morgan_Blvd = 6400,
        Largo_Town_Center = 6500
    }
```

Now, wherever we want to use a value from the `SilverLine` enum, we simply need to declare a value type by the same name and assign a value, such as the following:

```
SilverLine nextStop = SilverLine.Federal_Triangle;
nextStop = SilverLine.Smithsonian;
```

In the example we just saw, our code initializes a `SilverLine` value to show the Silver Line's next stop as station 4100, using `SilverLine.Federal_Triangle`. Once the doors close on the platform, we need to update this value to show our train is moving to station 4200, so we update the value to `SilverLine.Smithsonian`.

Java

Although Java does not permit us to define structs explicitly, we can define enums. However, the definition may not appear as you expect:

```
public enum SilverLine
{
    WIEHLE_RESTON_EAST,
    SPRING_HILL,
    GREENSBORO,
    TYSONS_CORNER,
    MCCLEAN,
    EAST_FALLS_CHURCH,
    BALLSTON_MU,
    VIRGINIA_SQ_GMU,
    CLARENDON,
    COURTHOUSE,
    ROSSLYN,
    FOGGY_BOTTOM_GWU,
    FARRAGUT_WEST,
    MCPHERSON_SQ,
    METRO_CENTER,
    FEDERAL_TRIANGLE,
    SMITHSONIAN,
    LENFANT_PLAZA,
    FEDERAL_CENTER_SW,
    CAPITAL_SOUTH,
```

```
        EASTERN_MARKET,
        POTOMAC_AVE,
        STADIUM_ARMORY,
        BENNING_ROAD,
        CAPITAL_HEIGHTS,
        ADDISON_ROAD,
        MORGAN_BLVD,
        LARGO_TOWN_CENTER
    }
```

You may notice that we have not explicitly assigned integer values to each of these entries. This is because Java will not allow us to do so. Remember that Java does not support structs, so enums in this language are not really primitives at all but rather objects of their own type. Therefore, they do not play by the same rules as enums in other languages, and some argue that Java enums are more robust because of it.

Unfortunately for our planned use of this structure, this limitation will be a small hurdle because we cannot map the station names directly to their associated ID value. One option here would be to add a `public static` method, which will operate on the string value of `this`, and use that value to map the string to an integer value behind the scenes. This may be a somewhat verbose solution, but when you consider the fact that this is even possible, it opens a whole new world of alternative solutions to the overall business problem.

Objective-C

Just as Objective-C does not support structures, it also does not directly support enums. Luckily, we can use the underlying C language enum in this case as well. Here's how:

```
    typedef enum NSUInteger
    {
        Wiehle_Reston_East = 1000,
        Spring_Hill = 1100,
        Greensboro = 1200,
        Tysons_Corner = 1300,
        McClean = 1400,
        East_Falls_Church = 2000,
        Ballston_MU = 2100,
        Virginia_Sq_GMU = 2200,
        Clarendon = 2300,
        Courthouse = 2400,
        Rosslyn = 3000,
        Foggy_Bottom_GWU = 3100,
        Farragut_West = 3200,
        McPherson_Sq = 3300,
        Metro_Center = 4000,
        Federal_Triangle = 4100,
```

```
          Smithsonian = 4200,
          LEnfant_Plaza = 5000,
          Federal_Center_SW = 5100,
          Capital_South = 5200,
          Eastern_Market = 5300,
          Potomac_Ave = 5400,
          Stadium_Armory = 6000,
          Benning_Road = 6100,
          Capital_Heights = 6200,
          Addison_Road = 6300,
          Morgan_Blvd = 6400,
          Largo_Town_Center = 6500
    } SilverLine;
```

First, note that we have integrated the `typedef` keyword into this definition, which means that we will not need to add the declaration of the `SilverLine` enum as an object on a separate line in our code. Also note the `enum` keyword, which is required to declare an enum in C. Note that we are explicitly declaring that this enum is of value type `NSUInteger`. We are using `NSUInteger` here because we do not want to support signed values, but if we did, then we could just as easily have chosen `NSInteger` for this purpose. Finally, note that the actual name of the `enum` variable comes after the definition.

Otherwise, our enum definition is similar to that of most other C-based languages, with just a couple of caveats. First, enums must be declared in a header (`*.h`) file if you intend to use it *outside* the scope of the current file. In either case, the enum must also be declared them *outside* the `@interface` or `@implementation` tags or your code will not compile. Finally, the name of your enum must be unique among all other objects within the workspace.

Swift

Structs in Swift have more in common with those of C# than those of Objective-C due to their wide flexibility. In our example here, we will not add any additional methods or `init` functions, but we could if we needed to:

```
public enum SilverLine : Int
{
    case Wiehle_Reston_East = 1000
    case Spring_Hill = 1100
    case Greensboro = 1200
    case Tysons_Corner = 1300
    case McClean = 1400
    case East_Falls_Church = 2000
    case Ballston_MU = 2100
    case Virginia_Sq_GMU = 2200
```

```
        case Clarendon = 2300
        case Courthouse = 2400
        case Rosslyn = 3000
        case Foggy_Bottom_GWU = 3100
        case Farragut_West = 3200
        case McPherson_Sq = 3300
        case Metro_Center = 4000
        case Federal_Triangle = 4100
        case Smithsonian = 4200
        case LEnfant_Plaza = 5000
        case Federal_Center_SW = 5100
        case Capital_South = 5200
        case Eastern_Market = 5300
        case Potomac_Ave = 5400
        case Stadium_Armory = 6000
        case Benning_Road = 6100
        case Capital_Heights = 6200
        case Addison_Road = 6300
        case Morgan_Blvd = 6400
        case Largo_Town_Center = 6500
    }
```

Note the inclusion of the `Int` declaration in our definition. This is not strictly required in most cases, unless we intend to explicitly set values for our entries as we have done here. This lets the compiler know in advance what types to expect for the purpose of type checking. If we had chosen to leave out the explicit values, we could have optionally left off the `Int` declaration as well.

Summary

In this chapter, you learned the basic definition of the struct data structure, as well as how to create structs in applicable languages. We also examined some common applications of structs including the very common enum data type. Finally, we looked at some previous code examples to check whether we could improve on them using struct objects instead of custom classes.

9
Trees: Non-Linear Structures

Tree structures are essentially collections of nodes, typically including constraints that prevent more than one reference to each node, and stipulate that no references point to the root node. This structure simulates a hierarchical tree-like structure that can be either ordered or unordered based on the value contained in each node. Also, nodes can contain either value types or instances of objects, depending on the purpose of the tree.

Trees are incredibly useful data structures in programming, although their applications can be somewhat limited. Even when a structure is in use, you may not always recognize their presence since many other data structures are built on top of them. In this chapter we are going to examine the tree data structure in detail, and in later chapters we will examine other structures that typically use the tree structure as a foundation.

In this chapter we will cover the following topics:

- Definition of the tree data structure
- Tree data structure versus the tree data type
- Terminology associated with trees
- Common operations
- Creating trees
- Recursion
- Traversal

Tree data structure versus tree data type

In fact, there is both a tree data type as well as a tree data structure, and the two are quite different. So before we go any further, it is important to make a distinction between a tree data structure and a tree data type.

For starters, a data type is only an arrangement of data without any definition of how a collection of that data is to be implemented. On the other hand, a data structure is precisely concerned with detailing how to take a particular data type and create a usable, concrete implementation of that type.

In the case of trees, a tree data type must have a value and some concept of children where each of those children is also a tree. A tree data structure is a group of nodes that are linked according to the pattern of a tree data type.

The two diagrams following show the two types of tree:

- Ordered Tree:

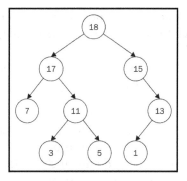

- Unordered Tree:

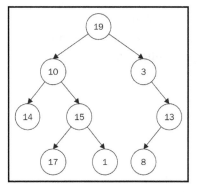

Therefore each node is a tree, with the potential for child nodes that are also trees. In this chapter, we will be focusing on the concrete implementation of a tree data structure.

Tree terminology

Many of the terms and definitions used in trees are unique to these data structures. Therefore, before we can examine tree data structures we need to take the time to learn the language.

Here are some of the most common and important terms:

- **Node**: Any object or value stored in the tree represents a node. In the preceding figure, the root and all of its children and descendants are independent nodes.
- **Root**: The root is the base node of the tree. Ironically, this node is typically depicted at the top of a graphic representation of the tree. Note that a root node, even if it has zero descendants, represents an entire tree by itself.
- **Parent**: A parent node is any node which contains *1...n* child nodes. The parent is only the parent in respect to one of its children. Also note that any parent node can have *0...n* children depending on the rules associated with the tree's structure.
- **Child**: Any node other than the root node is a child to one (and only one) other node. The root node of any tree that is not a sub-tree of another structure is the only node that is not itself a child.
- **Siblings**: Siblings, also referred to as children, represent the collection of all of the child nodes to one particular parent. For example, referring to the preceding figure, the collection of two nodes below the root represents siblings.
- **Leaf**: Any node that has no child nodes is called a leaf.
- **Edge**: An edge is the route, or reference, between a parent and child node.
- **Descendant**: The descendants of a node are any of the nodes that can be reached from that node following edges away from the root node.
- **Ancestor**: The ancestors of a node are any of the nodes that can be reached from that node following edges toward the root node.
- **Path**: A path is described as a list of edges between a node and one of its descendants.
- **Height of tree**: The height of a tree represents the number of edges between the root node and the leaf that is furthest from the root node.
- **Depth**: The number of edges between that node and the root node represents the depth of a node. The root node, therefore, has a depth equal to zero.

Common operations

Tree data structures can consistent of $1...n$ nodes., which means that even a single node without a parent or any children is still considered a tree. Therefore, many of the common operations associated with trees can be defined in terms of a single node, or from the perspective of the same. Here is a list of the most common operations associated with trees

- **Data**: The data operation is associated with a single node, and returns the object or value contained in that node.
- **Children**: The children operation returns the collection of siblings associated with this parent node.
- **Parent**: Some tree structures provide a mechanism to "climb" the tree, or traverse the structure from any particular node back toward the root.
- **Enumerate**: An enumeration operation will return a list or some other collection containing every descendant of a particular node, including the root node itself.
- **Insert**: An insert operation allows a new node to be added as a child of an existing node in the tree. The insert operation can be somewhat complicated when the tree structure has a limit to the number of children that can be associated with a particular parent. When the maximum number of children permitted is already in place, one of those children must be relocated as a child of the new node being inserted.
- **Graft**: Graft is a similar operation to insert, except that the node being inserted has descendants of its own, meaning it is a multi-layer tree. As with the insert operation, graft can be somewhat complicated when the tree structure has a limit to the number of children that can be associated with a particular parent. When the maximum number of children permitted is already in place, one of those children must be logically relocated as a child of a leaf of the new tree being inserted.
- **Delete**: The delete operation will remove a specified node from the tree. If the node being deleted has descendants, those nodes must be relocated to the deleted node's parent in some fashion, otherwise the operation is classified as a prune.
- **Prune**: Prune operations will remove a node and all of its descendants from a tree.

Instantiating trees

Considering how commonly the tree is seen in computer science, it is somewhat surprising that *none* of the languages we are discussing provides a simple and versatile concrete implementation of the tree structure for general use. Therefore, we are going to create implementations of our own.

Tree structures

Before we begin, we need to detail a few characteristics our tree structure will possess. For starters, we are going to create an ordered tree so we are not going to allow duplicate values to be added, which will simplify our implementation. Also, we are going to restrict each node to two child nodes. Technically this means we are defining a binary tree structure, but for now we are going to ignore the specific advantages and applications of such a structure and examine that definition in more detail later. Next, our structure is going to implement *data* and *children* operations by simply exposing the underlying objects contained in each node. We will not be implementing the parent operation because we have no need to traverse the tree backward at this time.

The *insert* operation will be implemented as two separate methods supporting raw data and an existing node, while the *graft* operation will only support existing nodes. Due to our decision not to permit duplicates, the *graft* operation will act similarly to a union operation within a set data structure in that the resulting tree will only consist of unique values from the two input trees. Each of these three operations will return Boolean values indicating whether the operation succeeded.

The *delete* operation will also provide two methods supporting raw data and existing nodes, while the *prune* operation will only support existing nodes. Each of these three methods will remove the node from the tree and return that node to the caller. In this way, the *delete* and *prune* operations will act similarly to a *pop* function in a queue or stack.

We will need to implement *search* operations that will return matching nodes but will not remove the node from the tree. In this way, the search functions will act similarly to a *peek* function in a queue or stack.

Our *enumerate* operation will be implemented as a recursive function. We will examine recursion in more detail later, but for now we'll just implement the method. Finally, we will implement some form of *copy* operation.

C#

C# provides enough functionality for us to create a versatile tree data structure with surprisingly little code. First we need to build a class to represent the nodes of a tree. Here's what a concrete implementation of a `Node` class might look like in C#:

```
public Int16 Data;
public Node Left;
public Node Right;
```

A `Node` represents two basic components including the data contained in the node, and a collection of child nodes that are referenced by our node. In our implementation we have a public field for our node's data, which in this case is an integer. We also have a public field for each of the two child nodes called `Left` and `Right`.

```
public List<Node> Children
{
    get
    {
        List<Node> children = new List<Node>();
        if (this.Left != null)
        {
            children.Add(this.Left);
        }
        if (this.Right != null)
        {
            children.Add(this.Right);
        }
        return children;
    }
}
```

We have added one additional getter called `Children` that returns a `List<Node>` containing any child nodes that exist in this node. This property is not so much for convenience as an integral part of our various recursive functions that come later.

```
public Node(Int16 data)
{
    this.Data = data;
}
```

Our Node class defines one custom constructor, which accepts a single parameter of type Int. This parameter populates our Data field as it is the only required field in our structure, since child nodes are always optional.

```
public bool InsertData(Int16 data)
{
    Node node = new Node (data);
    return this.InsertNode(node);
}

public bool InsertNode(Node node)
{
    if (node == null || node.Data == this.Data)
    {
        return false;
    }
    else if (node.Data < this.Data)
    {
        if (this.Left == null)
        {
            this.Left = node;
            return true;
        }
        else
        {
            return this.Left.InsertNode(node);
        }
    }
    else
    {
        if (this.Right == null)
        {
            this.Right = node;
            return true;
        }
        else
        {
            return this.Right.InsertNode(node);
        }
    }
}
```

Our first two methods support inserting data and inserting nodes. The InsertData(Int data) method provides our *insert* functionality for raw node data. Therefore, this method takes the data point and creates a new Node object from it before passing that object to the InsertNode(Node node) method.

The `InsertNode(Node node)` method provides the *Insert* functionality for an existing `Node` object. The method first checks whether `node` is `null`, or the `Data` value of `node` matches that of the current node. If so, we return `false`, which prevents duplicates from being added to our tree. Next we check if the value is less than our current node's data value. If so, we first check if the `Left` node exists and if not we assign the newly inserted node to that open position. Otherwise, this new node must be inserted somewhere below the `Left` node so we recursively call `InsertNode(Node node)` on the `Left` node. That recursive call will start the process over again, confirming that `Left` does not contain this value and so on.

If the value of the inserted `Node` is greater than our current node, the entire process repeats but starting with the `Right` node. Eventually, we either find the value already exists in our tree, or we find a leaf with an available child position that can accept the inserted `Node`. This method has a worst case complexity of **O**(*log(n)*).

Using this method, we could theoretically merge entire trees together with a single call. Unfortunately, `InsertNode(Node node)` will not prevent duplicates from being entered into our tree if values existing in our current tree also exist as descendants of the inserted node. The *graft* operation is required for this functionality.

```
public bool Graft(Node node)
{
    if (node == null)
    {
        return false;
    }

    List<Node> nodes = node.ListTree();
    foreach (Node n in nodes)
    {
        this.InsertNode(n);
    }

    return true;
}
```

The `Graft(Node node)` method leverages the existing `InsertNode(Node node)`. The method first confirms that `node` is not `null`, and returns `false` if it is. Next, the method creates a new `List<Node>` collection by calling `ListTree()` on `node`. We will examine `ListTree()` in a moment, but for now know that `ListTree()` will return a list containing `node` and every one of its descendants.

```
public Node RemoveData(Int16 data)
{
    Node node = new Node (data);
    return this.RemoveNode(node);
}

public Node RemoveNode(Node node)
{
    if (node == null)
    {
        return null;
    }

    Node retNode;
    Node modNode;
    List<Node> treeList = new List<Node>();

    if (this.Data == node.Data)
    {
        //Root match
        retNode = new Node(this.Data);
        modNode = this;
        if (this.Children.Count == 0)
        {
            return this; //Root has no childen
        }
    }
    else if (this.Left.Data == node.Data)
    {
        retNode = new Node(this.Left.Data);
        modNode = this.Left;
    }
    else if (this.Right.Data == node.Data)
    {
        retNode = new Node(this.Right.Data);
        modNode = this.Right;
    }
    else
    {
        foreach (Node child in this.Children)
        {
```

```
                    if (child.RemoveNode(node) != null)
                    {
                        return child;
                    }
                }

            //No match in tree
            return null;
        }

        //Reorder the tree
        if (modNode.Left != null)
        {
            modNode.Data = modNode.Left.Data;
            treeList.AddRange(modNode.Left.ListTree());
            modNode.Left = null;
        }
        else if (modNode.Right != null)
        {
            modNode.Data = modNode.Right.Data;
            treeList.AddRange(modNode.Right.ListTree());
            modNode.Right = null;
        }
        else
        {
            modNode = null;
        }
        foreach (Node n in treeList)
        {
            modNode.InsertNode(n);
        }

        //Finished
        return retNode;
    }
```

The next two methods support deleting data and deleting nodes. The `RemoveData(Int data)` method provides our *delete* functionality for raw node data. Therefore, this method takes the data point and creates a new `Node` object from it, before passing that object to the `RemoveNode(Node node)` method.

The RemoveNode(Node node) method provides the *delete* functionality for an existing Node object. The method first confirms that node is not null, and returns null if it is. Otherwise, the method sets up three objects including retNode which represents the node that will be returned; modNode which represents the node that will be modified to accommodate the removed node; and treelist which will be used to reorder the tree when a node is removed.

Following this, the method is broken down into two major components. The first searches for a match to the node parameter. The first if block checks if the current node data matches the node. If the node matches, retNode is created using this.Data and modNode is set to this. Before the execution moves on, the method checks if this has any children. If not, we have a single node tree so our method simply returns this. This logic prevents us from trying to completely eliminate the tree, which can only be done by another class that instantiates the root Node object. The next two if else blocks check if node matches Left or Right, respectively. In either case, retNode is created using the Data from the matching child, and modNode is set to the matching child. If we still don't find a match, the method recursively calls RemoveNode(Node node) on each of the two child nodes. If any of those calls return a Node object, that object is returned to the caller. When all else fails, our method returns null, meaning there is no match for node.

Due to how the algorithm is written, the contents of the first if block can only execute when the root of the tree is being examined. That's because, by the time we begin calling the method recursively on the children, we already know their Data values don't match that of node. From this point forward, our method is always looking forward to the children for a match. In terms of recursion, we refer to the first if statement as the **base case** of our algorithm. We will examine recursion in greater detail later in this chapter.

The second component of RemoveNode(Node node) reorders the remaining nodes so our sorting is not lost in the process of removing node. This component first checks whether Left is not null, meaning there is a branch of nodes to the left of this node. If Left happens to be null, Right is checked next. If both Left and Right are null, we've gotten off easy as this is a leaf with no descendants that need to be reordered.

If either `Left` or `Right` has an object, there are descendants that need to be addressed. In either case, the block of code moves the `Data` value from the child node and assigns it to `modNode.Data`, which if you recall is the node we actually want to remove. By moving the data in this fashion we are simultaneously deleting the node and moving its child `Data` up to take its place. Following this, our method creates a `List<Node>` collection by calling `ListTree()` on the child node. This operation returns the child node and every one of its descendants. Then the block completes by setting the child to `null`, effectively deleting the entire branch.

Finally, the method loops through the `treeList` collection and calls `InsertNode(Node node)` with every `Node` in the list. This approach ensures that the data value of our child node will not be duplicated in the final tree, plus our final tree will be properly ordered before the operation has completed.

Although many algorithms could perform this reorder, and perhaps more than a few of those more efficient than this, for now we just need to make sure that our final tree structure still contains every node but the one that was deleted and it is properly ordered. That being said, the `RemoveNode(Node node)` method has a *painfully* expensive complexity cost of $O(n^2)$.

```
public Node Prune(Node root)
{
    Node matchNode;
    if (this.Data == root.Data)
    {
        //Root match
        Node b = this.CopyTree();
        this.Left = null;
        this.Right = null;
        return b;
    }
    else if (this.Left.Data == root.Data)
    {
        matchNode = this.Left;
    }
    else if (this.Right.Data == root.Data)
    {
        matchNode = this.Right;
    }
    else
    {
        foreach (Node child in this.Children)
        {
            if (child.Prune(root) != null)
            {
```

```
                    return child;
                }
            }

        //No match in tree
        return null;
    }

    Node branch = matchNode.CopyTree ();
    matchNode = null;

    return branch;
}
```

The `Prune (Node root)` method operates in a similar fashion to `RemoveNode (Node node)`. We start by confirming that `root` is not `null` and returning `null` if it is. Next we establish our base case and look for a match in `this`. If our root node matches, the method creates a copy of the entire tree named `b`, then sets `Left` and `Right` to `null` to delete all descendants of the root before returning `b`. As in `RemoveNode (Node node)`, this logic prevents us from trying to completely eliminate the tree, which can only be done by another class that instantiates the root `Node` object.

If the root node does not match `root`, our method checks `Left` and `Right` and finally it recursively checks `Children`. If all else fails, we still return `null` denoting that a match could not be found.

If a match is found in `Left` or `Right`, `matchNode` is set to the matching node and that node is later copied to `Node branch`. Finally, `matchNode` is set to `null`, which deletes the node and its descendants from the tree, and branch is finally returned. This method has a worst case complexity of $O(n)$.

```
public Node FindData(Int16 data)
{
    Node node = new Node (data);
    return this.FindNode (node);
}

public Node FindNode(Node node)
{
    if (node.Data == this.Data)
    {
        return this;
    }

    foreach (Node child in this.Children)
    {
```

```
                    Node result = child.FindNode(node);
                    if (result != null)
                    {
                        return result;
                    }
                }

                return false;
            }
```

Our Node class implements *search* functionality using the FindData(Int data) and FindNode(Node node) methods. FindData(Int data) allows us to pass in a raw Int value, which creates a new Node object and passes that to FindNode(Node node).

The FindNode(Node node) method in turn checks if the search node data matches the current node's data. If so, we return true because we have a match. Otherwise, the method recursively calls FindNode(Node node) on each node in the Children collection until a match is found, or we reach the end of the tree. In that case, we return false denoting that the data does not exist in the tree. This method has a worst case complexity of **O**(*log(n)*).

```
        public Node CopyTree()
        {
            Node n = new Node (this.Data);
            if (this.Left != null)
            {
                n.Left = this.Left.CopyTree();
            }

            if(this.Right != null)
            {
                n.Right = this.Right.CopyTree();
            }
            return n;
        }
```

The CopyTree() method duplicates the current node, then sets Left and Right to copies of this using recursive method calls. When the method returns the copied node, the copy represents a complete duplicate of the entire tree, branch, or node.

```
        public List<Node> ListTree()
        {
            List<Node> result = new List<Node>();
            result.Add(new Node(this.Data()));
            foreach (Node child in this.Children)
            {
                result.AddRange(child.ListTree());
            }
```

```
        return result;
    }
```

Finally, we come to the *enumeration* functionality provided by the `ListTree()` method. This method simply creates a new `List<Node>` collection, adds a new `Node` based on the `Data` in `this` to the collection, then recursively calls `ListTree()` on each node in the `Children` collection until we have gathered every node in the tree. Finally, the method returns `result` to the caller.

 This simple class represents each of the nodes in our tree. However, you may be wondering why a node class implements all of the functionality of a tree data structure. If you recall the discussion on terminology, a root node without any descendants represents an entire tree. This means any definition of a node must necessarily provide all of the functionality of the entire tree, in and of itself. Any subsequent implementations of a tree structure will then be built with a single `Node` object as its core. This node will have children, which will in turn also have children, and so on, thus providing an entire tree structure encapsulated within a single field.

Java

Java also provides the basic tools necessary to build a robust implementation of our `Node` class with little effort. Here's an example of what that implementation might look like:

```java
public int Data;
public Node left;
public Node right;

public List<Node> getChildren()
{
    List<Node> children = new LinkedList<Node>();
    if (this.Left != null)
    {
        children.add(this.Left);
    }
    if (this.Right != null)
    {
        children.add(this.Right);
    }
    return children;
}
```

As with C#, our Java `Node` class includes a public field for our node's data, as well as public fields for each of the two child nodes called `Left` and `Right`. Our Java `Node` likewise includes a public method called `getChildren()` that returns a `LinkedList<Node>` containing any child nodes that exist in this node.

```java
public Node(int data)
{
    this.Data = data;
}
```

Our `Node` class defines one custom constructor, that accepts a single parameter of type `int` which is used to populate the `Data` field.

```java
public boolean insertData(int data)
{
    Node node = new Node (data);
    return this.insertNode(node);
}

public boolean insertNode(Node node)
{
    if (node == null || node.Data == this.Data)
    {
        return false;
    }
    else if (node.Data < this.Data)
    {
        if (this.Left == null)
        {
            this.Left = node;
            return true;
        }
        else
        {
            return this.Left.insertNode(node);
        }
    }
    else
    {
        if (this.Right == null)
        {
            this.Right = node;
            return true;
        }
        else
        {
            return this.Right.insertNode(node);
```

```
            }
          }
      }
```

Our first two methods support inserting data and inserting nodes. The `insertData(int data)` method provides our *insert* functionality for raw node data. Therefore, this method takes the data point and creates a new `Node` object from it before passing that object to the `insertNode(Node node)` method.

`insertNode(Node node)` provides the *insert* functionality for an existing `Node` object. The method first checks if `node` is `null`, or the `Data` value of `node` matches that of the current node. If so, we return `false`, which prevents duplicates from being added to our tree. Next we check if the value is less than our current node's data value. If so, we first check if the `Left` node exists and if not we assign the newly inserted node to that open position. Otherwise, this new node must be inserted somewhere below the `Left` node so we recursively call `insertNode(Node node)` on the `Left` node. That recursive call will start the process over again, confirming that `Left` does not contain this value and so on.

If the value of the inserted `Node` is greater than our current node, the entire process repeats using the `Right` node. Eventually, we will determine the value already existed in our tree, or we find a leaf with an available child position that can accept the inserted `Node`. This method has a worst case complexity of **O***(log(n))*.

```
public boolean graft(Node node)
{
    if (node == null)
    {
        return false;
    }

    List<Node> nodes = node.listTree();
    for (Node n : nodes)
    {
        this.insertNode(n);
    }
    return true;
}
```

The `graft(Node node)` method leverages the existing `insertNode(Node node)`. The method first confirms that `node` is not `null`, and returns `false` if it is. Next, the method creates a new `List<Node>` collection by calling `listTree()` on `node` which returns a list containing `node` and every one of its descendants.

```
public Node removeData(int data)
{
    Node node = new Node(data);
    return this.removeNode(node);
}

public Node removeNode(Node node)
{
    if (node == null)
    {
        return null;
    }

    Node retNode;
    Node modNode;
    List<Node> treeList = new LinkedList<Node>();

    if (this.Data == node.Data)
    {
        //Root match
        retNode = new Node(this.Data);
        modNode = this;
        if (this.getChildren().size() == 0)
        {
            return this; //Root has no childen
        }
    }
    else if (this.Left.Data == node.Data)
    {
        //Match found
        retNode = new Node(this.Left.Data);
        modNode = this.Left;
    }
    else if (this.Right.Data == node.Data)
    {
        //Match found
        retNode = new Node(this.Right.Data);
        modNode = this.Right;
    }
    else
    {
        for (Node child : this.getChildren())
```

```
        {
            if (child.removeNode(node) != null)
            {
                return child;
            }
        }

        //No match in tree
        return null;
    }

    //Reorder the tree
    if (modNode.Left != null)
    {
        modNode.Data = modNode.Left.Data;
        treeList.addAll(modNode.Left.listTree());
        modNode.Left = null;
    }
    else if (modNode.Right != null)
    {
        modNode.Data = modNode.Right.Data;
        treeList.addAll(modNode.Right.listTree());
        modNode.Right = null;
    }
    else
    {
        modNode = null;
    }

    for (Node n : treeList)
    {
        modNode.insertNode(n);
    }

    //Finished
    return retNode;
}
```

The next two methods support deleting data and deleting nodes. The `removeData(Int data)` method provides our *delete* functionality for raw node data. Therefore, this method takes the data point and creates a new `Node` object from it, before passing that object to the `removeNode(Node node)` method.

removeNode(Node node) provides the *delete* functionality for an existing Node object. The method first confirms that node is not null, and returns null if it is. Otherwise, the method sets up three objects including retNode which represents the node that will be returned; modNode, which represents the node that will be modified to accommodate the removed node; treelist, that will be used to reorder the tree when a node is removed.

The next block begins by searching for a match to the node parameter. The first if block checks if the current node matches the node. If the node matches, retNode is created using this.Data and modNode is set to this. Before the execution moves on, the method checks if this has any children. If not, we have a single node tree so our method simply returns this. The next two if else blocks check if node matches Left or Right, respectively. In both cases, retNode is created using Data from the matching child, and modNode is set to the matching child. If we still don't find a match, the method recursively calls removeNode(Node node) on each of the two child nodes. If any of those calls return a Node object, that object is returned to the caller. When all else fails, our method returns null meaning there is no match for node in our tree.

The second block of removeNode(Node node) reorders the remaining nodes so our sorting is not lost in the process of removing node. This component first checks if Left is not null, meaning there is a branch of nodes to the left of this node. If Left happens to be null, Right is checked next. If both Left and Right are null, we're done.

If either Left or Right is not null, the method moves the Data value from the child node and assigns it to modNode.Data. Following this, our method creates a List<Node> collection by calling listTree() on the child node. Then the block wraps up by setting the child to null, effectively deleting the entire branch.

Finally, the method loops through the treeList collection and calls insertNode(Node node) with every Node in the list. The RemoveNode(Node node) method has a cost of $O(n^2)$.

```
public Node prune(Node root)
{
    if (root == null)
    {
        return null;
    }

    Node matchNode;
    if (this.Data == root.Data)
    {
        //Root match
        Node b = this.copyTree();
```

```
            this.Left = null;
            this.Right = null;
            return b;
        }
        else if (this.Left.Data == root.Data)
        {
            matchNode = this.Left;
        }
        else if (this.Right.Data == root.Data)
        {
            matchNode = this.Right;
        }
        else
        {
            for (Node child : this.getChildren())
            {
                if (child.prune(root) != null)
                {
                    return child;
                }
            }

            //No match in tree
            return null;
        }

        Node branch = matchNode.copyTree();
        matchNode = null;

        return branch;
    }
```

The prune(Node root) method operates in a similar fashion to removeNode(Node node). We start by confirming that root is not null and returning null if it is. Next we establish our base case and look for a match in this. If our root node matches, the method creates a copy of the entire tree named b, then sets Left and Right to null to delete all descendants of the root before returning b.

If the root node does not match root, our method checks Left and Right, and finally it recursively checks Children. If all else fails, we return null since there is no match for root in our tree.

If a match is found in `Left` or `Right`, `matchNode` is set to the matching node and that node is later copied to `Node branch`. Finally, `matchNode` is set to `null`, which deletes the node and its descendants from the tree and branch is finally returned. This method has a cost of **O**(*n*).

```
public Node findData(int data)
{
    Node node = new Node (data);
    return this.findNode(node);
}

public Node findNode(Node node)
{
    if (node.Data == this.Data)
    {
        return this;
    }

    for (Node child : this.getChildren())
    {
        Node result = child.findNode(node);
        if (result != null)
        {
            return result;
        }
    }

    return null;
}
```

Our `Node` class implements *search* functionality using the `findData(Int data)` and `findNode(Node node)` methods. `findData(Int data)` allows us to pass in a raw `int` value, which creates a new `Node` object and passes that to `findNode(Node node)`.

The `findNode(Node node)` method in turn checks if the search node data matches the current node's data. If so, we return `true` because we have a match. Otherwise, the method recursively calls `findNode(Node node)` on each node in the `Children` collection until a match is found, or we reach the end of the tree. In that case, we return `false`, denoting that the data does not exist in the tree. This method has a cost of **O**(*log(n)*):

```
public Node copyTree()
{
    Node n = new Node(this.Data);
    if (this.Left != null)
    {
        n.Left = this.Left.copyTree();
```

```
        }
        if(this.Right != null)
        {
            n.Right = this.Right.copyTree();
        }
        return n;
    }
```

The copyTree() method duplicates the current node, then sets Left and Right to copies of the same using recursive method calls. When the method returns the copied node, the copy represents a complete duplicate of the entire tree, branch or node.

```
    public List<Node> listTree() {
        List<Node> result = new LinkedList<Node>();
        result.add(new Node(this.Data));
        for (Node child : this.getChildren())
        {
            result.addAll(child.listTree());
        }
        return result;
    }
```

Finally, we come to the *enumeration* functionality provided by the listTree() method. This method simply creates a new LinkedList<Node> collection, adds a new Node to the collection based on the Data in this, then recursively calls listTree() on each node in the Children collection until we have gathered every node in the tree. Finally, the method returns result to the caller.

Objective-C

As with other data structure implementations in Objective-C, we have to think a little out-of-the-box to build our Node class. In some ways, Objective-C makes our job simpler but that isn't always the case. Here's what a Node implementation might look like in Objective-C:

```
    -(instancetype)initNodeWithData:(NSInteger)data
    {
        if (self = [super init])
        {
            _data = data;
        }
        return self;
    }
```

Our EDSNode class defines one initializer, which accepts a single parameter of type NSInetger. This parameter populates our _data field as it is the only required field in our structure since child nodes are always optional.

```
-(NSInteger)data
{
    return _data;
}

-(EDSNode*)left
{
    return _left;
}

-(EDSNode*)right
{
    return _right;
}

-(NSArray*)children
{
    return [NSArray arrayWithObjects:_left, _right, nil];
}
```

The EDSNode node has three public properties for the data and two child nodes left and right, as well as an array property named children representing the collection of child nodes:

```
-(BOOL)insertData:(NSInteger)data
{
    EDSNode *node = [[EDSNode alloc] initNodeWithData:data];
    return [self insertNode:node];
}

-(BOOL)insertNode:(EDSNode*)node
{
    if (!node || [self findNode:node])
    {
        return NO;
    }
    else if (node.data < _data)
    {
        if (!_left)
        {
            _left = node;
            return YES;
        }
    }
```

```
        else
        {
            return [_left insertNode:node];
        }
    }
    else
    {
        if (!_right)
        {
            _right = node;
            return YES;
        }
        else
        {
            return [_right insertNode:node];
        }
    }
}
```

Our first two methods support inserting data and inserting nodes. The `insertData:` method provides our *insert* functionality for raw node data. Therefore, this method takes the data point and creates a new `EDSNode` object from it before passing that object to the `insertNode:` method.

`insertNode:` provides the *insert* functionality for an existing `EDSNode` object. The method first checks if `node` is `nil`, or the `data` value of `node` matches that of the current node. If so, we return `NO`. Next we check if the value of `data` is less than our current node's `data` value. If so, we first check if the `left` node exists and if not we assign the newly inserted node to that available position. Otherwise, this new node must be inserted somewhere below the `left` node so we recursively call `insertNode:` on the `left` node. If the value of the inserted `EDSNode` is greater than our current node, the entire process repeats with the `right` node. Eventually, we either confirm the value already exists in our tree, or we find a leaf with an available child position that can accept the inserted `EDSNode`. This method has a worst case complexity of **O**(*log(n)*):

```
-(BOOL)graft:(EDSNode*)node
{
    if (!node)
    {
        return NO;
    }
    NSArray *nodes = [node listTree];
    for (EDSNode *n in nodes)
    {
        [self insertNode:n];
    }
```

```
        return true;
    }
```

The `graft:` method leverages the existing `insertNode:`. The method first confirms that node is not `nil`, and returns `false` if it is. Next, the method creates a new `NSArray` collection by calling `listTree` on node. We will examine the `listTree` method in more detail in a moment, but for now just be aware that this method will return a list containing the node object and every one of its descendants.

```
-(EDSNode*) removeData: (NSInteger) data
{
    EDSNode *node = [[EDSNode alloc] initNodeWithData:data];
    return [self removeNode:node];
}

-(EDSNode*) removeNode: (EDSNode*) node
{
    if (!node)
    {
        return NO;
    }
    EDSNode *retNode;
    EDSNode *modNode;
    NSMutableArray *treeList = [NSMutableArray array];
    if (self.data == node.data)
    {
        //Root match
        retNode = [[EDSNode alloc] initNodeWithData:self.data];
        modNode = self;
        if ([self.children count] == 0)
        {
            return self; //Root has no childen
        }
    }
    else if (_left.data == node.data)
    {
        //Match found
        retNode = [[EDSNode alloc] initNodeWithData:_left.data];
        modNode = _left;
    }
    else if (_right.data == node.data)
    {
        //Match found
        retNode = [[EDSNode alloc] initNodeWithData:_right.data];
        modNode = _right;
    }
    else
```

```
    {
        for (EDSNode *child in self.children)
        {
            if ([child removeNode:node])
            {
                return child;
            }
        }
        //No match in tree
        return nil;
    }
    //Reorder the tree
    if (modNode.left)
    {
        modNode.data = modNode.left.data;
        [treeList addObjectsFromArray:[modNode.left listTree]];
        modNode.left = nil;
    }
    else if (modNode.right)
    {
        modNode.data = modNode.right.data;
        [treeList addObjectsFromArray:[modNode.right listTree]];
        modNode.right = nil;
    }
    else
    {
        modNode = nil;
    }
    for (EDSNode *n in treeList)
    {
        [modNode insertNode:n];
    }
    //Finished
    return retNode;
}
```

The next two methods support deleting data and deleting nodes. The `removeData:` method provides our *delete* functionality for raw node data. Therefore, this method takes the data point and creates a new `EDSNode` object from it, before passing that object to the `removeNode:` method.

The `removeNode:` method provides the *delete* functionality for an existing `Node` object. The method first confirms that `node` is not `nil`, and returns `nil` if it is. Otherwise, the method sets up three objects including `retNode` which represents the node that will be returned; `modNode` that represents the node that will be modified to accommodate the removed node, and `treelist` which will be used to reorder the tree when a node is removed.

Following this, the method is broken down into two major components. The first searches for a match to the `node` parameter. The first `if` block checks if `self.data` matches `node.data`. If the node matches, `retNode` is created using `this.data` and `modNode` is set to `this`. Before the execution moves on, the method checks if `this` has any children. If not, we have a single node tree so our method simply returns `this`. This logic prevents us from trying to completely eliminate the tree, which can only be done by another class that instantiates the root `EDSNode` object. The next two `if else` blocks check if node matches `left` or `right`, respectively. In either case, `retNode` is created using the `data` from the matching child, and `modNode` is set to the matching child. If we still don't find a match, the method recursively calls `removeNode:` on each of the two child nodes. If any of those calls return a `Node` object, that object is returned to the caller. When all else fails, our method returns `nil` meaning, there is no match for `node`.

The second half of `removeNode:` reorders the remaining nodes so our sorting is not lost in the process of removing node. This component first checks if `left` is not `nil`, meaning there is a branch of nodes to the left of this node. If `left` happens to be `nil`, `Right` is checked next. If both `left` and `right` are `nil`, we are done.

If either `left` or `right` has an object, our code moves `data` from the child node and assigns it to `modNode.data`. Following this, our method creates a `NSArray` by calling `listTree` on the child node. The method then sets the child to `nil`, effectively deleting the entire branch. Finally, the method loops through the `treeList` collection and calls `insertNode:` with every `EDSNode` in the list. The `removeNode:` method has a cost of $O(n^2)$:

```
- (EDSNode*) prune: (EDSNode*) root
{
    if (!root)
    {
        return nil;
    }
    EDSNode *matchNode;
    if (self.data == root.data)
    {
        //Root match
        EDSNode *b = [self copyTree];
        self.left = nil;
```

```
            self.right = nil;
            return b;
        }
        else if (self.left.data == root.data)
        {
            matchNode = self.left;
        }
        else if (self.right.data == root.data)
        {
            matchNode = self.right;
        }
        else
        {
            for (EDSNode *child in self.children)
            {
                if ([child prune:root])
                {
                    return child;
                }
            }
            //No match in tree
            return nil;
        }
        EDSNode *branch = [matchNode copyTree];
        matchNode = nil;
        return branch;
    }
```

The prune: method starts by confirming that root is not nil and returning nil if it is. Next we establish our base case and look for a match in this. If our root node matches, the method creates a copy of the entire tree named b, then sets left and right to nil to delete all descendants of the root before returning b. If the root node does not match root, our method checks left and right, and last it recursively checks children. If all else fails, we still return nil denoting that a match could not be found.

If a match is found in left or right, matchNode is set to the matching node and that node is later copied to EDSNode branch. Finally, matchNode is set to nil, which deletes the node and its descendants from the tree, and branch is finally returned. This method has a worst-case complexity of **O**(*n*):

```
-(EDSNode*)findData:(NSInteger)data
{
    EDSNode *node = [[EDSNode alloc] initNodeWithData:data];
    return [self findNode:node];
}
```

```
- (EDSNode*) findNode: (EDSNode*) node
{
    if (node.data == self.data)
    {
        return self;
    }
    for (EDSNode *child in self.children)
    {
        EDSNode *result = [child findNode:node];
        if (result)
        {
            return result;
        }
    }
    return nil;
}
```

Our `EDSNode` class implements *search* functionality using the `findData:` and `findNode:` methods. `findData:` allows us to pass in a raw `NSInteger` value, which creates a new `EDSNode` object and passes that to `findNode:`.

The `findNode:` method in turn checks if the search node data matches the current node's data. If so, we return `YES` because we have a match. Otherwise, the method recursively calls `findNode:` on each node in the `children` collection until a match is found, or we reach the end of the tree. In that case, we return `NO` denoting that the data does not exist in the tree. This method has a worst case complexity of **O**(*log(n)*):

```
- (EDSNode*) copyTree
{
    EDSNode *n = [[EDSNode alloc] initNodeWithData:self.data];
    if (self.left)
    {
        n.left = [self.left copyTree];
    }
    if(self.right)
    {
        n.right = [self.right copyTree];
    }
    return n;
}
```

The `copyTree` method duplicates the current node, then sets `left` and `right` to copies of this using recursive method calls. When the method returns the copied node, the copy represents a complete duplicate of the entire tree, branch, or node:

```
- (NSArray*)listTree
{
    NSMutableArray *result = [NSMutableArray array];
    [result addObject:[[EDSNode alloc] initNodeWithData:self.data]];
    for (EDSNode *child in self.children) {
        [result addObjectsFromArray:[child listTree]];
    }
    return [result copy];
}
```

Finally, we come to the *enumeration* functionality, which is provided by the `listTree:` method. This method simply creates a new `NSArray` collection, adds a new `EDSNode` based on the `data` in `this` to the collection, then recursively calls `listTree` on each node in the `children` collection until we have gathered every node in the tree. Finally, the method returns `result` to the caller.

Swift

Our Swift `Node` class is similar in structure and functionality to the C# and Java implementations. Here's what an example of the `Node` class might look like in Swift:

```
public var data: Int
public var left: Node?
public var right: Node?

public var children: Array<Node> {
    return [left!, right!]
}
```

Our Swift `Node` has three public properties for the data and two child nodes `left` and `right`, as well as an array property named `children` representing the collection of child nodes:

```
public init (nodeData: Int)
{
    data = nodeData
}
```

Our `EDSNode` class defines one initializer, which accepts a single parameter of type `NSInetger`. This parameter populates our `_data` field as it is the only required field in our structure since child nodes are always optional:

```
public func insertData(data: Int) -> Bool
{
    return insertNode(node: Node(nodeData:data))
}

public func insertNode(node: Node?) -> Bool
{
    if (node == nil)
    {
        return false
    }
    if ((findNode(node: node!)) != nil)
    {
        return false
    }
    else if (node!.data < data)
    {
        if (left == nil)
        {
            left = node
            return true
        }
        else
        {
            return left!.insertNode(node: node)
        }
    }
    else
    {
        if (right == node)
        {
            right = node
            return true
        }
        else
        {
            return right!.insertNode(node: node)
        }
    }
}
```

Our first two methods support inserting data and inserting nodes. The `insertData:` method provides our *insert* functionality for raw node data. Therefore, this method takes the data point and creates a new `EDSNode` object from it before passing that object to the `insertNode:` method.

The `insertNode:` method provides the *insert* functionality for an existing `EDSNode` object. The method first checks if `node` is `nil`, or the `data` value of `node` matches that of the current node. If so, we return `NO`. Next we check if the value of `data` is less than our current node's `data` value. If so, we first check if the `left` node exists and if not we assign the newly inserted node to that available position. Otherwise, this new node must be inserted somewhere below the `left` node so we recursively call `insertNode:` on the `left` node. If the value of the inserted `EDSNode` is greater than our current node, the entire process repeats with the `right` node. Eventually, we either confirm the value already exists in our tree, or we find a leaf with an available child position that can accept the inserted `EDSNode`. This method has a worst case complexity of **O**(*log(n)*):

```
public func graft(node: Node?) -> Bool
{
    if (node == nil)
    {
        return false
    }
    let nodes: Array = node!.listTree()
    for n in nodes
    {
        self.insertNode(node: n)
    }
    return true
}
```

The `graft:` method functions leverages the existing `insertNode:`. The method first confirms that `node` is not `nil`, and returns `false` if it is. Next, the method creates a new `NSArray` collection by calling `listTree` on `node`. We will examine `listTree` in a moment, but for now know that `listTree` will return a list containing `node` and every one of its descendants:

```
public func removeData(data: Int) -> Node?
{
    return removeNode(node: Node(nodeData:data))
}

public func removeNode(node: Node?) -> Node?
{
    if (node == nil)
    {
```

```
            return nil
    }
    var retNode: Node
    var modNode: Node?
    var treeList = Array<Node>()
    if (self == node!)
    {
        //Root match
        retNode = Node(nodeData: self.data)
        modNode = self
        if (children.count == 0)
        {
            return self //Root has no childen
        }
    }
    else if (left! == node!)
    {
        //Match found
        retNode = Node(nodeData: left!.data)
        modNode = left!
    }
    else if (right! == node!)
    {
        //Match found
        retNode = Node(nodeData: right!.data)
        modNode = right!
    }
    else
    {
        for child in self.children
        {
            if (child.removeNode(node: node) != nil)
            {
                return child
            }
        }
        //No match in tree
        return nil
    }
    //Reorder the tree
    if ((modNode!.left) != nil)
    {
        modNode! = modNode!.left!
        treeList = modNode!.left!.listTree()
        modNode!.left = nil
    }
    else if ((modNode!.right) != nil)
    {
```

```
                modNode! = modNode!.right!
                treeList = modNode!.right!.listTree()
                modNode!.right = nil
        }
        else
        {
                modNode = nil
        }
        for n in treeList
        {
                modNode!.insertNode(node: n)
        }
        //Finished
        return retNode
    }
```

The next two methods support deleting data and deleting nodes. The `removeData:` method provides our *delete* functionality for raw node data. Therefore, this method takes the data point and creates a new `EDSNode` object from it, before passing that object to the `removeNode:` method.

The `removeNode:` method provides the *delete* functionality for an existing `Node` object. The method first confirms that `node` is not `nil`, and returns `nil` if it is. Otherwise, the method sets up three objects including `retNode` which represents the node that will be returned; `modNode`, that represents the node that will be modified to accommodate the removed node; `treelist`, that will be used to reorder the tree when a node is removed.

Following this, the method is broken down into two major components. The first searches for a match to the `node` parameter. The first `if` block checks if `self.data` matches `node.data`. If the node matches, `retNode` is created using `this.data` and `modNode` is set to `this`. Before the execution moves on, the method checks if `this` has any children. If not, we have a single node tree so our method simply returns `this`. This logic prevents us from trying to completely eliminate the tree, which can only be done by another class that instantiates the root `EDSNode` object. The next two `if else` blocks check if node matches `left` or `right`, respectively. In either case, `retNode` is created using the `data` from the matching child, and `modNode` is set to the matching child. If we still don't find a match, the method recursively calls `removeNode:` on each of the two child nodes. If any of those calls return a `Node` object, that object is returned to the caller. When all else fails, our method returns `nil` meaning there is no match for `node`.

The second half of `removeNode:` reorders the remaining nodes so our sorting is not lost in the process of removing node. This component first checks if `left` is not nil, meaning there is a branch of nodes to the left of this node. If `left` happens to be `nil`, `right` is checked next. If both `left` and `right` are `nil` we are done.

If either `left` or `right` has an object, our code moves `data` from the child node and assigns it to `modNode.data`. Following this, our method creates a `NSArray` by calling `listTree` on the child node. The method then sets the child to `nil`, effectively deleting the entire branch. Finally, the method loops through the `treeList` collection and calls `insertNode:` with every `EDSNode` in the list. The `removeNode:` method has a cost of $O(n^2)$:

```
public func prune(root: Node?) -> Node?
{
    if (root == nil)
    {
        return nil
    }
    var matchNode: Node?
    if (self == root!)
    {
        //Root match
        let b = self.copyTree()
        self.left = nil
        self.right = nil
        return b
    }
    else if (self.left! == root!)
    {
        matchNode = self.left!
    }
    else if (self.right! == root!)
    {
        matchNode = self.right!
    }
    else
    {
        for child in self.children
        {
            if (child.prune(root: root!) != nil)
            {
                return child
            }
        }
        //No match in tree
        return nil;
    }
```

```
        let branch = matchNode!.copyTree()
        matchNode = nil

        return branch
    }
```

The `prune:` method starts by confirming that `root` is not `nil` and returning `nil` if it is. Next we establish our base case and look for a match in `this`. If our root node matches, the method creates a copy of the entire tree named `b`, then sets `left` and `right` to `nil` to delete all descendants of the root before returning `b`. If the root node does not match `root`, our method checks `left` and `right`, and finally it recursively checks `children`. If all else fails, we still return `nil` denoting that a match could not be found.

If a match is found in `left` or `right`, `matchNode` is set to the matching node and that node is later copied to `EDSNode branch`. Finally, `matchNode` is set to `nil`, which deletes the node and its descendants from the tree, and branch is finally returned. This method has a worst case complexity of **O**(*n*):

```
    public func findData(data: Int) -> Node?
    {
        return findNode(node: Node(nodeData:data))
    }

    public func findNode(node: Node) -> Node?
    {
        if (node == self)
        {
            return self
        }
        for child in children
        {
            let result = child.findNode(node: node)
            if (result != nil)
            {
                return result
            }
        }
        return nil
    }
```

Our `EDSNode` class implements *search* functionality using the `findData:` and `findNode:` methods. `findData:` allows us to pass in a raw `NSInteger` value, which creates a new `EDSNode` object and passes that to `findNode:`.

The `findNode:` method in turn checks if the search node data matches the current node's data. If so, we return `YES` because we have a match. Otherwise, the method recursively calls `findNode:` on each node in the `children` collection until a match is found, or we reach the end of the tree. In that case, we return `NO` denoting that the data does not exist in the tree. This method has a worst case complexity of **O***(log(n))*.

```
public func copyTree() -> Node
{
    let n = Node(nodeData: self.data)
    if (self.left != nil)
    {
        n.left = self.left!.copyTree()
    }
    if(self.right != nil)
    {
        n.right = self.right!.copyTree()
    }
    return n
}
```

The `copyTree` method duplicates the current node, then sets `left` and `right` to copies of this using recursive method calls. When the method returns the copied node, the copy represents a complete duplicate of the entire tree, branch, or node:

```
public func listTree() -> Array<Node>
{
    var result = Array<Node>()
    result.append(self)
    for child in children
    {
        result.append(contentsOf: child.listTree())
    }
    return result
}
```

Our Swift `Node` class implements the *enumeration* functionality with the `listTree:` method. This method simply creates a new `NSArray` collection, adds a new `EDSNode` based on the `data` in `this` to the collection, then recursively calls `listTree` on each node in the `children` collection until we have gathered every node in the tree. Finally, the method returns `result` to the caller:

```
public func == (lhs: Node, rhs: Node) -> Bool {
```

```
            return (lhs.data == rhs.data)
    }
```

Finally, since our class implements the `Equatable` protocol, we need to override the `==` operator with respect to `Node`. This method allows us to compare data tags for our `Node` objects by simply comparing the nodes themselves; this makes our resulting code more concise and readable.

Recursion

Although many programmers and even computer science students have a difficult time understanding recursion, the concept is actually quite simple. Plainly stated, recursion is repeatedly performing the same operation by having the method of that operation invoke itself. Therefore, any function that calls an instance of itself is a **recursive function**. As a matter of fact, if a function `f()` calls another function `g()` which in turn may call function `f()` again, this is still a recursive function because `f()` eventually calls itself. Recursion is an excellent tool for solving complex problems where the solution to the problem is based on the solution to smaller examples of the same problem.

The concept of recursion, or recursive functions, is so powerful that almost every modern computer language supports it by providing the ability for a method to call itself. However, before you define a recursive function, you should be aware any function that calls itself could very easily become an **infinite loop** that will crash your application. Any recursive function is useless if there is no way to make it stop. To avoid this your algorithm must define a **base case,** or a value that marks the end of your processing and allows the recursive function to return. Lets examine the quintessential recursion example, the **Fibonacci sequence**.

The Fibonacci sequence is a series of integers where each integer in the list is the sum of the previous two integers. This definition is easily converted to the algorithm $x_n = x_{n-1} + x_{n-2}$ where n is the value of any integer in the list. For example, for the list of integers *[1, 1, 2, 3, 5, 8, 13, 21, 34, ..., x_i]*, where $x_n = 8$, $x_{n-1} = 5$ and $x_{n-2} = 3$ so *5 + 3 = 8*. Likewise, where *n = 21*, x_{n-1} *= 13* and $x_{n-2} = 8$ so *13 + 8 = 21*. This pattern is consistent throughout the list of integers where n > 2.

So we have a repeatable pattern where $n > 2$, but what if $n = 2$? In that case $x_n = 1$, $x_{n-1} = 1$ and $x_{n-2} = undefined$, which means our algorithm breaks down. At $n = 1$ we run into a similar problem. Therefore, we need to define the base case for $n = 1$ and $n = 2$, or x_1 and x_2. In the Fibonacci sequence, $x_1 = 1$ and $x_2 = 1$. If we were to take this algorithm with the base case values, we can create a recursive function to return the list of Fibonacci integers for any value of n. In this method we will define two base case values for $n = 0$ and $n = 1$, but when $n > 1$ our method calls itself and returns the value. Here's one example in C#:

```csharp
public static int Fibonacci(int n)
{
    if (n == 0) return 0; //Base case
    if (n == 1) return 1; //Base case
    return Fibonacci(n - 1) + Fibonacci(n - 2);
}
```

Recursion is a great tool to have under your belt, but don't abuse it! It has been my experience that many programmers fall into two categories. On one hand, there are programmers who either don't fully understand recursion or simply choose to never use it. On the other hand, some programmers try to use it to solve every problem, which is only forgivable if you're programming in a language LISP.

The truth is, you should use recursion where it is appropriate, and it's appropriate when it feels natural. When you are trying to solve a problem where recursion fits you will most likely recognize it instinctively. You will either be able to distinguish the recursive nature of the problem, or no matter how hard you try you will not be able to develop an iterative solution that handles all of the base cases.

One final consideration for recursive functions is readability. While writing your function, keep in mind that other programmers will have to read your work. If you find yourself struggling to understand the function minutes after you wrote it, imagine how someone who is removed from the problem domain will feel while they are reading it. Therefore, review your code carefully to ensure that it is as readable and understandable as possible. Your peers will thank you.

Traversal

There are several ways to traverse the nodes in a tree data structure, but which one you choose will be based largely on how the nodes of your tree are implemented. For example, our Node class includes references from parents to children, but not the reverse. Nor does it provide references to any siblings or cousins of the same order, or level, of the tree. Therefore, our traversal pattern is limited to stepping through the tree by means of following edges, or references, from parents to children. This type of traversal is called **walking the tree**.

Our node construction would have also allowed us to examine either child prior to examining the parent. If we had structured our search patterns to check the left child node, then the right child node, and finally the node itself, we would have implemented an *in-order traversal*. If our nodes contained links between objects of the same order, we could examine all parents of a particular order prior to examining any children. This approach is called a **pre-order walk**. If we were to also include links from the child nodes to their respective parents, we could perform the inverse operation, whereby we examine all of the children of a particular order prior to examining any parents. This approach is called a post-order walk. Both of these approaches could be categorized as a **level-order walk**, which performs a breadth-first search over the entire tree, checking nodes level by level.

Summary

In this chapter we learned about tree data structures, and how they differ from tree data types. We took the time to examine the terminology associated with trees including a visual representation of tree data structures. Next we evaluated the most common operations when working with trees and their complexity cost. Following this we created our own simple binary tree data structure class from scratch, and discussed how the recursive operations are used to traverse the tree. We examined the meaning of recursion and how to write recursive functions of your own using the Fibonacci sequence as an example of this process. Finally, we examined the various ways that tree data structures can be traversed depending on how the nodes in the tree are related to one another.

10
Heaps: Ordered Trees

Heaps are a special category of the tree data structure, that are ordered with respect to the value of the tree's nodes or the keys associated with each node. This ordering is either ascending in a min heap, meaning that the root node is smaller in value or priority than it's child nodes, or descending in a max heap, meaning that the root node is larger in value or priority than it's child nodes. Note that heap data structures should not be confused with the heap memory of a computer system, which is the name typically used for system's dynamically allocated memory.

In this chapter we will cover the following topics:

- Defining the heap data structure
- Array implementation
- Creating heaps
- Common operations

Heap implementations

Like trees, heaps are typically implemented using either linked lists or linked nodes, or an array. Since we examined the linked node approach in Chapter 9, *Trees: Nonlinear Structures*, in this chapter, we'll examine an array implementation of a heap called a **binary heap**.

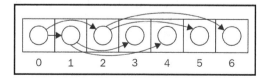

A binary heap is a tree structure where all levels of the tree are filled completely, with the possible exception of the last or deepest level. In the case of the deepest level the nodes are filled from left to right until the level is full. As you can see from the preceding figure, in an array-based implementation each parent node has two child nodes that are located at $2i + 1$ and $2i + 2$, where i is the index of the parent node and the first node of the collection is found at index 0.

 Alternate implementations skip the 0 index of the array to simplify the arithmetic of finding child and parent nodes for a given index. In this design, the child nodes for any given index i are located at $2i$ and $2i + 1$.

Heap operations

Not all implementations of the heap data structures expose the same operational methods. However, the more common operations should be available or made available as needed by the developer.

- **Insert**: The Insert operation adds a new node to the heap. This operation must also re-order the heap to ensure that the newly added node maintains the heap property. This operation has an **O**(*log n*) operational cost.
- **FindMax**: The FindMax operation is synonymous with a max heap, and returns the largest value or highest-priority object in the collection. In an array-based implementation, this is typically the object at either index 0 or index 1, depending on the design. This is equivalent to the *peek* operation in a stack or queue, which is important when using a heap to implement a priority queue. This operation has an **O**(*1*) operational cost.
- **FindMin**: The FindMin operation is related to a min heap, and returns the smallest value or lowest-priority object in the collection. In an array-based implementation this is typically the object at either index 0 or index 1, depending on the design. This operation has an **O**(*1*) operational cost.
- **ExtractMax**: The ExtractMax operation is related to a max heap, and both returns the largest value or highest-priority object in the collection and removes it from the collection. This is equivalent to the *pop* operation in a stack or queue structure. As with FindMax, this is typically the object at either index 0 or index 1 depending on the design. This operation will also re-order the heap to maintain the heap property. This operation has an **O**(*log n*) operational cost.

- **ExtractMin**: The ExtractMin operation is related to a min heap, and both returns the smallest value or lowest-priority object in the collection and removes it from the collection. As with FindMin, this is typically the object at either index 0 or index 1 depending on the design. This operation will also re-order the heap to maintain the heap property. This operation has an **O**(*log n*) operational cost.
- **DeleteMax**: The DeleteMax operation is related to a max heap, and simply removes the largest value or highest priority object in the collection. As with FindMax, this is typically the object at either index 0 or index 1 depending on the design. This operation will also re-order the heap to maintain the heap property. This operation has an **O**(*log n*) operational cost.
- **DeleteMin**: The DeleteMin operation is related to a min heap, and simply removes the smallest value or lowest priority object in the collection. As with FindMin, this is typically the object at either index 0 or index 1 depending on the design. This operation will also re-order the heap to maintain the heap property. This operation has an **O**(*log n*) operational cost.
- **Count**: The Count operation returns the total number of nodes in the heap. This operation has an O(*1*) operational cost.
- **Children**: The Children operation will return the two child nodes for the provided node or node index. This operation has an **O**(*2*) operational cost since two calculations must be performed to gather the child nodes.
- **Parent**: The Parent operation will return the parent node for any given node or node index. This operation has an **O**(*1*) operational cost.

This list of operations may remind you somewhat of the tree data structure discussed in `Chapter 9`, *Trees: Non-linear Structures*. It is important to note that, although a binary heap is quite similar to a binary search tree, the two should not be confused. Like a binary search tree, a heap data structure organizes each node of the collection. The heap orders nodes priority based on some arbitrary property of the node or the environment, while the values of each node are not necessarily ordered at all. In a binary search tree, on the other hand, the values of the nodes themselves are ordered.

Instantiating heaps

Since heaps are a form of tree data structure, it is unsurprising that we will not find a native concrete implementation in the languages we are discussing. However, the heap data structure is actually quite simple to implement. Therefore, we are going to build our own heap structure, specifically a min heap.

Min heap structure

Before we begin, we need to detail a few characteristics our heap structure will possess. For starters, we are going to implement the heap using an array, and the first node will occupy the 0 index in this array. This decision is important because it affects the formula we use to calculate each node's parent and Children. Next, we will need an object to represent the nodes in our heap. Since this is going to be a very simple object for our demonstration, we'll define its class in-line with our heap implementation.

Since this is a min heap, we will only need to implement the `min` operations. Therefore, our implementation must expose methods for `FindMin` (peek), `ExtractMin` (pop), and `DeleteMin`. The heap's *Insert, Count, Children,* and *Parent* operations will each be implemented as single methods.

Our min heap implementation will also need two supporting methods to re-order the collection whenever a node is added or removed. We'll call these methods `OrderHeap` and `SwapNodes`, and their functions should be self-explanatory.

 Note that an implementation of a max heap is almost identical to a `min` heap except that you switch around the variables in a few operations. We'll examine those differences in-line with our implementations.

C#

C# provides enough functionality for us to create a versatile heap data structure with very little code. First we need to build the simple class that represents the nodes of the heap:

```
public class HeapNode
{
    public int Data;
}
```

This class is very simple, containing only a `public` property to store our integer data. Since this class' contents are consistent in each of the following language examples, we will only examine it here.

Next we can implement our heap functions. Here's what a concrete implementation of the `MinHeap` class might look like in C#:

```
List<HeapNode> elements;
public int Count
{
    get
```

```
    {
        return elements.Count;
    }
}

public MinHeap()
{
    elements = new List<HeapNode>();
}
```

Our `MinHeap` class includes two public fields. The first is a `List<HeapNode>` named `elements` that represents our heap collection. The second is a `Count` field that will return the total number of elements in the collection. Finally, our constructor simply initializes the `elements` collection.

```
public void Insert(HeapNode item)
{
    elements.Add(item);
    OrderHeap();
}
```

The `Insert(HeapNode item)` method accepts a new `HeapNode` object and adds it to the collection. Once the object has been added, the method calls `OrderHeap()` to make sure the new object is placed in the correct position to maintain the heap property.

```
public void Delete(HeapNode item)
{
    int i = elements.IndexOf(item);
    int last = elements.Count - 1;

    elements[i] = elements[last];
    elements.RemoveAt(last);
    OrderHeap();
}
```

The `Delete(HeapNode item)` method accepts a `HeapNode` item to be removed from the collection. The method first finds the index of the item to be removed, then gets the index of the last object in the collection. Next, the method deletes the matching node by overwriting its position with a reference to the last node in the heap and then the last node is removed. Finally, the `OrderHeap()` method is called to ensure the final collection satisfies the heap property.

```
public HeapNode ExtractMin()
{
    if (elements.Count > 0)
    {
```

```
            HeapNode item = elements[0];
            Delete(item);
            return item;
        }

        return null;
    }
```

The `ExtractMin()` method first confirms that the `elements` collection has at least one element. If not, the method returns `null`. Otherwise, the method creates a new instance of `HeapNode` called `item` and sets it to the root object in the collection, which is the smallest object or the object with the lowest priority. Next, the method calls `Delete(item)` to remove the node from the collection. Finally, since the `ExtractMin` function must return an object, the method returns `item` to the caller.

```
        public HeapNode FindMin()
        {
            if (elements.Count > 0)
            {
                return elements[0];
            }

            return null;
        }
```

The `FindMin()` method is very similar to the `ExtractMin()` method, except that it does not remove the returned minimum value from the collection. The method first confirms that the element's collection has at least one element. If not, the method returns `null`. Otherwise the method returns the root object in the collection, which is the smallest object or the object with the lowest priority.

```
        private void OrderHeap()
        {
            for (int i = elements.Count - 1; i > 0; i--)
            {
                int parentPosition = (i - 1) / 2;

                if (elements[parentPosition].Data > elements[i].Data)
                {
                    SwapElements(parentPosition, i);
                }
            }
        }

        private void SwapElements(int firstIndex, int secondIndex)
        {
```

```
            HeapNode tmp = elements[firstIndex];
            elements[firstIndex] = elements[secondIndex];
            elements[secondIndex] = tmp;
    }
```

The private `OrderHeap()` method is the heart of the `MinHeap` class. This is the method responsible for maintaining the heap property of the collection. The method first establishes a `for` loop based on the length of the elements collection, and begins iterating through the collection from the end to the beginning.

Since we know that the two children of any object at index i are located at indices *2i + 1* and *2i + 2*, we likewise know that the parent of any object at index i is found at *(i − 1) / 2*. This formula only works because the resulting value is defined as an integer, meaning that any floating-point values are truncated and only the whole number value is retained. This algorithm, implemented in the `OrderHeap()` method via the `int parentPosition = (i - 1) / 2;` code, is what ensures the heap data structure retains its binary nature.

Using the `min` heap property formula, the `for` loop first identifies the parent index for the current node. Next, the value of the current node's `Data` field is compared to that of the parent; if the parent is larger, the method calls `SwapElements(parentPosition, i)`. Once each of the nodes has been evaluated, the method is complete and the heap property is consistent throughout the collection.

Note that, by switching the two operands of the `if` statement, or by simply changing the comparator from > to <, or, our collection would effectively change from a min heap to a max heap. Using this knowledge, it would be very simple indeed to create a heap collection that could be defined as either a `min` heap or a `max` heap at *runtime*.

The `SwapElements(int firstIndex, int secondIndex)` method's function is self-explanatory. Each of the nodes at the given indices is swapped to enforce the heap property.

```
        public List<HeapNode> GetChildren(int parentIndex)
        {
            if (parentIndex >= 0)
            {
                List<HeapNode> children = new List<HeapNode>();
                int childIndexOne = (2 * parentIndex) + 1;
                int childIndexTwo = (2 * parentIndex) + 2;
                children.Add(elements[childIndexOne]);
                children.Add(elements[childIndexTwo]);
```

```
            return children;
        }

        return null;
    }
```

Using the same rule, which states that the two children of any object at index i are located at indices *2i + 1* and *2i + 2*, the GetChildren(int parentIndex) method gathers and returns the two child nodes for a given parent index. The method first confirms that parentIndex is not less than 0, otherwise it returns null. If the parentIndex is valid, the method creates a new List<Heapnode> and populates it using the calculated child indices before returning the children collection.

```
    public HeapNode GetParent(int childIndex)
    {
        if (childIndex > 0 && elements.Count > childIndex)
        {
            int parentIndex = (childIndex - 1) / 2;
            return elements[parentIndex];
        }

        return null;
    }
```

Finally, GetParent(int childIndex) works on the same principle as GetChildren. If the given childIndex is greater than 0 the node has a parent. The method confirms that we are not searching for the root node and also confirms that the index is not out of bounds for the collection. If either check fails, the method returns null. Otherwise, the method determines the node's parent index and then returns the node found at that index.

Java

Java also provides the basic tools necessary to build a robust implementation of our MinHeap class with little code. Here's how that class might look in Java:

```
    List<HeapNode> elements;

    public int size()
    {
        return elements.size();
    }

    public MinHeap()
    {
        elements = new ArrayList<HeapNode>();
    }
```

Our `MinHeap` class includes one public field of abstract type `List<HeapNode>` named `elements` that represents our heap collection. The class also include a method named `size()`, which will return the total number of elements in the collection. Finally, our constructor simply initializes the `elements` collection as an `ArrayList<HeapNode>`:

```
public void insert(HeapNode item)
{
    elements.add(item);
    orderHeap();
}
```

The `insert(HeapNode item)` method accepts a new `HeapNode` object and adds it to the collection. Once the object has been added, the method calls `orderHeap()` to make sure the new object is placed in the correct position to maintain the heap property.

```
public void delete(HeapNode item)
{
    int i = elements.indexOf(item);
    int last = elements.size() - 1;

    elements.set(i, elements.get(last));
    elements.remove(last);
    orderHeap();
}
```

The `delete(HeapNode item)` method accepts a `HeapNode` item to be removed from the collection. The method first finds the index of the item to be removed, then gets the index of the last object in the collection. Next, the method deletes the matching node by overwriting its position with a reference to the last node in the heap and then the last node is removed. Finally, `orderHeap()` is called to ensure the final collection satisfies the heap property.

```
public HeapNode extractMin()
{
    if (elements.size() > 0)
    {
        HeapNode item = elements.get(0);
        delete(item);
        return item;
    }

    return null;
}
```

The extractMin() method first confirms that the elements collection has at least one element. If not, the method returns null. Otherwise the method creates a new instance of HeapNode called item and sets it to the root object in the collection, which is the smallest object or the object with the lowest priority. Next, the method calls delete(item) to remove the node from the collection. Finally, since the ExtractMin function must return an object, the method returns item to the caller.

```
public HeapNode findMin()
{
    if (elements.size() > 0)
    {
        return elements.get(0);
    }

    return null;
}
```

The findMin() method is very similar to the extractMin() method, except that it does not remove the returned minimum value from the collection. The method first confirms that the elements collection has at least one element. If not, the method returns null. Otherwise the method returns the root object in the collection by calling elements.get(0).

```
private void orderHeap()
{
    for (int i = elements.size() - 1; i > 0; i--)
    {
        int parentPosition = (i - 1) / 2;

        if (elements.get(parentPosition).Data > elements.get(i).Data)
        {
            swapElements(parentPosition, i);
        }
    }
}

private void swapElements(int firstIndex, int secondIndex)
{
    HeapNode tmp = elements.get(firstIndex);
    elements.set(firstIndex, elements.get(secondIndex));
    elements.set(secondIndex, tmp);
}
```

The private orderHeap() method is responsible for maintaining the heap property of the collection. The method first establishes a for loop based on the length of the elements collection, and begins iterating through the collection from the end to the beginning.

Using the min heap property formula, the `for` loop first identifies the parent index for the current node. Next, the value of the current node's `Data` field is compared to that of the parent, and if the parent is larger, the method calls `swapElements(parentPosition, i)`. Once each of the nodes has been evaluated, the method is complete and the heap property is consistent throughout the collection.

The `swapElements(int firstIndex, int secondIndex)` method's function is self-explanatory. Each of the nodes at the given indices is swapped to enforce the heap property.

```
public List<HeapNode> getChildren(int parentIndex)
{
    if (parentIndex >= 0)
    {
        ArrayList<HeapNode> children = new ArrayList<HeapNode>();
        int childIndexOne = (2 * parentIndex) + 1;
        int childIndexTwo = (2 * parentIndex) + 2;
        children.add(elements.get(childIndexOne));
        children.add(elements.get(childIndexTwo));

        return children;
    }

    return null;
}
```

Using the same rule, which states that the two children of any object at index i are located at indices *2i + 1* and *2i + 2*, the `getChildren(int parentIndex)` method gathers and returns the two child nodes for a given parent index. The method first confirms that `parentIndex` is not less than 0, otherwise it returns `null`. If the `parentIndex` is valid, the method creates a new `ArrayList<Heapnode>` and populates it using the calculated child indices before returning the `children` collection.

```
public HeapNode getParent(int childIndex)
{
    if (childIndex > 0 && elements.size() > childIndex)
    {
        int parentIndex = (childIndex - 1) / 2;
        return elements.get(parentIndex);
    }

    return null;
}
```

Finally, `getParent(int childIndex)` works on the same principle as `getChildren`. If the given `childIndex` is greater than 0 the node has a parent. The method confirms that we are not searching for the root node and also confirms that the index is not out of bounds for the collection. If either check fails, the method returns `null`. Otherwise, the method determines the node's parent index and then returns the node found at that index.

Objective-C

Using an `NSMutableArray` as the core structure, Objective-C can also easily implement the min heap data structure. Here's how the `EDSMinHeap` class might look in Objective-C:

```
@interface EDSMinHeap()
{
    NSMutableArray<EDSHeapNode*> *_elements;
}

@implementation EDSMinHeap

-(instancetype)initMinHeap{
    if (self = [super init])
    {
        _elements = [NSMutableArray array];
    }
    return self;
}
```

Using the class cluster `NSMutableArray`, we create an ivar for our class called `_elements`. Our initializer instantiates this array, giving us the underlying data structure to build our `EDSMinHeap` class on.

```
-(NSInteger)getCount
{
    return [_elements count];
}
```

Our `EDSMinHeap` class includes one public property named `Count`, and the `getCount()` accessor returns the `count` property of the `_elements` array.

```
-(void)insert:(EDSHeapNode*)item
{
    [_elements addObject:item];
    [self orderHeap];
}
```

The `insert:` method accepts a new `EDSHeapNode` object and adds it to the array. Once the object has been added, the method calls `orderHeap` to make sure the new object is placed in the correct position to maintain the heap property:

```
- (void) delete: (EDSHeapNode*) item
{
    long i = [_elements indexOfObject:item];
    _elements[i] = [_elements lastObject];
    [_elements removeLastObject];
    [self orderHeap];
}
```

The `delete:` method accepts an `EDSHeapNode` item to be removed from the collection. The method first finds the index of the item to be removed using `indexOfObject:`, then deletes the matching node by overwriting its position with a reference to the `lastObject` in the heap. Next, the last node is removed using `removeLastObject`. Finally, `orderHeap:` is called to ensure the final collection satisfies the heap property.

```
- (EDSHeapNode*) extractMin
{
    if ([_elements count] > 0)
    {
        EDSHeapNode *item = _elements[0];
        [self delete:item];
        return item;
    }
    return nil;
}
```

The `extractMin` method first confirms that the `_elements` collection has at least one element. If not, the method returns `nil`. Otherwise, the method creates a new instance of `EDSHeapNode` called `item` and sets it to the root object in the collection, which is the smallest object or the object with the lowest priority. Next, the method calls `delete:` to remove the node from the collection. Finally, since the *ExtractMin* function must return an object, the method returns `item` to the caller.

```
- (EDSHeapNode*) findMin
{
    if ([_elements count] > 0)
    {
        return _elements[0];
    }
    return nil;
}
```

The findMin method is very similar to the extractMin method, except that it does not remove the returned minimum value from the collection. The method first confirms that the elements collection has at least one element. If not, the method returns nil. Otherwise the method returns the first object in the collection, which is the root node.

```
- (void) orderHeap
{
    for (long i = [_elements count] - 1; i > 0; i--)
    {
        long parentPosition = (i - 1) / 2;
        if (_elements[parentPosition].data > _elements[i].data)
        {
            [self swapElement:parentPosition withElement:i];
        }
    }
}

- (void) swapElement:(long)firstIndex withElement:(long)secondIndex
{
    EDSHeapNode *tmp = _elements[firstIndex];
    _elements[firstIndex] = _elements[secondIndex];
    _elements[secondIndex] = tmp;
}
```

The private orderHeap method is responsible for maintaining the heap property of the collection. The method first establishes a for loop based on the length of the elements collection, and begins iterating through the collection from the end to the beginning.

Using the min heap property formula, the for loop first identifies the parent index for the current node. Next, the value of the current node's data property is compared to that of the parent, and if the parent is larger, the method calls swapElement:withElement:. Once each of the nodes has been evaluated, the method is complete and the heap property is consistent throughout the collection.

The swapElement:withElement: method's function is self-explanatory. Each of the nodes at the given indices is swapped to enforce the heap property.

```
- (NSArray<EDSHeapNode*>*) childrenOfParentIndex:(NSInteger)parentIndex
{
    if (parentIndex >= 0)
    {
        NSMutableArray *children = [NSMutableArray array];
        long childIndexOne = (2 * parentIndex) + 1;
        long childIndexTwo = (2 * parentIndex) + 2;
        [children addObject:_elements[childIndexOne]];
        [children addObject:_elements[childIndexTwo]];
```

```
            return children;
        }
        return nil;
    }
```

Using the rule that states the two children of any object at index i are located at indices *2i + 1* and *2i + 2*, the `childrenOfParentIndex:` method gathers and returns the two child nodes for a given parent index. The method first confirms that `parentIndex` is not less than 0, otherwise it returns `nil`. If the `parentIndex` is valid, the method creates a new `NSMutableArray` and populates it using nodes from the calculated child indices before returning the `children` collection.

```
    -(EDSHeapNode*)parentOfChildIndex:(NSInteger)childIndex
    {
        if (childIndex > 0 && [_elements count] > childIndex)
        {
            long parentIndex = (childIndex - 1) / 2;
            return _elements[parentIndex];
        }
        return nil;
    }
```

Finally, `parentOfChildIndex:` works on the same principle as `childrenOfParentIndex:`. If the given `childIndex` is greater than 0, the node has a parent. The method confirms that we are not searching for the root node and also confirms that the index is not out of bounds for the collection. If either check fails, the method returns `nil`. Otherwise, the method determines the node's parent index and then returns the node found at that index.

Swift

Our Swift `MinHeap` class is similar in structure and functionality to the C# and Java implementations. Here's what an example of the `MinHeap` class might look like in Swift:

```
    public var _elements: Array = [HeapNode]()
    public init() {}

    public func getCount() -> Int
    {
        return _elements.count
    }
```

Using the `Array` class we create a private property for our class called `_elements`. Since our property is declared and instantiated simultaneously, and there is no other custom code requiring instantiation, we can exclude the explicit public initializer and rely on the default initializer. Our class also provides a public method called `getCount()`, which returns the size of the `_elements` array.

```
public func insert(item: HeapNode)
{
    _elements.append(item)
    orderHeap()
}
```

The `insert(HeapNode item)` method accepts a new `HeapNode` object and adds it to the collection. Once the object has been added the method calls `orderHeap()` to make sure the new object is placed in the correct position to maintain the heap property.

```
public func delete(item: HeapNode)
{
    if let index = _elements.index(of: item)
    {
        _elements[index] = _elements.last!
        _elements.removeLast()
        orderHeap()
    }
}
```

The `delete(HeapNode item)` method accepts a `HeapNode` item to be removed from the collection. The method first finds the `index` of the item to be removed, then deletes the matching node by overwriting its position with a reference to the `last` object in the heap. Finally, the `orderHeap()` method is called to ensure the final collection satisfies the heap property.

```
public func extractMin() -> HeapNode?
{
    if (_elements.count > 0)
    {
        let item = _elements[0]
        delete(item: item)
        return item
    }
    return nil
}
```

The `extractMin()` method first confirms that the `elements` collection has at least one element. If not, the method returns `nil`. Otherwise the method creates a new variable called `item` and sets it to the root object in the collection, which is the smallest `HeapNode` or the `HeapNode` with the lowest priority. Next, the method calls `delete(item: Heapnode)` to remove the node from the collection. Finally, the method returns `item` to the caller.

```
public func findMin()  -> HeapNode?
{
    if (_elements.count > 0)
    {
        return _elements[0]
    }
    return nil
}
```

The `findMin()` method is very similar to the `extractMin()` method, except that it does not remove the returned minimum value from the collection. The method first confirms that the elements collection has at least one element. If not, the method returns `nil`. Otherwise the method returns `_elements[0]`, which is the root object in the collection.

```
public func orderHeap()
{
    for i in (0..<(_elements.count)  - 1).reversed()
    {
        let parentPosition = (i - 1) / 2

        if (_elements[parentPosition].data! > _elements[i].data!)
        {
            swapElements(first: parentPosition, second: i)
        }
    }
}

public func swapElements(first: Int, second: Int)
{
    let tmp = _elements[first]
    _elements[first]  = _elements[second]
    _elements[second]  = tmp
}
```

The private `orderHeap()` method is responsible for maintaining the heap property of the collection. The method first establishes a `for` loop based on the length of the elements collection, and begins iterating through the collection from the end to the beginning.

Using the min heap property formula, the `for` loop first identifies the parent index for the current node. Next, the value of the current node's `data` field is compared to that of the parent, and if the parent is larger, the method calls `swapElements(first: Int, second: Int)`. Once each of the nodes has been evaluated, the method is complete and the heap property is consistent throughout the collection.

The `swapElements(int firstIndex, int secondIndex)` method's function is self-explanatory. Each of the nodes at the given indices is swapped to enforce the heap property:

```
public func getChildren(parentIndex: Int) -> [HeapNode]?
{
    if (parentIndex >= 0)
    {
        var children: Array = [HeapNode]()
        let childIndexOne = (2 * parentIndex) + 1;
        let childIndexTwo = (2 * parentIndex) + 2;
        children.append(_elements[childIndexOne])
        children.append(_elements[childIndexTwo])
        return children;
    }
    return nil;
}
```

Using the same rule that states the two children of any object at index i are located at indices *2i + 1* and *2i + 2*, the `getChildren(parentIndex: Int)` method gathers and returns the two child nodes for a given parent index. The method first confirms that `parentIndex` is not less than 0, otherwise it returns `nil`. If the `parentIndex` is valid, the method creates a new `Array` of `HeapNode` objects and populates it using the calculated child indices before returning the `children` collection:

```
public func getParent(childIndex: Int) -> HeapNode?
{
    if (childIndex > 0 && _elements.count > childIndex)
    {
        let parentIndex = (childIndex - 1) / 2;
        return _elements[parentIndex];
    }
    return nil;
}
```

Finally, `getParent(childIndex: Int)` works on the same principle as `getChildren`. If the given `childIndex` is greater than 0 the node has a parent. The method confirms that we are not searching for the root node and also confirms that the index is not out of bounds for the collection. If either check fails, the method returns `nil`. Otherwise, the method determines the node's parent index and then returns the node found at that index.

Common applications

Heap data structures are actually quite common, although you may not always realize you are working with one. Here are some of the most common applications for the heap data structure:

- **Selection algorithms**: A selection algorithm is used to determine the kth smallest or largest element in a collection, or the median valued object of a collection. In a typically collection, this operation costs O(n). However, in an ordered heap implemented with an array finding the kth element is an **O**(1) operation because we can find the element by simply examining the k index in the array.

- **Priority queue**: Priority queues are an abstract data structure similar to standard queues except that the nodes contain an additional value representing the priority of that object in relation to others in the collection. Due to the natural sorting of the heap data structure, priority queues are often implemented using the heap.

Summary

In this chapter, we learned about heap data structures. We examined the most common operations when working with heaps and their complexity cost. Following this we created our own simple min heap data structure class from scratch, and discussed how the min heap property formula is used to calculate parents or children for any given node index. Finally, we examined the most common applications for heap data structures.

11
Graphs: Values with Relationships

The final data structure that we will examine is the **Graph**. Graphs are sets of objects with no specifically structured relationship, where each object can have links to one or many other objects in the collection. Objects in graphs are typically referred to as nodes, vertices, or points. Links, or the relationships between the objects, are referred to as edges, lines, or arcs. These links can be simple references or they can be objects with values of their own. More formally stated, graphs are a pair of sets (N, E), where N is the set of nodes and E is the set of edges in the collection.

One excellent example of graph applications would be visualizing the relationships between individuals in a social media database. In such a database, each person in the database represents one node, and each of their links to other people in their circle of acquaintances represents an edge. In such a circle of acquaintances, it would be perfectly reasonable to see circular or even intertwined relationships between nodes as one person can share many of the same friends or coworkers as another person. Tree and heap structures would very rapidly break down when attempting to rationalize these sets, while the graph data structure was practically designed with such scenarios in mind.

In this chapter, we will cover the following topics:

- Definition of the graph data structure
- Visual conception of the graph structure
- Common operations
- Graph implementations

Visual graph concepts

It is sometimes easier to grasp the concept of graph data structures using visual representations of some collections. Consider the following diagram:

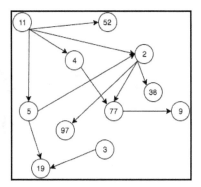

This is a basic graph consisting of eleven nodes and twelve edges. Sets N and E can be described as follows:

$N = \{2, 3, 4, 5, 9, 11, 19, 38, 52, 77, 97\}$

$E = \{2{:}38, 2{:}77, 2{:}97, 3{:}19, 4{:}77, 5{:}2, 5{:}19, 11{:}2, 11{:}4, 11{:}5, 11{:}52, 77{:}9\}$

Note that, in this example, there are only unidirectional edges between nodes. This is perfectly acceptable, but graphs are much more powerful when bidirectional nodes are permitted. Consider the following example:

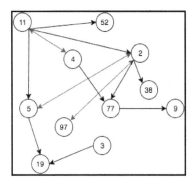

This is the same graph we saw earlier, but set E now contains several new reciprocal edges between existing nodes. Sets N and E can now be described as follows:

N = {2, 3, 4, 5, 9, 11, 19, 38, 52, 77, 97}

E = {2:5, 2:38, 2:77, 2:97, 3:19, 4:11, 4:77, 5:2, 5:19, 11:2, 11:4, 11:5, 11:52, 77:9, 97:2}

Finally, edges between nodes can also be defined with a particular value. Consider the following example:

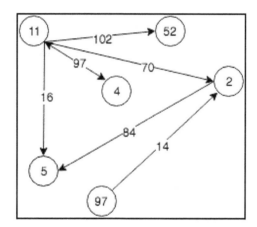

In this figure, we see a graph with a set of six nodes and seven edges. In this case, however, the edges are further defined by a specific value. This value is not limited to integers, but it can be represented by any type or custom object you need. Sets N and E for this graph can be described as follows:

N = {2, 4, 5, 52, 97}

E = {2:5(84), 4:11(97), 11:2(70), 11:4(97), 11:5(16), 11:52(102), 97:2(14)}

Graph operations

Since graphs support bidirectional references between nodes and nodes can virtually have unlimited neighbors, it is necessary to define two basic objects in order to implement the collection. These include the nodes that make up the graph as well as the graph collection itself. Optionally, an edge object may be required if the implementation supports edges that contain a value. Therefore, note that some of these common graph operations will have components in more than one class:

- **AddNode**: This operation is sometimes calledthe **AddVertex** or **AddPoint** operation, and is dependent on the language used to define the graph. The AddNode operation simply inserts new nodes into the graph without defining any edges or references to neighboring nodes. Since a node does not necessarily need to have neighbors to exist in the graph, the AddNode operation represents an **O**(1) operation. Also note that the AddNode operation is exclusively implemented in the graph collection object.

- **RemoveNode**: This operation issometimes called the **RemoveVertex** or RemovePoint operation, and it is dependent on the language used to define the graph. The RemoveNode operation deletes the node from the graph and removes any edges or references to and from neighboring nodes. This operation has an **O**($n + k$) operational cost, where n is the number of nodes in our graph and k is the number of edges. The RemoveNode operation is exclusively implemented in the graph collection object.

    This may seem expensive for a simple remove operation, but keep in mind that references in a graph can be bidirectional, meaning that our node could potentially have edges to every other node in the graph while every other node in the graph could simultaneously have edges pointing back to our node.

This is primarily a concern with graphs designed to support edges that contain a value. In that case, each edge must be individually examined to determine if it points to the node being removed, and it must be handled accordingly if that is the case. In graphs where edges are merely pointers between objects, setting an object to `null` or `nil` will effectively eliminate any edges that point to it, potentially reducing this operation's cost to **O**(1).

- **AddEdge**: This operation is sometimes called the **AddArc** or **AddLine** operation, and it is dependent on the language used to define the node. The AddEdge operation simply adds a new edge from node x to node y. The AddEdge operation is implemented in both the collection object and the node object. At the node level, only the target node y must be passed as a parameter; while at the graph level, both x and y must be provided. If the graph supports edges with values, the new value must also be passed as a parameter, to the graph operation. Since graphs support bidirectional relationships between nodes, there is no need to first confirm that an edge already exists from node y to node x. This means adding a new edge between nodes is a simple process with an **O**(1) operational cost.

- **RemoveEdge**: This operation is sometimes calledthe **RemoveArc** or **RemoveLine** operation, and it is dependent on the language used to define the node. The RemoveEdge operation simply removes an existing edge from node x to node y if it exists. At the node level, only the target node y must be passed as a parameter, while at the graph level, both x and y must be provided. If the graph supports edges with values, the new value must also be passed as a parameter to the graph operation. Since graphs support bidirectional relationships between nodes, removing an edge from node x to node y as an operation is completely independent of existing edges from node y to node x; and this process, therefore, has an **O**(1) operational cost.

- **GetNodeValue**: The GetNodeValue operation issometimes called the **GetVertexValue** or **GetPointValue** operation, and this is dependent on the language used to define the node. This operation returns the value associated with the node, whether it is a primitive or some custom object type, and the operation has an **O**(1) operational cost. This operation can be defined at either the graph or node level, but if it is defined as a part of the graph object, the node to be interrogated must be passed into the operation as a parameter.

- **SetNodeValue**: The SetNodeValue operation is sometimes called the **SetVertexValue** or **SetPointValue** operation, and it is dependent on the language used to define the node. This operation sets the value of the node and has an **O**(1) operational cost. Again, this operation can be defined at either the graph or node level but, if it is defined as a part of the graph object, the node to be set must be passed into the operation as a parameter.

- **Adjacent**: The Adjacent operation checks whether an edge exists from node x to node y, and typically returns a Boolean value representing the result. This operation is typically defined at the graph level and requires both node x and node y to be provided. This simple operation has an **O**(1) operational cost.

- **Neighbors**: This operation functions similarly to the children operation in a tree data structure. The Neighbors operation returns a list containing all of the nodes y where there is an edge from node x to node y. This operation is typically defined at the graph level and requires node x be provided. This operation has an **O**(1) operational cost.

- **Count**: As with many other collections, graphs typically expose a count operation that returns the number of nodes contained in the collection. Although dependent on the implementation, this operation typically has an **O**(1) operational cost.

- **GetEdgeValue**: This operation is sometimescalled the GetArcValue or GetLineValue operation, and it is dependent on the language used to define the node. In graphs that support edges with values, this operation returns the value associated with the edge, whether it is a primitive or some custom object type, and the operation has an **O**(1) operational cost. This operation can also be defined as a part of the node object, in which case the edge to be interrogated must be passed into the operation as a parameter.

- **SetEdgeValue**: This operation issometimes called the **SetArcValue** or **SetLineValue** operation, and this is dependent on the language used to define the edge. This operation sets the value of the edge and has an **O**(1) operational cost. Again, this operation can be defined as a part of the node object, in which case the edge to be set must be passed into the operation as a parameter.

Graph implementations

As with heaps, graphs are a form of tree data structure and, therefore, we will not find a native concrete implementation in the languages we are discussing. However, the graph data structure is surprisingly easy to implement, so we will build our own `Graph` class from scratch.

The graph data structure

Before we begin, we need to detail a few characteristics that our graph structure will possess. Our graph will support nodes that have no edges to or from other nodes. Our graph will also support exclusive and bidirectional edges. For the sake of brevity, the edges in our graph collection will not support edge values, but adding values to edges is a simple matter if you decide to use them in your custom implementations.

Our graph will be made up of two classes. The first is the `Graph` class itself, which in our implementation will contain most of the standard graph operations. The next is a `GraphNode` class, which will represent the nodes of our collection. Note that this class could also be named `GraphVertex` or `GraphPoint`, but in keeping with our tree `Node` class example from `Chapter 9`, *Trees: Non-linear Structures*, we will stick with nodes.

The `Graph` class will be based on an array or list that contains the root references to the nodes. Each `GraphNode` object will also contain an array or list that holds the references to other nodes. In this implementation, these references represent the edges in our data structure. This class will support instantiation from scratch or by passing in an existing list of `GraphNode` objects. Operations for adding and removing both nodes and edges will be implemented in the `Graph` class. The `Graph` class will also contain operations for checking node adjacency, node neighbors, and the total count of nodes in the collection.

C#

C# does not provide a concrete `Graph` or `GraphNode` class out of the box, so we will need to create our own. We will start with the `GraphNode` class. Here is what a basic implementation of a `GraphNode` class might look like in C#:

```
public class GraphNode
{
    public Int16 Value;

    private List<GraphNode> _neighbors;
    public List<GraphNode> Neighbors
    {
        get
        {
            return _neighbors;
        }
    }

    public GraphNode()
    {
        _neighbors = new List<GraphNode>();
    }

    public GraphNode(Int16 value)
    {
        _neighbors = new List<GraphNode>();
        Value = value;
    }
}
```

This class is very simple, containing a public field named `Value` to store our integer data and a `List<GraphNode>` object named `neighbors` that represents the edges between this node and its neighbors. The class also has two constructors both of which instantiate the `_neighbors` list. The overloaded `GraphNode(Int16 value)` constructor also allows a value to be defined at instantiation.

Next, we can implement our graph functions. Here's what a concrete implementation of a `Graph` class might look like in C#:

```
private List<GraphNode> _nodes;
public List<GraphNode> Nodes
{
    get
    {
        return _nodes;
    }
}

public Graph(List<GraphNode> nodes)
{
    if (nodes == null)
    {
        _nodes = new List<GraphNode>();
    }
    else
    {
        _nodes = nodes;
    }
}
```

Our `Graph` class includes one public field, a `List<GraphNode>` collection named `Nodes` that exposes read-only access to the private `List<GraphNode> _nodes` field. This field maintains the list of edges to neighboring nodes. Finally, our constructor accepts one parameter of the type `List<Graphnode>` and sets `_nodes` to this value if it is not null; otherwise, it initializes the `_nodes` collection:

```
public void AddNode(GraphNode node)
{
    _nodes.Add(node);
}

public void AddNodeForValue(Int16 value)
{
    _nodes.Add(new GraphNode(value));
}
```

The first two public methods in `Graph` are `AddNode(GraphNode node)` and `AddNodeForValue(Int16 value)`, which add two versions of the AddNode functionality to our class. The first adds a pre-existing node to the _nodes collection, while the second instantiates a new node using `value`, then adds that node to the _nodes collection. Both of these methods add nodes without defining any edges and, therefore, these operations have an **O**(1) cost:

```
public bool RemoveNode(Int16 value)
{
    GraphNode nodeToRemove = _nodes.Find(n => n.Value == value);
    if (nodeToRemove == null)
    {
        return false;
    }
    _nodes.Remove(nodeToRemove);

    foreach (GraphNode node in _nodes)
    {
        int index = node.Neighbors.IndexOf(nodeToRemove);
        if (index != -1)
        {
            node.Neighbors.RemoveAt(index);
        }
    }
    return true;
}
```

The `RemoveNode(Int16 value)` method provides the RemoveNode functionality to our class. This method accepts one parameter of type `Int16` and named `value`, representing the node that the caller is asking to remove. The method begins by using a **LINQ** statement to examine each of the nodes in the collection, searching for a match to `value`. If no match is found, the method returns `false`. Otherwise, the matching node is removed from the _nodes collection and the method execution continues.

The second half of this method loops through each of the nodes in the collection, examining each node's neighbors to find a match for `nodeToRemove`. A match found means an edge exists from the `node` object to the `nodeToRemove` object and returns an index value for that match. By removing the `nodeToRemove` object from the `node.Neighbors` collection using `index`, we eliminate the reference and delete the edge.

As we examined in the discussion on graph operations, the RemoveNode operation has an operational cost of $O(n + k)$, where n is the number of nodes in the collection and k is the number of edges. In the RemoveNode(Int16 value) method, the first half represents n and the second half represents k in that equation:

```
public void AddEdge(GraphNode from, GraphNode to)
{
    from.Neighbors.Add(to);
}

public void AddBidirectedEdge(GraphNode from, GraphNode to)
{
    from.Neighbors.Add(to);
    to.Neighbors.Add(from);
}
```

The AddEdge(GraphNode from, GraphNode to) and AddBidirectedEdge(GraphNode from, GraphNode to) methods provide the AddEdge functionality to the Graph class. The first method is the standard AddEdge operation, while the second method exists more as a convenience in case the caller wants to immediately add bidirectional references. The first method has an $O(1)$ operational cost, while the second technically has a more unusual $O(2)$ operational cost:

```
public bool Adjacent(GraphNode from, GraphNode to)
{
    return from.Neighbors.Contains(to);
}
```

The Adjacent(GraphNode from, GraphNode to) method returns a Boolean value denoting whether an edge exists between two nodes, from and to. Hopefully the signature makes the direction of this edge clear but, for clarity, this method only confirms that an edge exists from the from node and to the to node, but not the reciprocal. Since this method is based on the contains function, it has an $O(n)$ operational cost where n is the number of edges contained in from.Neighbors:

```
public List<GraphNode> Neighbors(Int16 value)
{
    GraphNode node = _nodes.Find(n => n.Value == value);
    if (node == null)
    {
        return null;
    }
    else
    {
        return node.Neighbors;
    }
```

```
    }
```

The `Neighbors(Int16 value)` method provides the Neighbors functionality to our class. This method accepts one parameter of type `Int16` and named `value`, representing the node the caller is asking to examine. The method begins by using a LINQ statement to examine each of the nodes in the collection searching for a match to `value`. If no match is found, the method returns `null`. Otherwise, the method returns the matching node's `Neighbors` collection. If the `GraphNode` object was known in advance, this operation would have an O(1) operational cost. However, since we are examining the entire collection of _nodes at the `Graph` level based on the value of a specific node, this implementation has an O(*n*) operational cost:

```
public int Count
{
    get
    {
        return _nodes.Count;
    }
}
```

Finally, the `Count` field is a read-only value that returns the total number of nodes contained in the collection by returning _nodes.Count. This field provides the Count functionality to our `Graph` class and has an O(1) operational cost.

Java

Like C#, Java does not provide a concrete `Graph` or `GraphNode` class out-of-the-box, so we will need to create our own. Again, we will start with the `GraphNode` class. Here is what a basic implementation of a `GraphNode` class will look like in Java:

```
public class GraphNode
{
    public int Value;

    private LinkedList<GraphNode> _neighbors;
    public LinkedList<GraphNode> GetNeighbors()
    {
        return _neighbors;
    }

    public GraphNode()
    {
        _neighbors = new LinkedList<GraphNode>();
    }

    public GraphNode(int value)
```

```
        {
                _neighbors = new LinkedList<GraphNode>();
                Value = value;
        }
    }
```

This class is very simple, containing a public field named `Value` to store our integer data and a private `LinkedList<GraphNode>` object named `_neighbors` that represents the edges between this node and its neighbors. There is also a public method called `GetNeighbors()` that exposes the private `_neighbors` list. The class also has two constructors, both of which instantiate the `_neighbors` list. The overloaded `GraphNode(Int16 value)` constructor also allows a value to be defined at instantiation.

Next, we can implement our graph functions. Here's what a concrete implementation of a `Graph` class will look like in Java:

```
        private LinkedList<GraphNode> _nodes;
        public LinkedList<GraphNode> GetNodes()
        {
                return _nodes;
        }

        public Graph(){
            _nodes = new LinkedList<GraphNode>();
        }

        public Graph(LinkedList<GraphNode> nodes)
        {
                _nodes = nodes;
        }
```

Our `Graph` class includes one private field, a `List<GraphNode>` collection named `_nodes` and a method named `GetNodes()`, which exposes read-only access to the private `List<GraphNode>` `_nodes` field. This field maintains a list of edges between the current node and its neighboring nodes. Finally, our constructor accepts one parameter of the type `List<Graphnode>`, and sets `_nodes` to this value if it is not `null`; otherwise, it initializes the `_nodes` collection:

```
        public void AddNode(GraphNode node)
        {
                _nodes.add(node);
        }

        public void AddNodeForValue(int value)
        {
                _nodes.add(new GraphNode(value));
```

```
        }
```

The first two public methods in `Graph` are `AddNode(GraphNode node)` and
`AddNodeForValue(int value)`, which add two versions of the AddNode functionality to
our class. The first adds a pre-existing node to the _nodes collection, while the second
instantiates a new node using `value` and then adds that node to the _nodes collection. Both
of these methods add nodes without defining any edges, and therefore these operations
have an **O**(1) cost:

```
public boolean RemoveNode(int value)
{
    GraphNode nodeToRemove = null;
    for (GraphNode node : _nodes)
    {
        if (node.Value == value)
        {
            nodeToRemove = node;
            break;
        }
    }

    if (nodeToRemove == null)
    {
        return false;
    }

    _nodes.remove(nodeToRemove);

    for (GraphNode node : _nodes)
    {
        int index = node.GetNeighbors().indexOf(nodeToRemove);
        if (index != -1)
        {
            node.GetNeighbors().remove(index);
        }
    }
    return true;
}
```

The `RemoveNode(int value)` method provides the `RemoveNode` functionality to our
class. This method accepts one parameter of type `int` named `value`, representing the node
the caller is asking to remove. The method begins by looping through each of the nodes,
searching for a match for `value`. If no match is found, the method returns `false`.
Otherwise, the matching node is removed from the _nodes collection using the `remove(E)`
function and method execution continues.

The second half of this method loops through each of the nodes in the collection, examining each node's neighbors to find a match for `nodeToRemove`. A match found means an edge exists from `node` and `nodeToRemove` and returns an index value for that match. By removing `nodeToRemove` from that `node.Neighbors` using `index`, we eliminate the reference and delete the edge.

The operational cost in Java is the same as that in C#. The `RemoveNode` operation has a cost of $O(n + k)$, where n is the number of nodes in the collection and k is the number of edges. In the `RemoveNode(int value)` method, the first half represents n and the second half represents k in that equation:

```
public void AddEdge(GraphNode from, GraphNode to)
{
    from.GetNeighbors().add(to);
}

public void AddBidirectedEdge(GraphNode from, GraphNode to)
{
    from.GetNeighbors().add(to);
    to.GetNeighbors().add(from);
}
```

The `AddEdge(GraphNode from, GraphNode to)` and `AddBidirectedEdge(GraphNode from, GraphNode to)` methods provide the `AddEdge` functionality to the `Graph` class. The first method is the standard AddEdge operation, while the second is more of a convenience method in case the caller wants to immediately add bidirectional references. The first method has an $O(1)$ operational cost, while the second technically has a more unusual $O(2)$ operational cost:

```
public boolean Adjacent(GraphNode from, GraphNode to)
{
    return from.GetNeighbors().contains(to);
}
```

The `Adjacent(GraphNode from, GraphNode to)` method returns a Boolean value denoting whether an edge exists between two nodes, `from` and `to`. Hopefully, the signature makes the direction of this edge clear, but for clarity, this method only confirms that an edge exists from the `from` node and to the `to` node, but not the reciprocal. Since this method is based on the `contains` function, it has an $O(n)$ operational cost, where n is the number of edges contained in `from.Neighbors`:

```
public LinkedList<GraphNode> Neighbors(int value)
{
    GraphNode node = null;
    for (GraphNode n : _nodes)
```

```
    {
        if (n.Value == value)
        {
            return node.GetNeighbors();
        }
    }

    return null;
}
```

The `Neighbors(int value)` method provides the Neighbors functionality to our class. This method accepts one parameter of type `int` and named `value`, representing the node the caller is asking to examine. The method begins by looping through the collection of nodes, searching for a match for `value`. If no match is found, the method returns `null`. Otherwise, the method returns the matching node's `Neighbors` collection using `GetNeighbors()`. If the `GraphNode` object was known in advance, this operation will have an **O**(1) operational cost. However, since we are examining the entire collection of `_nodes` at the `Graph` level based on the value of a specific node, this implementation has an **O**(n) operational cost:

```
public int GetCount()
{
    return _nodes.size();
}
```

Finally, the `GetCount()` method exposes read-only access to the total number of nodes contained in the collection by returning `_nodes.size()`. This field provides the Count functionality to our `Graph` class and has an **O**(1) operational cost.

Objective-C

Objective-C does not provide a concrete `Graph` or `GraphNode` class, but it does provide the basic components necessary to build them. Here is what a basic implementation of a `EDSGraphNode` class will look like in Objective-C:

```
@interface EDSGraphNode()
{
    NSInteger _value;
    NSMutableArray *_neighbors;
}
-(instancetype)initGraphNode
{
    if (self = [super init])
    {
        _neighbors = [NSMutableArray array];
    }
```

```
        return self;
    }

    -(instancetype)initGraphNodeWithValue:(NSInteger)value
    {
        if (self = [super init])
        {
            _value = value;
            _neighbors = [NSMutableArray array];
        }
        return self;
    }

    -(NSMutableArray*)neighbors
    {
        return _neighbors;
    }

    -(NSInteger)value
    {
        return _value;
    }
```

This class contains two ivar properties named _value and _neighbors. The _value property is an NSInteger object and stores our integer data, while _neighbors is an NSMutableArray object that represents the edges between this node and its neighbors. The class has two initializers, both of which instantiate the _neighbors list. The initGraphNode: method simply instantiates the _neighbors array, while the initGraphNodeWithValue: also sets _value to the passed value property.

Next, we can implement our graph functions. Here's what a concrete implementation of a EDSGraph class will look like in Objective-C:

```
@interface EDSGraph()
{
    NSMutableArray<EDSGraphNode*>* _nodes;
}

-(NSMutableArray<EDSGraphNode*>*)nodes
{
    return _nodes;
}

-(instancetype)initGraphWithNodes:(NSMutableArray<EDSGraphNode *>
*)nodes
{
    if (self = [super init])
```

```
        {
            if (nodes)
            {
                _nodes = nodes;
            }
            else
            {
                _nodes = [NSMutableArray array];
            }
        }
        return self;
    }
```

Our `EDSGraph` class includes one ivar property, an `NSMutableArray<EDSGraphNode*>*` named `_nodes` that maintains the list of edges to neighboring nodes. There is also a method named `nodes` that exposes read-only access to the private `_nodes` property. Finally, our initializer `initGraphWithNodes:(NSMutableArray<EDSGraphNode *> *)nodes` accepts one array of `EDSGraphnode` and sets `_nodes` to this value if it is not `nil`. Otherwise, the initializer method initializes the `_nodes` collection:

```
    -(NSInteger) countOfNodes
    {
        return [_nodes count];
    }
```

The `countOfNodes` method exposes read-only access to the total number of nodes contained in the collection by returning `[_nodes count]`. This method provides the Count functionality to our `EDSGraph` class and has an **O**(1) operational cost:

```
    -(void) addNode:(EDSGraphNode*)node
    {
        [_nodes addObject:node];
    }

    -(void) addNodeForValue:(NSInteger)value
    {
        EDSGraphNode *node = [[EDSGraphNode alloc]
  initGraphNodeWithValue:value];
        [_nodes addObject:node];
    }
```

The first two public methods in `EDSGraph` are `addNode:` and `addNodeForValue:` that add two versions of the `AddNode` functionality to our class. The first adds a pre-existing node to the `_nodes` collection, while the second instantiates a new node using `value` and then adds that node to the `_nodes` collection. Both of these methods add nodes without defining any edges, and therefore these operations have an **O**(1) cost:

```
- (BOOL) removeNodeForValue: (NSInteger) value
{
    EDSGraphNode *nodeToRemove;
    for (EDSGraphNode *n in _nodes)
    {
        if (n.value == value)
        {
            nodeToRemove = n;
            break;
        }
    }
    if (!nodeToRemove)
    {
        return NO;
    }
    [_nodes removeObject:nodeToRemove];
    for (EDSGraphNode *n in _nodes)
    {
        long index = [n.neighbors indexOfObject:nodeToRemove];
        if (index != -1)
        {
            [n.neighbors removeObjectAtIndex:index];
        }
    }
    return YES;
}
```

The `removeNodeForValue:` method provides the RemoveNode functionality to our class. This method accepts one parameter of type `NSInteger` and named `value`, representing the node the caller is asking to remove. The method begins by looping through the collection of nodes searching for a match for `value`. If no match is found, the method returns `NO`. Otherwise, the matching node is removed from the `_nodes` collection using `removeObject:` and the method execution continues.

The second half of this method loops through each of the nodes in the collection, examining each node's neighbors to find a match for `nodeToRemove`. A match found means an edge exists from `node` and `nodeToRemove` and returns an index value for that match. By removing `nodeToRemove` from that `node.Neighbors` using `index`, we eliminate the reference and delete the edge.

As we examined in the discussion on graph operations, the `RemoveNode` operation has an operational cost of $O(n + k)$, where n is the number of nodes in the collection and k is the number of edges. In the `removeNodeForValue:` method, the first half represents n and the second half represents k in that equation:

```
- (void) addEdgeFromNode: (EDSGraphNode*) from toNode: (EDSGraphNode*) to
{
    [from.neighbors addObject:to];
}

    - (void) addBidirectionalEdgeFromNode: (EDSGraphNode*) from
toNode: (EDSGraphNode*) to
{
    [from.neighbors addObject:to];
    [to.neighbors addObject:from];
}
```

The `addEdgeFromNode:toNode:` and `addBidirectionalEdgeFromNode:toNode:` methods provide the AddEdge functionality to the `Graph` class. The first method is the standard AddEdge operation, while the second is more of a convenience method in case the caller wants to immediately add bidirectional references. The first method has an $O(1)$ operational cost, while the second has an $O(2)$ operational cost:

```
- (BOOL) adjacent: (EDSGraphNode*) from toNode: (EDSGraphNode*) to
{
    return [from.neighbors containsObject:to];
}
```

The `adjacent:toNode:` method returns a `BOOL` value denoting whether an edge exists between two nodes, `from` and `to`. Hopefully, the signature makes the direction of this edge clear, but for clarity, this method only confirms that an edge exists from the `from` node and to the `to` node, but not the reciprocal. Since this method is based on the `containsObject:` function, it has an $O(n)$ operational cost, where n is the number of edges contained in `from.neighbors`:

```
- (NSMutableArray<EDSGraphNode*>*) neighborsOfValue: (NSInteger) value
{
    for (EDSGraphNode *n in _nodes)
    {
        if (n.value == value)
        {
            return n.neighbors;
        }
    }
    return nil;
}
```

The `neighborsOfValue:` method provides the Neighbors functionality to our class. This method accepts one parameter of type `NSInteger` and named `value`, representing the node the caller is asking to examine. The method begins by looping through the collection of nodes searching for a match for `value`. If no match is found, the method returns `nil`. Otherwise, the method returns the matching node's `neighbors` collection. If the `EDSGraphNode` object was known in advance, this operation would have an **O**(1) operational cost. However, since we are examining the entire collection of _nodes at the `EDSGraph` level based on the value of a specific node, this implementation has an **O**(*n*) operational cost.

Swift

Like its counterparts, Swift does not provide a concrete `Graph` or `GraphNode` class by default, so we will need to create our own. We will start with the `GraphNode` class. Here is what a basic implementation of a `GraphNode` class might look like in Swift:

```
public class GraphNode : Equatable
{
    public var neighbors: Array = [GraphNode]()
    public var value : Int
    public init(val: Int) {
        value = val
    }
}

public func == (lhs: GraphNode, rhs: GraphNode) -> Bool {
    return (lhs.value == rhs.value)
}
```

This class extends `Equatable`. This is necessary to support searching by value and by object. The class contains two public properties. The first is an array of `GraphNode` objects named `neighbors` that represents the edges between the node and its neighboring nodes. The second is an `Int` variable named `value`, and it is used to store our integer data for the object. The class has one custom constructor that accepts `Int` and assigns that value to the `value` variable. Finally, the class defines an overloaded comparison operator to support the `Equatable` functionality.

Next, we can implement our graph functions. Here's what a concrete implementation of a `Graph` class might look like in Swift:

```
public var nodes: Array = [GraphNode]()

public init(nodes: Array<GraphNode>)
{
```

```
        self.nodes = nodes
    }
```

Our `Graph` class includes one public `Array` property named `nodes`. This property maintains the list of edges to neighboring nodes. The class has one custom constructor that accepts one parameter of the type `Array<GraphNode>` and sets `_nodes` to this value if it is not `nil`. Since the `nodes` object is initialized when it is declared, there is no need to initialize it here:

```
public func count() -> Int
{
    return nodes.count
}
```

The first method in this class is `count()`, which exposes read-only access to the total number of nodes contained in the collection by returning `nodes.count`. This method provides the Count functionality to our `Graph` class and has an **O**(1) operational cost:

```
public func addNode(node: GraphNode)
{
    nodes.append(node)
}

public func addNodeForValue(value: Int)
{
    let node = GraphNode(val: value)
    nodes.append(node);
}
```

The next two public methods in `Graph`, `AddNode(node: GraphNode)` and `AddNodeForValue(value: Int)`, add two versions of the `AddNode` functionality to our class. The first adds a pre-existing node to the `nodes` collection, while the second instantiates a new node using `value` and then adds that node to the `nodes` collection. Both of these methods add nodes without defining any edges, and therefore these operations have an **O**(1) cost:

```
public func removeNodeForValue(value: Int) -> Bool
{
    var nodeToRemove: GraphNode? = nil
    for n in nodes
    {
        if (n.value == value)
        {
            nodeToRemove = n;
            break
        }
    }
```

```
        }

        if (nodeToRemove == nil)
        {
            return false
        }
        if let index = nodes.index(of: nodeToRemove!)
        {
            nodes.remove(at: index)
            for n in nodes
            {
                if let foundIndex = n.neighbors.index(of: nodeToRemove!)
                {
                    n.neighbors.remove(at: foundIndex)
                }
            }
            return true
        }
        return false
    }
```

The `removeNodeForValue(value: Int)` method provides the `RemoveNode` functionality to our class. This method accepts one parameter of type `Int` and named `value` representing the node the caller is asking to remove. The method begins by looping through each of the nodes in the collection searching for a match to the `value`, object. If no match is found, the method returns `false`. Otherwise, the matching node is removed from the `nodes` collection and method execution continues.

The second half of this method loops through each of the nodes in the collection, examining each node element's neighbors to find a match for `nodeToRemove`. A match found means an edge exists between the `node` and `nodeToRemove` objects and returns an index value for that match. By removing `nodeToRemove` from `node.neighbors` using `index`, we eliminate the reference and delete the edge.

As we examined in the discussion on graph operations, the `RemoveNode` operation has an operational cost of $O(n + k)$, where n is the number of nodes in the collection and k is the number of edges. In the `removeNodeForValue(value: Int)` method, the first half represents n and the second half represents k in that equation:

```
        public func addEdgeFromNodeToNode(from: GraphNode, to: GraphNode)
        {
            from.neighbors.append(to)
        }

        public func addBidirectionalEdge(from: GraphNode, to: GraphNode)
        {
```

```
        from.neighbors.append(to)
        to.neighbors.append(from)
    }
```

The `addEdgeFromNodeToNode(from: GraphNode, to: GraphNode)` and
`addBidirectedEdge(from: GraphNode, to: GraphNode)` methods provide the
`AddEdge` functionality to the `Graph` class. The first method is the standard AddEdge
operation, while the second is more of a convenience method in case the caller wants to
immediately add bidirectional references. The first method has an **O**(1) operational cost,
while the second technically has an **O**(2) operational cost:

```
public func adjacent(from: GraphNode, to: GraphNode) -> Bool
{
    if from.neighbors.index(of: to) != nil
    {
        return true
    }
    else
    {
        return false
    }
}
```

The `adjacent(from: GraphNode, to: GraphNode)` method returns a `Bool` value
denoting whether an edge exists between two nodes, `from` and `to`. Hopefully, the signature
makes the direction of this edge clear, but for clarity, this method only confirms that an
edge exists from the `from` node and to the `to` node, but not the reciprocal. Since this
method is based on the `contains` function, it has an **O**(*n*) operational cost, where *n* is the
number of edges contained in `from.Neighbors`:

```
public func neighborsOfValue(value: Int) -> Array<GraphNode>?
{
    for n in nodes
    {
        if (n.value == value)
        {
            return n.neighbors
        }
    }

    return nil
}
```

The `neighborsOfValue(value: Int)` provides the Neighbors functionality to our class. This method accepts one parameter of type `Int` and named `value` representing the node the caller is asking to examine. The method begins by looping through the collection of nodes searching for a match to `value`. If no match is found, the method returns `nil`. Otherwise, the method returns the matching node's `neighbors` collection. If the `GraphNode` object was known in advance, this operation would have an **O**(1) operational cost. However, since we are examining the entire collection of `nodes` at the `Graph` level based on the value of a specific node, this implementation has an **O**(n) operational cost.

Summary

In this chapter, you learned about graph data structures. We used visual representations of graphs to gain a better understanding of how they are structured and how they can be used. Next, we examined the most common operations when working with graphs and discussed their typical complexity cost. Following this, we created our own simple graph node object and graph data structure class from scratch in each of the four languages we have examined in this book.

12
Sorting: Bringing Order Out Of Chaos

Being able to build the right data structure or collection class for a particular application is only half the battle. Unless the data sets in your problem domain are very small, any collection of your data will benefit from a little organization. Organizing the elements in your list or collection by a particular value or set of values is known as **sorting**.

Sorting your data is not strictly necessary, but doing so makes searching or lookup operations much more efficient. Likewise, when you need to merge multiple collections of data together, having the various collections sorted in advance of the merge can greatly improve the efficiency of the merge operation.

If your data is a collection of numeric values, then sorting can be something as simple as arranging it in ascending or descending order. However, if your data consists of complex objects, you can sort the collection by a particular value. In this case, the field or property by which the data is sorted is referred to as a **key**. For example, if you have a collection of car objects and you want to sort them by their make, such as Ford, Chevrolet or Dodge, then the make is the key. However, if you wanted to sort by multiple keys, say the make and model, then the make becomes the *primary key*, while the model becomes the *secondary key*. Further extensions of this pattern would result in *tertiary keys*, *Quaternary keys*, and so on.

Sorting algorithms come in many shapes and sizes, and many of them are specifically suited to particular types of data structures. Although an exhaustive examination of known or even just popular sorting algorithms is beyond the scope of this book, in this chapter, we will focus on those algorithms that are either fairly common or are well suited to some of the data structures we have already examined. In each case, we will review examples in each of the four languages we have been looking at and discuss the complexity cost.

In this chapter, we will cover the following:

- Selection sort
- Insertion sort
- Bubble sort
- Quick sort
- Merge sort
- Bucket sort
- Counting sort

Selection sort

A selection sort can be described as an in-place comparison. This algorithm divides a collection or list of objects into two parts. The first is a subset of objects that have already been sorted, ranging from *0* to *i*, where *i* is the next object to be sorted. The second is a subset of objects that have not been sorted, ranging from *i* to *n*, where *n* is the length of the collection.

The selection sort algorithm works by taking the smallest or largest value in a collection and placing it at the beginning of the unsorted subarray by swapping it with the object at the current index. For example, consider ordering a collection in ascending order. At the outset, the sorted subarray will consist of 0 members, while the unsorted subarray will consist of all the members in the set. The selection sort algorithm will find the smallest member in the unsorted subarray and place it at the beginning of the unsorted subarray.

At this point, the sorted subarray consists of one member, while the unsorted subarray consists of all the remaining members in the original set. This process will repeat until all members of the unsorted subarray have been placed in the sorted subarray.

Given the following set of values:

S = {50, 25, 73, 21, 3}

Our algorithm will find the smallest value in *S[0...4]*, which in this case is 3, and place it at the beginning of *S[0...4]*:

S = {3, 25, 73, 21, 50}

The process is repeated for *S[1...4]*, which returns the value 21:

S = *{3, 21, 73, 25, 50}*

The next evaluation at *S[2...4]* returns a value of 25:

S = *{3, 21, 25, 73, 50}*

Finally, the function repeats again for *S[3...4]* which returns the smallest value of 50:

S = *{3, 21, 25, 50, 73}*

There is no need to examine the last object in the collection because it, by necessity, is already the largest remaining value. This is a small consolation, however, because the selection sort algorithm still has an $O(n^2)$ complexity cost. Moreover, this worst-case complexity score doesn't tell the whole tale in this particular case. The selection sort is always an $O(n^2)$ complexity, even under the best of circumstances. Therefore, the selection sort is quite possibly the slowest and most inefficient sorting algorithm you may encounter.

 Each of the code examples in this chapter will examine algorithms in the form of those methods most essential to the operation, with these being detached from their parent classes. Additionally, in each case the collection of objects being sorted will be defined at the class level, outside of the example code shown here. Likewise, the subsequent object instantiation and population of those collections will be defined outside the example code. To see the full class examples, please use the code examples accompanying this text.

C#

```csharp
public void SelectionSort(int[] values)
{
    if (values.Length <= 1)
    return;
    int j, minIndex;
    for (int i = 0; i < values.Length - 1; i++)
    {
        minIndex = i;
        for (j = i + 1; j < values.Length; j++)
        {
            if (values[j] < values[minIndex])
            {
                minIndex = j;
            }
        }
        Swap(ref values[minIndex], ref values[i]);
```

```
            }
    }

    void Swap(ref int x, ref int y)
    {
        int t = x;
        x = y;
        y = t;
    }
```

Each of our implementations of the `SelectionSort` method begins by confirming that the `values` array has at least two members. If not, the method returns as there are not enough members to sort. Otherwise, we create two nested loops. The outer `for` loop moves the boundary of the unsorted array one index at a time, while the inner `for` loop is used to find the minimum value within the unsorted boundary. Once we have a minimum value, the method swaps the member at `i` with the member identified as the current minimum. Since C# does not support passing primitives by reference by default we must explicitly invoke the `ref` keyword on both the `swap(ref int x, ref int y)` method signature as well as the called parameter. Although it may seem like more work to create a separate `swap` method for this purpose, the swap functionality is common to several popular sorting algorithms and having this code in a separate method saves us some keystrokes later on.

Nested for loops

Remember that nested loops will automatically increase the complexity of an algorithm exponentially. Any algorithm with a `for` loop has a complexity cost of $O(n)$, but once you nest another `for` loop within the first the complexity cost increases to $O(n^2)$. Nesting another `for` loop within the second makes the cost $O(n^3)$, and so on.

Also note that nesting `for` loops in any implementation will be a red flag to an observant reviewer and you should always be ready to justify such a design. Only nest for loops when you absolutely must.

Java

```java
public void selectionSort(int[] values)
{
    if (values.length <= 1)
        return;

    int j, minIndex;
    for (int i = 0; i < values.length - 1; i++)
    {
```

```
            minIndex = i;
            for (j = i + 1; j < values.length; j++)
            {
                if (values[j] < values[minIndex])
                {
                    minIndex = j;
                }
            }

            int temp = values[minIndex];
            values[minIndex] = values[i];
            values[i] = temp;
        }
    }
```

The Java implementation is nearly identical in design to the C# implementation, except for the name of the array `length` function. However, Java does not support passing primitives by reference at all. Although it is possible to emulate this behavior by passing the primitive to an instance of a mutable wrapper class, most developers agree that this is a bad idea. Instead, our Java implementation performs the swap directly inside the `for` loop.

Objective-C

```
- (void) selectionSort: (NSMutableArray<NSNumber*>*) values
{
    if ([values count] <= 1)
        return;
    NSInteger j, minIndex;
    for (int i = 0; i < [values count] - 1; i++)
    {
        minIndex = i;
        for (j = i + 1; j < [values count]; j++)
        {
            if ([values[j] intValue] < [values[minIndex] intValue])
            {
                minIndex = j;
            }
        }
        NSNumber *temp = (NSNumber*) values[minIndex];
        values[minIndex] = values[i];
        values[i] = temp;
    }
}
```

Since `NSArray` can only store objects, we need to cast our values to `NSNumber`, and when we evaluate the members we need to explicitly examine the `intValue` object. Like Java, we opt to not create a separate swap method and pass the values by reference. Otherwise, implementations.

Swift

```
open func selectionSort( values: inout [Int])
{
    if (values.count <= 1)
    {
        return
    }
    var minIndex: Int
    for i in 0..<values.count
    {
        minIndex = i
        for j in i+1..<values.count
        {
            if (values[j] < values[minIndex])
            {
                minIndex = j
            }
        }
        swap(x: &values[minIndex], y: &values[i])
    }
}

open func swap( x: inout Int, y: inout Int)
{
    let t: Int = x
    x = y
    y = t
}
```

Swift does not permit C-style `for` loops so our method must use the Swift 3.0 equivalent. Also, since Swift considers arrays to be `struct` implementations instead of class implementations, the `values` parameter cannot be simply passed by reference. Therefore, our Swift implementation includes the `inout` decorator on the `values` parameter. Otherwise, the functionality is fundamentally the same as its predecessors. This rule also applies in our `swap( x: inout Int, y: inout Int)` method, which is used to swap the values during the sort.

Insertion sort

An **insertion sort** is a very simple algorithm that looks at an object in a collection and compares its key to the keys prior to itself. You can visualize this process as how many of us order a hand of playing cards, individually removing and inserting cards from left to right in ascending order.

For example, consider the case of ordering a collection in ascending order. An insertion sort algorithm will examine an object at index i and determine if it's key is lower in value or priority than the object at index $i - 1$. If so, the object at i is removed and inserted at $i - 1$. At this point, the function will repeat and continue to loop in this manner until the object key at $i - 1$ is not lower than the object key at i.

Given the following set of values:

$S = \{50, 25, 73, 21, 3\}$

Our algorithm will begin examining the list at $i = 1$. We do this because at $i = 0$, $i - 1$ is a non-existent value and would require special handling.

Since 25 is less than 50, it is removed and reinserted at $i = 0$. Since we're at index 0, there is nothing left to examine to the left of 25, so this iteration is complete:

$S = \{25, 50, 73, 21, 3\}$

Next we examine $i = 2$. Because 73 is not less than 50, this value doesn't need to move. Since we have already sorted everything to the left of $i = 2$, this iteration is immediately completed. At $i = 3$, the value 21 is less than 73 and so it is removed and reinserted at $i = 2$. Checking again, 21 is less than 50, so the value 21 is removed and reinserted at index 1. Finally, 21 is less than 25, so the value 21 is removed and reinserted at $i = 0$. Since we're now at index 0, there is nothing left to examine to the left of 21, so this iteration are complete:

$S = \{21, 25, 50, 73, 3\}$

Finally, we come to $i = 4$, the end of the list. Since 3 is less than 21, the value 3 is removed and reinserted at $i = 3$. Next, 3 is less than 73, so the value 3 is removed and reinserted at $i = 2$. At $i = 2$, 3 is less than 50 so the value 3 is removed and reinserted at $i = 1$. At $i = 1$, 3 is less than 25 so the value 3 is removed and reinserted at $i = 0$. Since we're now at index 0, there is nothing left to examine to the left of 3 so this iteration, and our sorting function, are complete:

$S = \{3, 21, 25, 50, 73\}$

As you can see this algorithm is simple but also potentially expensive for larger lists of objects or values. The insertion sort has a worst-case and even an *average*-case complexity of $O(n^2)$. However, unlike selection sort, insertion sort has improved efficiency when sorting lists that were previously sorted. As a result, it enjoys a best-case complexity of $O(n)$, making this algorithm a slightly better choice than selection sort.

C#

```csharp
public void InsertionSort(int[] values)
{
   if (values.Length <= 1)
      return;
   int j, value;
   for (int i = 1; i < values.Length; i++)
   {
      value = values[i];
      j = i - 1;

      while (j >= 0 && values[j] > value)
      {
         values[j + 1] = values[j];
         j = j - 1;
      }
      values[j + 1] = value;
   }
}
```

Each of our implementations of the `InsertionSort` method begins by confirming that the `values` array has at least two members. If not, the method returns as there are not enough members to sort. Otherwise, two integer variables are declared named `j` and `value`. Next a `for` loop is created that iterates through the members of the collection. The index `i` is used to track the position of the last sorted member. Within this for loop, `value` is assigned to the last sorted member while `j` is used to track the position in the current iteration through the unsorted members. Our `while` loop continues until `j` is equal to `0` and the value at index `j` is greater than the value at index `i`. In every iteration of the `while` loop, we swap the member at position `j` with the member at position `j + 1`, then the loop decrements the value of `j` by 1 to move back through the collection. Finally, the last step is to set the member stored in `value` at position `j + 1`.

Java

```java
public void insertionSort(int[] values)
{
    if (values.length <= 1)
        return;
```

```
int j, value;
for (int i = 1; i < values.length; i++)
{
    value = values[i];
    j = i - 1;

    while (j >= 0 && values[j] > value)
    {
        values[j + 1] = values[j];
        j = j - 1;
    }
    values[j + 1] = value;
}
}
```

The Java implementation is nearly identical in design to the C# implementation, except for the name of the array `length` function.

Objective-C

```
-(void)insertionSort:(NSMutableArray<NSNumber*>*)values
{
    if ([values count] <= 1)
        return;
    NSInteger j, value;
    for (int i = 1; i < [values count]; i++)
    {
        value = [values[i] intValue];
        j = i - 1;
        while (j >= 0 && [values[j] intValue] > value)
        {
            values[j + 1] = values[j];
            j = j - 1;
        }
        values[j + 1] = [NSNumber numberWithInteger:value];
    }
}
```

Since NSArray can only store objects, we need to cast our values to the NSNumber variable, and when we evaluate the members we need to explicitly examine the intValue variable. Otherwise, this implementation is fundamentally the same as the C# or Java implementations.

Swift

```swift
open func insertionSort( values: inout [Int])
{
    if (values.count <= 1)
    {
        return
    }
    var j, value: Int
    for i in 1..<values.count
    {
        value = values[i];
        j = i - 1;

        while (j >= 0 && values[j] > value)
        {
            values[j + 1] = values[j];
            j = j - 1;
        }
        values[j + 1] = value;
    }
}
```

Swift does not permit C-style `for` loops, so our method must use the Swift 3.0 equivalent. Also, since Swift considers arrays to be struct implementations instead of class implementations, the `values` parameter cannot be simply passed by reference. Therefore, our Swift implementation includes the `inout` decorator on the `values` parameter. Otherwise, the functionality is fundamentally the same as its predecessors.

Bubble sort

Bubble sort is another simple algorithm that steps through the list of values or objects to be sorted and compares adjacent items or their keys to determine if they are in the wrong order. The name comes from the way that unordered items seem to bubble to the top of the list. However, some developers sometimes refer to this as a **sinking sort**, as objects could just as easily appear to be dropping down through the list.

Overall, the bubble sort is just another inefficient comparison sort. However, it does have one distinct advantage over other comparison sorts, in that: inherently determine whether or not the list has been sorted. Bubble sort accomplishes this by not performing comparisons on objects that were sorted in previous iterations and by stopping once the collection proves ordered.

For example, consider the case of ordering a collection in ascending order. A bubble sort algorithm will examine an object at index i and determine if its key is lower in value or priority than the object at index $i + 1$, in which case the two objects are swapped.

Given the following set of values:

$S = \{50, 25, 73, 21, 3\}$
The bubble sort algorithm will compare $\{i = 0, i = 1\}$. Since 50 is greater than 25, the two are swapped. Next the method compares $\{i = 1, i = 2\}$. In this case 50 is less than 73, so nothing changes. At $\{i = 2, i = 3\}$, 73 is greater than 21 so they are swapped. Finally, at $\{i = 3, i = 4\}$, 73 is greater than 3, so they are swapped as well. After our first iteration, our set now looks like this:

$S = \{25, 50, 21, 3, 73\}$

Let's examine another iteration. In this iteration, our algorithm will begin by comparing $\{i = 0, i = 1\}$, and since 25 is less than 50 nothing changes. Next we examine $\{i = 1, i = 2\}$. Since 50 is greater than 21 the two are swapped. At $\{i = 2, i = 3\}$, 50 is greater than 3 so the two are swapped. Since $i = 4$ was sorted in the previous iteration, the loop halts and resets to position $i = 0$ for the next iteration. After the second iteration our set looks like this:

$S = \{25, 21, 3, 50, 73\}$

This shows us that iterations through the set consist of $n - j$ comparisons, where n is the number of items in the set and j is the current iteration count. Therefore, after each iteration the bubble sort becomes *slightly* more efficient. Plus, once the set proves to be sorted the iterations stop altogether. Although bubble sort has a worst case and an average case complexity of $O(n^2)$, the ability to limit the sorting to objects that have not been sorted provides the algorithm with a best case complexity of $O(n)$, making this approach slightly better than selection sort but about equal to insertion sort. In certain circumstances where the list is already sorted, the bubble sort is also slightly more efficient than **quick sort**, which we will discuss later. However, bubble sort is still a terribly inefficient algorithm that is unsuitable for all but small collections of objects.

C#

```
public void BubbleSort(int[] values)
{
    bool swapped;
    for (int i = 0; i < values.Length - 1; i++)
    {
        swapped = false;
        for (int j = values.Length - 1; j > i; j--)
        {
            if (values[j] < values[j - 1])
```

```
        {
            Swap(ref values[j], ref values[j - 1]);
            swapped = true;
        }
    }

    if (swapped == false)
        break;
    }
}
```

Each of our implementations of the `BubbleSort` method begins by declaring a Boolean value named `swapped`. This value is critical to the optimized bubble sort method as it is used to track whether any objects were swapped during the current iteration. If `true`, there is no guarantee that the list is guaranteed so at least one more iteration is required. If `false`, no objects were swapped meaning that the list is ordered and the algorithm can stop now.

Next we create a `for` loop that iterates through the members of the collection. This loop effectively tracks our current iteration. Inside this loop, we immediately set `swapped` variable to `false` and then create another inner loop, which moves backward through the collection performing comparisons on the pair of objects. If the pair of objects is determined to be out of order, the `BubbleSort()` method calls the same `swap()` method examined in the selection sort discussion and then changes swapped to true. Otherwise, the execution continues to the next iteration of `j`. Once the inner loop is completed, the method checks the `swapped` variable to determine if any objects were ordered. If false, the execution continues to the next iteration of `i`. Otherwise, the method breaks out of the outer loop and the execution is finished.

Java

```
public void bubbleSort(int[] values)
{
    boolean swapped;
    for (int i = 0; i < values.length - 1; i++)
    {
        swapped = false;
        for (int j = values.length -1; j > i; j--)
        {
            if (values[j] < values[j - 1])
            {
                int temp = values[j];
                values[j] = values[j - 1];
                values[j - 1] = temp;
                swapped = true;
            }
        }
```

```
            }

        if (swapped == false)
            break;
    }
}
```

The Java implementation is nearly identical in design to the C# implementation, except for the name of the array `length` function. However, Java does not support passing primitives by reference at all. Although it is possible to emulate this behavior by passing the primitive to an instance of a mutable wrapper class, most developers agree that this is a bad idea. Instead, our Java implementation performs the swap directly inside the `for` loop.

Objective-C

```
-(void)bubbleSortArray:(NSMutableArray<NSNumber*>*)values
{
    bool swapped;
    for (NSInteger i = 0; i < [values count] - 1; i++)
    {
        swapped = false;
        for (NSInteger j = [values count] - 1; j > i; j--)
        {
            if (values[j] < values[j - 1])
            {
                NSInteger temp = [values[j] intValue];
                values[j] = values[j - 1];
                values[j - 1] = [NSNumber numberWithInteger:temp];
                swapped = true;
            }
        }
        if (swapped == false)
            break;
    }
}
```

Since the `NSArray` variable can only store objects, we need to cast our values to `NSNumber`, and when we evaluate the members we need to explicitly examine the `intValue`. Like Java, we opt to not create a separate swap method, and pass the values by reference. Otherwise, this implementation is fundamentally the same as the C# or Java implementations.

Swift

```
open func bubbleSort( values: inout [Int])
{
    var swapped: Bool
    for i in 0..<values.count - 1
    {
        swapped = false
        for j in ((i + 1)..<values.count).reversed()
        {
            if (values[j] < values[j - 1])
            {
                swap(x: &values[j], y: &values[j - 1])
                swapped = true
            }
        }
        if (swapped == false)
        {
            break
        }
    }
}
```

Swift does not permit C-style `for` loops so our method must use the Swift 3.0 equivalent. Also, since Swift considers arrays to be struct implementations instead of class implementations, the `values` parameter cannot be simply passed by reference. Therefore, our Swift implementation includes the `inout` decorator on the `values` parameter. Otherwise, the functionality is fundamentally the same as its predecessors. This rule also applies in our `swap( x: inout Int, y: inout Int)` method, which is used to swap the values during the sort.

Quick sort

The quick sort is one of a set of algorithms known as **divide-and-conquer**. Divide and conquer algorithms work by recursively breaking down a set of objects into two or more sub sets until each sub set becomes simple enough to solve directly. In the case of quick sort, the algorithm picks an element called a **pivot**, and then sorts by moving all smaller items prior to it and greater items after it. Moving elements before and after the pivot is the primary component of a quick sort algorithm and is referred to as a **partition**. The partition is recursively repeated on smaller and smaller sub sets until each sub set contains the 0 or 1 element, at which point the set is ordered.

Choosing the correct pivot point is critical in maintaining quick sort's improved performance. For example, choosing the smallest or largest element in the list will result in $O(n^2)$ complexity. Although there is no bulletproof approach for choosing the best pivot, there are fundamentally four approaches your design can take:

- Always pick the *first* object in the collection.
- Always pick the *median* object in the collection.
- Always pick the *last* object in the collection.
- Choose an object at *random* from the collection.

In the following examples, we will take the third approach and choose the last object in the collection as the pivot.

Although the quick sort algorithm has a worst case complexity of $O(n^2)$ like other sorts we have examined thus far, it has a much improved average- and best-case complexity of $O(n \log(n))$, cost making it, on average, better than the selection, insertion and bubble sort approaches.

C#

```csharp
public void QuickSort(int[] values, int low, int high)
{
  if (low < high)
  {
    int index = Partition(values, low, high);

    QuickSort(values, low, index -1);
    QuickSort(values, index +1, high);
  }
}

int Partition(int[] values, int low, int high)
{
  int pivot = values[high];
  int i = (low - 1);
  for (int j = low; j <= high -1; j++)
  {
    if (values[j] <= pivot)
    {
      i++;

      Swap(ref values[i], ref values[j]);
    }
  }
  i++;
```

```
    Swap(ref values[i], ref values[high]);
    return i;
}
```

Each of our implementations of the `QuickSort` method begins by checking if the low index is less than the high index. If `false`, the sub set is empty or has one item so it is ordered by definition and the method returns. If `true`, the method first determines the `index` of the next division of sub sets by calling the `Partition(int[] values, int low, int high)` method. Next, the `QuickSort(int[] values, int low, int high)` method is called recursively on the lower and upper sub sets, which are defined based on `index`.

The real magic in this algorithm occurs in the `Partition(int[] values, int low, int high)` method. Here, an `index` variable is defined for the pivot, which in our case is the last object in the collection. Next, `i` is defined as the `low` index −1. Our algorithm then loops through the list from `low` to `high` −1. Within the loop, if the value at `i` is less than or equal to the pivot, we increment `i`, so we have the index of the first unsorted object in the collection, then we swap that unsorted object with the object at `j` which is less than the pivot.

Once the loop is completed we increment `i` one more time because *i + 1* is the first object in the collection that is greater than the pivot while every object prior to *i + 1* is less than the pivot. Our method swaps the value at *i* and the pivot object at index `high` so the pivot is also properly ordered. Finally, the method returns `i`, which is the index of the next break point for the `QuickSort(int[] values, int low, int high)` method.

Java

```java
public void quickSort(int[] values, int low, int high)
{
    if (low < high)
    {
        int index = partition(values, low, high);

        quickSort(values, low, index - 1);
        quickSort(values, index + 1, high);
    }
}

int partition(int[] values, int low, int high)
{
    int pivot = values[high];
    int i = (low - 1);
    for (int j = low; j <= high - 1; j++)
    {
        if (values[j] <= pivot)
```

```
        {
            i++;

            int temp = values[i];
            values[i] = values[j];
            values[j] = temp;
        }
    }

    i++;
    int temp = values[i];
    values[i] = values[high];
    values[high] = temp;

    return i;
}
```

The Java implementation is nearly identical in design to the C# implementation, except for the name of the array `length` function. However, Java does not support passing primitives by reference at all. Although it is possible to emulate this behavior by passing the primitive to an instance of a mutable wrapper class, most developers agree that this is a bad idea. Instead, our Java implementation performs the swap directly inside the `for` loop and the method itself.

Objective-C

```
    -(void)quickSortArray:(NSMutableArray<NSNumber*>*)values
forLowIndex:(NSInteger)low andHighIndex:(NSInteger)high
    {
        if (low < high)
        {
            NSInteger index = [self partitionArray:values forLowIndex:low
andHighIndex:high];
            [self quickSortArray:values forLowIndex:low andHighIndex:index
 - 1];
            [self quickSortArray:values forLowIndex:index + 1
andHighIndex:high];
        }
    }

    -(NSInteger)partitionArray:(NSMutableArray<NSNumber*>*)values
forLowIndex:(NSInteger)low andHighIndex:(NSInteger)high
    {
        NSInteger pivot = [values[high] intValue];
        NSInteger i = (low - 1);
        for (NSInteger j = low; j <= high - 1; j++)
        {
```

```
            if ([values[j] intValue] <= pivot)
            {
                i++;
                NSInteger temp = [values[i] intValue];
                values[i] = values[j];
                values[j] = [NSNumber numberWithInteger:temp];
            }
        }
        i++;
        NSInteger temp = [values[i] intValue];
        values[i] = values[high];
        values[high] = [NSNumber numberWithInteger:temp];
        return i;
    }
```

Since the `NSArray` variable can only store objects, we need to cast our values to `NSNumber`, and when we evaluate the members we need to explicitly examine the `intValue`. Like Java, we opt to not create a separate swap method and pass the values by reference. Otherwise, this implementation is fundamentally the same as the C# or Java implementations.

Swift

```
    open func quickSort( values: inout [Int], low: Int, high: Int)
    {
        if (low < high)
        {
            let index: Int = partition( values: &values, low: low, high:
high)
            quickSort( values: &values, low: low, high: index - 1)
            quickSort( values: &values, low: index + 1, high: high)
        }
    }

    func partition( values: inout [Int], low: Int, high: Int) -> Int
    {
        let pivot: Int = values[high]
        var i: Int = (low - 1)
        var j: Int = low
        while j <= (high - 1)
        {
            if (values[j] <= pivot)
            {
                i += 1
                swap(x: &values[i], y: &values[j])
            }
            j += 1
        }
        i += 1
```

```
            swap(x: &values[i], y: &values[high])
            return i;
    }
```

Swift does not permit C-style `for` loops so our Swift 3.0 version of the `mergeSort:` method is somewhat limited in this case. Therefore, our `for` loop will be replaced by a `while` loop. As such, we are define `j` as the `low` index value and increment `j` explicitly within each iteration of the `while` loop. Also, since Swift considers arrays to be struct implementations instead of class implementations, the `values` parameter cannot be simply passed by reference. Therefore, our Swift implementation includes the `inout` decorator on the `values` parameter. Otherwise, the functionality is fundamentally the same as its predecessors. This rule also applies in our `swap(x: inout Int, y: inout Int)` method, which is used to swap the values during the sort.

Merge sort

Merge sort is another popular version of the divide and conquer algorithm. It is a very efficient, general-purpose sort algorithm. The algorithm gets is named from the fact that it divides the collection in half, recursively sorts each half, and then merges the two sorted halves back together. Each half of the collection is repeatedly halved until there is only one object in the half, at which point it is sorted by definition. As each sorted half is merged, the algorithm compares the objects to determine where to place each sub set.

As far as divide and conquer algorithms are concerned, merge sort is one of the most efficient algorithms. The algorithm has a worst-, average- and best- case complexity of $\mathbf{O}(n \log(n))$, making it an improvement over quick sort even in the worst circumstances.

C#

```
public void MergeSort(int[] values, int left, int right)
{
  if (left == right)
    return;

  if (left < right)
  {
    int middle = (left + right) / 2;

    MergeSort(values, left, middle);
    MergeSort(values, middle + 1, right);

    int[] temp = new int[values.Length];
    for (int n = left; n <= right; n++)
```

```
      {
        temp[n] = values[n];
      }

      int index1 = left;
      int index2 = middle + 1;
      for (int n = left; n <= right; n++)
      {
        if (index1 == middle + 1)
        {
          values[n] = temp[index2++];
        }
        else if (index2 > right)
        {
          values[n] = temp[index1++];
        }
        else if (temp[index1] < temp[index2])
        {
          values[n] = temp[index1++];
        }
        else
        {
          values[n] = temp[index2++];
        }
      }
    }
  }
```

In each of our implementations of the MergeSort method, the left and right parameters define the beginning and end of a collection within the overall values array. When the method is initially called, the left parameter should be 0 and the right parameter should be the index of the final object in the values collection.

The method begins by checking whether the left index is equal to the right index. If true, the sub set is empty or has one item so it is ordered by definition and the method returns. Otherwise, the method checks whether the left index is less than the right index. If false, the method returns as this sub set is already ordered.

If `true`, the method execution begins in earnest. First, the method determines the mid point of the current sub set as this will be needed to divide the sub set into two new halves. The `middle` variable is declared and defined by adding `left` and `right` and dividing the sum by 2. Next, the `MergeSort(int[] values, int left, int right)` method is called recursively on each of the two halves by passing the values array and using `left`, `right`, and `middle` as guidelines. Following this, the method creates a new array called `temp` of the same size as `values`, and populates only the indices that correlate to the current sub set. Once the `temp` array is populated, the method creates two `int` variables called `index1` and `index2`, which represent the starting points of the two halves in the current sub set.

Finally, we get to the `for` loop, which iterates through the sub set from start to finish (`left` to `right`) and orders the values found there. The logic in each of these `if` statement is self-explanatory, but it helps to understand the reasoning behind these particular comparisons:

- The first comparison is only `true` when the left sub set has been exhausted of values, at which time the `values[n]` array is set to the value at `temp[index2]`. Following this, using the post-increment operator, the `index2` variable is incremented by 1 to move the pointer within the right sub set one index to the right.
- The second comparison is only `true` when the right sub set has been exhausted of values, at which time the `values[n]` array is set to the value at `temp[index1]`. Following this, using the post-increment operator, `index1` variable is incremented by 1 to move the pointer within the left sub set one index to the right.
- The third and final comparison is only evaluated when there are values in both the left and right subsets that have not yet been ordered. This comparison is `true` when the value at the `temp[index1]` array is less than the value at `temp[index2]`, at which time the `values[n]` array is set to `temp[index1]`. Again, following this, using the post-increment operator, the `index1` variable is incremented by 1 to move the pointer within the left sub set one index to the right.
- Finally, when all other logical options are false, the default behavior assumes that the value at `temp[index1]` array is greater than the value at `temp[index2]`, so the else block sets the value at the `values[n]` array to `temp[index2]`. Following this, using the post-increment operator, the `index2` variable is incremented by 1 to move the pointer within the right sub set one index to the right.

Java

```java
public void mergeSort(int[] values, int left, int right)
{
    if (left == right)
        return;

    if (left < right)
    {
        int middle = (left + right) / 2;

        mergeSort(values, left, middle);
        mergeSort(values, middle + 1, right);
        int[] temp = new int[values.length];
        for (int n = left; n <= right; n++)
        {
            temp[n] = values[n];
        }

        int index1 = left;
        int index2 = middle + 1;
        for (int n = left; n <= right; n++)
        {
            if (index1 == middle + 1)
            {
                values[n] = temp[index2++];
            }
            else if (index2 > right)
            {
                values[n] = temp[index1++];
            }
            else if (temp[index1] < temp[index2])
            {
                values[n] = temp[index1++];
            }
            else
            {
                values[n] = temp[index2++];
            }
        }
    }
}
```

The Java implementation is nearly identical in design to the C# implementation, except for the name of the array `length` function.

Objective-C

```objc
-(void)mergeSort:(NSMutableArray*)values withLeftIndex:(NSInteger)left
andRightIndex:(NSInteger)right
{
    if (left == right)
        return;
    if (left < right)
    {
        NSInteger middle = (left + right) / 2;
        [self mergeSort:values withLeftIndex:left
andRightIndex:middle];
        [self mergeSort:values withLeftIndex:middle + 1
andRightIndex:right];
        NSMutableArray *temp = [NSMutableArray arrayWithArray:values];
        NSInteger index1 = left;
        NSInteger index2 = middle + 1;
        for (NSInteger n = left; n <= right; n++)
        {
            if (index1 == middle + 1)
            {
                values[n] = temp[index2++];
            }
            else if (index2 > right)
            {
                values[n] = temp[index1++];
            }
            else if (temp[index1] < temp[index2])
            {
                values[n] = temp[index1++];
            }
            else
            {
                values[n] = temp[index2++];
            }
        }
    }
}
```

The Objective-C implementation of `mergeSort:withLeftIndex:andRightIndex:` is fundamentally identical to the C# and Java implementations.

Swift

```swift
open func mergeSort( values: inout [Int], left: Int, right: Int)
{
    if (values.count <= 1)
    {
        return
    }

    if (left == right)
    {
        return
    }
    if (left < right)
    {
        let middle: Int = (left + right) / 2
        mergeSort(values: &values, left: left, right: middle)
        mergeSort(values: &values, left: middle + 1, right: right)
        var temp = values
        var index1: Int = left
        var index2: Int = middle + 1
        for n in left...right
        {
            if (index1 == middle + 1)
            {
                values[n] = temp[index2]
                index2 += 1
            }
            else if (index2 > right)
            {
                values[n] = temp[index1]
                index1 += 1
            }
            else if (temp[index1] < temp[index2])
            {
                values[n] = temp[index1]
                index1 += 1
            }
            else
            {
                values[n] = temp[index2]
                index2 += 1
            }
        }
    }
}
```

Swift does not permit C-style `for` loops so our method but the Swift 3.0 equivalent is somewhat limited for this case. Since Swift considers arrays to be struct implementations instead of class implementations, the `values` parameter cannot be simply passed by reference. This is not necessarily a problem for this merge sort implementation because whenever the method is called recursively the entire `values` array is passed as a parameter. However, to make the method more consistent with other algorithms being discussed here, and to avoid the need to declare a return type, this implementation still includes the `inout` decorator on the `values` parameter. Otherwise, the functionality is fundamentally the same as its predecessors.

Bucket sort

Bucket sort, also known as **bin sort**, is a type of distribution sorting algorithm. Distribution sorts are algorithms that scatter the original values into any sort of intermediate structures that are then ordered, gathered, and merged into the final output structure. It is important to note that, although bucket sort is considered a distribution sort, most implementations typically leverage a comparison sort to order the contents of the buckets.
This algorithm sorts values by distributing them throughout an array of arrays that are called **buckets**. Elements are distributed based on their value and the range of values assigned to each bucket. For example, if one bucket inclusively accepts a range of values from 5 to 10, and the original set consists of 3, 5, 7, 9, and 11, the values 5, 7, and 9 would be placed in this hypothetical bucket.

Once all of the values have been distributed to their respective buckets, the buckets themselves are then ordered by recursively calling the bucket sort algorithm again. Eventually, each of the buckets is sorted and then the sorted results are concatenated into a complete sorted collection.

Bucket sort can be much faster than other sorting algorithms because of how elements are assigned to the buckets, typically using an array for each bucket where the value represents the index. Although the algorithm still suffers from a worst case complexity of $\mathbf{O}(n^2)$, the average an best case complexity is a mere $O(n + k)$, where n is the number of elements in the original array, and k is the total number of buckets used to sort the collection.

C#

```csharp
public void BucketSort(int[] values, int maxVal)
{
  int[] bucket = new int[maxVal + 1];
  int num = values.Length;
  int bucketNum = bucket.Length;

  for (int i = 0; i < bucketNum; i++)
  {
    bucket[i] = 0;
  }

  for (int i = 0; i < num; i++)
  {
    bucket[values[i]]++;
  }

  int pos = 0;
  for (int i = 0; i < bucketNum; i++)
  {
    for (int j = 0; j < bucket[i]; j++)
    {
      values[pos++] = i;
    }
  }
}
```

Each of our implementations of the `BucketSort` method begins by creating the empty buckets based on the total number of elements in the `values` array. Next, a `for` loop is used to populate the buckets with a base value of 0. This is immediately followed by a second `for` loop that distributes the elements from values into the various buckets. Finally, a nested `for` loop is used to actually sort the elements in the buckets and in turn the `values` array.

Java

```java
public void BucketSort(int[] values, int maxVal)
{
    int[] bucket = new int[maxVal + 1];
    int num = values.length;
    int bucketNum = bucket.length;

    for (int i = 0; i < bucketNum; i++)
    {
        bucket[i] = 0;
    }
```

```
for (int i = 0; i < num; i++)
{
    bucket[values[i]]++;
}

int pos = 0;
for (int i = 0; i < bucketNum; i++)
{
    for (int j = 0; j < bucket[i]; j++)
    {
        values[pos++] = i;
    }
}
}
```

The Java implementation is nearly identical in design to the C# implementation, except for the name of the array `length` function.

Objective-C

```objc
-(void)bucketSortArray:(NSMutableArray<NSNumber*>*)values
withMaxValue:(NSInteger)maxValue
{
    NSMutableArray<NSNumber*>*bucket = [NSMutableArray array];
    NSInteger num = [values count];
    NSInteger bucketNum = maxValue + 1;
    for (int i = 0; i < bucketNum; i++)
    {
        [bucket insertObject:[NSNumber numberWithInteger:0] atIndex:i];
    }
    for (int i = 0; i < num; i++)
    {
        NSInteger value=[bucket[[values[i] intValue]] intValue]+ 1;
        bucket[[values[i] intValue]] = [NSNumber
numberWithInteger:value];
    }
    int pos = 0;
    for (int i = 0; i < bucketNum; i++)
    {
        for (int j = 0; j < [bucket[i] intValue]; j++)
        {
            values[pos++] = [NSNumber numberWithInteger:i];
        }
    }
}
```

Since the `NSArray` array can only store objects, we need to cast our values to the `NSNumber` array, and when we evaluate the members we need to explicitly examine the `intValue` variable. Otherwise, this implementation is fundamentally the same as the C# or Java implementations.

Swift

```swift
open func bucketSort( values: inout [Int], maxVal: Int)
{
    var bucket = [Int]()
    let num: Int = values.count
    let bucketNum: Int = bucket.count
    for i in 0..<bucketNum
    {
        bucket[i] = 0
    }
    for i in 0..<num
    {
        bucket[values[i]] += 1
    }
    var pos: Int = 0
    for i in 0..<bucketNum
    {
        for _ in 0..<bucket[i]
        {
            values[pos] = i
            pos += 1
        }
    }
}
```

Swift does not permit C-style `for` loops so our method must use the Swift 3.0 equivalent. Otherwise, the functionality is fundamentally the same as its predecessors.

Summary

In this chapter we discussed several of the more common sorting algorithms you might encounter in your day-to-day experience. We started with several comparison sorts including selection, insertion, and bubble. We noted that a selection sort is perhaps the most inefficient sorting algorithm you are likely to encounter in the real world, but that's not to say that it is completely academic. Insertion sort somewhat improves on selection, as does the bubble sorting algorithm. Next, we examined two divide and conquer sorting algorithms including quick sort and merge sort. Both of these approaches are much more efficient than comparison sorts. Finally, we explored a common and highly efficient distribution sort called the counting sort. The counting sort is the most efficient algorithm we examined, but it is not necessarily the best fit for every situation.

13
Searching: Finding What You Need

Sorting your collections can be costly, but often this represents a one-time cost after the collection has been created. However, this time and energy spent up front can significantly improve performance once in the life of your application's run cycle. Even adding a new object is a much less costly process when the object is added to an already sorted collection.

The real performance improvement comes when it is time to search your collections for specific elements or values. In this chapter, we will examine how sorted collections greatly improve search time, depending on the search algorithm you choose. We will not discuss all of the search algorithms you can choose from, but we will examine three of the most common ones:

- Linear search (sequential search)
- Binary search
- Jump search

Linear search

A search, also called a **sequential** search, is simply a loop through a collection with some kind of comparison function to locate a matching element or value. Most linear searches return a value representing the index of the matching object in the collection, or some impossible index value such as -1 when an object is not found. Alternative versions of this search could return the object itself or null if the object is not found.

This is the simplest form of search pattern and it carries an **O**(*n*) complexity cost. This complexity is consistent whether the collection is in random order or if it has already been sorted. In very small collections linear searches are perfectly acceptable and many developers make use of them daily. However, when working with very large collections it is often beneficial to find alternatives to this sequential search approach. This is particularly true when working with lists of very complex objects, such as spatial geometries, where search or analysis can be very processor-intensive operations.

Each of the code examples in this chapter will examine search algorithms in the form of the methods most essential to the operation, with these being detached from their parent classes. Additionally, in each case, the collection of objects being sorted will be defined at the class level, outside the example code shown here. Likewise, the subsequent object instantiation and population of those collections will be defined outside the example code. To see the full class examples, use the code examples accompanying this text.

C#

The first example of the linear search algorithm is in the `LinearSearchIndex(int[] values, int key)` method. As you can see, this method is very simple and almost self-explanatory. There are two major characteristics of this implementation worth mentioning. First, the method accepts the array of `values` and the search `key`. Second, the method returns the index `i` of any matching element, or simply −1 if the search key is not found.

```
public int LinearSearchIndex(int[] values, int key)
{
    for (int i = 0; i < values.Length - 1; i++)
    {
        if (values[i] == key)
        {
            return i;
        }
    }

    return -1;
}
```

The second example of a linear search is nearly identical to the first. However, in the `LinearSearchCustomer(Customer[] customers, int custId)` method, we are not searching for a value but rather for a key that represents the customer that the caller wants to retrieve. Note that the comparison is now searching the `customerId` field on the `Customer` object; if a match is found, the `Customer` at `customers[i]` is returned. If no match is found, the method returns `null`:

```
public Customer LinearSearchCustomer(Customer[] customers, int custId)
{
    for (int i = 0; i < customers.Length - 1; i++)
    {
        if (customers[i].customerId == custId)
        {
            return customers[i];
        }
    }

    return null;
}
```

Java

The Java implementation of each method is nearly identical in design to the C# implementation, except for the name of the array `length` function.

```
public int linearSearchIndex(int[] values, int key)
{
    for (int i = 0; i < values.length - 1; i++)
    {
        if (values[i] == key)
        {
            return i;
        }
    }

    return -1;
}

public Customer linearSearchCustomer(Customer[] customers, int custId)
{
    for (int i = 0; i < customers.length - 1; i++)
    {
        if (customers[i].customerId == custId)
        {
            return customers[i];
        }
    }
```

```
        return null;
    }
```

Objective-C

Since NSArray can only store objects, we need to cast our values to NSNumber, and when we evaluate the members we need to explicitly examine intValue. Otherwise, these implementations are fundamentally the same as the C# or Java implementations:

```
    - (NSInteger) linearSearchArray: (NSMutableArray<NSNumber*>*) values
byKey: (NSInteger) key
    {
        for (int i = 0; i < [values count] - 1; i++)
        {
            if ([values[i] intValue] == key)
            {
                return i;
            }
        }
        return -1;
    }


    -
    (EDSCustomer*) linearSearchCustomers: (NSMutableArray<NSNumber*>*) customers
byCustId: (NSInteger) custId
    {
        for (EDSCustomer *c in customers)
        {
            if (c.customerId == custId)
            {
                return c;
            }
        }
        return nil;
    }
```

Swift

Swift does not permit C-style for loops so our method must use the Swift 3.0 equivalent. Also, Swift does not allow a method to return nil unless the return type is explicitly declared as optional, so the linearSearchCustomer(customers: [Customer], custId: Int) method has a return type of Customer?. Otherwise, the functionality is fundamentally the same as its predecessors:

```
    open func linearSearhIndex( values: [Int], key: Int) -> Int
    {
        for i in 0..<values.count
```

```
    {
        if (values[i] == key)
        {
            return i
        }
    }

    return -1
}

open func linearSearchCustomer( customers: [Customer], custId: Int) ->
Customer?
    {
        for i in 0..<customers.count
        {
            if (customers[i].custId == custId)
            {
                return customers[i]
            }
        }
        return nil
    }
```

Binary search

When dealing with an unsorted collection, a sequential search is probably the most reasonable approach. However, when working with a sorted collection there are better methods of finding matches to search keys. One alternative is a binary search. A binary search is typically implemented as a recursive function and works on the principle of repeatedly dividing the collection in half and searching smaller and smaller chunks of the collection until a match is found or until the search has exhausted the remaining options and turns up empty.

For example, given the following set of ordered values:

$S = \{8, 19, 23, 50, 75, 103, 121, 143, 201\}$

Using a linear search to find the value 143 would have a complexity cost of **O(8)** since 143 is found at index 7 (position 8) in our collection. However, a binary search can take advantage of the sorted nature of the collection to improve upon this complexity cost.

We know that the collection consists of nine elements, so the binary search would begin by examining the median element at index 5 and comparing that to the key value of 143. Since *i[5] = 75*, and this is less than 143, the set is split and the range of possible matches is reduced to only include the upper half, leaving us with:

S = {103, 121, 143, 201}

With four elements, the median element is the element at position two. Position *i[2] = 121*, and this is less than 143 so the set is split and the range of possible matches is reduced to only include the upper quarter, leaving us with:

S = {143, 201}

With two elements, the median element is the element at position one. Since *i[1] = 143*, we have found a match and the value can be returned. This search only cost **O**(3), improving on the linear search time by almost 67%. Although individual results may vary, the binary search pattern is consistently more efficient than the linear search when the collection is sorted. This is a strong justification for taking the time to sort your collections before your application begins to use data supplied by them:

C#

The `BinarySort(int[] values, int left, int right, int key)` begins by checking if the `right` index is greater than or equal to the `left` index. If `false`, there are no elements within the prescribed range and the analysis has been exhausted so the method returns `-1`. We'll examine why in a moment. Otherwise, method execution continues because there is at least one object in the defined range.

Next, the method checks whether the value at the `middle` index matches our `key`. If `true`, the `middle` index is returned. Otherwise, the method checks whether the values at the `middle` index are greater than the `key` value. If `true`, `BinarySort(int[] values, int left, int right, int key)` is called recursively with bounds that select the lower half of the current range of elements. Otherwise, the value at the `middle` index is less than the `key`, so `BinarySort(int[] values, int left, int right, int key)` is called recursively with bounds that select the upper half of the current range of elements:

```
public int BinarySearch(int[] values, int left, int right, int key)
{
    if (right >= left)
    {
        int middle = left + (right - left) / 2;

        if (values[middle] == key)
        {
```

```
                    return middle;
            }
            else if (values[middle] > key)
            {
                return BinarySearch(values, left, middle - 1, key);
            }

            return BinarySearch(values, middle + 1, right, key);
        }

        return -1;
    }
```

Java

Apart from the name `binarySearch(int[] values, int left, int right, int key)`, the Java implementation is identical in design to the C# implementation:

```java
public int binarySearch(int[] values, int left, int right, int key)
{
    if (right >= left)
    {
        int mid = left + (right - left) / 2;

        if (values[mid] == key)
        {
            return mid;
        }
        else if (values[mid] > key)
        {
            return binarySearch(values, left, mid - 1, key);
        }
        return binarySearch(values, mid + 1, right, key);
    }

    return -1;
}
```

Objective-C

Since `NSArray` can only store objects, we need to cast our values to `NSNumber`, and when we evaluate the members we need to explicitly examine the `intValue`. Otherwise, these implementations are fundamentally the same as the C# or Java implementations:

```objc
- (NSInteger)binarySearchArray:(NSMutableArray<NSNumber*>*)values
withLeftIndex:(NSInteger)left
rightIndex:(NSInteger)right
andKey:(NSInteger)key
```

```
    {
        if (right >= left)
        {
            NSInteger mid = left + (right - left) / 2;
            if ([values[mid] intValue] == key)
            {
                return mid;
            }
            else if ([values[mid] intValue] > key)
            {
                return [self binarySearchArray:values withLeftIndex:left
    rightIndex:mid - 1 andKey:key];
            }
            return [self binarySearchArray:values withLeftIndex:mid + 1
    rightIndex:right andKey:key];
        }
        return -1;
    }
```

Swift

Fundamentally, the Swift implementation is the same as its predecessors:

```
    open func binarySearch( values: [Int], left: Int, right: Int, key: Int)
    -> Int
    {
        if (right >= left)
        {
            let mid: Int = left + (right - left) / 2

            if (values[mid] == key)
            {
                return mid
            }
            else if (values[mid] > key)
            {
                return binarySearch(values: values, left: left, right: mid
    - 1, key: key)
            }

            return binarySearch(values: values, left: mid + 1, right:
    right, key: key)
        }

        return -1
    }
```

Jump search

Another search algorithm that can improve performance with sorted arrays is the **jump search**. A jump search bears some similarity to both the linear search and binary search algorithms in that it searches blocks of elements from left to right beginning with the first block in the collection, and also because at each jump the algorithm compares the search key value to the value of the element at the current step. If the algorithm determines that the key could exist in the current subset of elements, the next step (no pun intended) is to examine each element in the current subset to determine if it is less than the key.

Once an element is found that is not less than the key , that element is compared to the key. If the element is equal to the key, it is returned; otherwise, it is greater than the key, which means that the key does not exist in the collection.

The jump length m is not an arbitrary value, but rather is calculated based on the length of the collection using the formula $m = \sqrt{n}$, where n is the total number of elements in the collection. The jump search begins by examining the value of the last object in the first block or subset.

For example, let's search for value *143* given the following set of ordered values:

$S = \{8, 19, 23, 50, 75, 103, 121, 143, 201\}$

Since our collection contains nine elements, $m = \sqrt{n}$ gives us a value of 3. Since $i[2] = 23$, and this is less than *143*, the algorithm jumps to the next block. Next, $i[4] = 103$ which is also less than *143* so this subset is excluded. Finally, $i[8] = 201$. Since *201* is greater than *143*, the key could possible exist in the third subset:

$S_3 = \{121, 143, 201\}$

Next, the algorithm checks each element in this subset to determine if it is less than *143*. And $i[6] = 121$, so the algorithm continues its examination. Also, $i[7] = 143$ which is not less than *143*, so the execution proceeds to the final step. Since $i[7] = 143$, we have found a match to our key and the value of i can be returned. This search cost **O**(5), which is only slightly better than the **O**(7) the linear search produced and slightly worse than the **O**(3) cost we found with a binary search. However, with much larger data sets the jump search is consistently more efficient than a linear and binary search when the collection is sorted.

Again, sorting the collection does represent some cost in time and performance up front, but the payoff over the life span of your application's run cycle is more than justifies the effort.

C#

Each of our implementations of the `BubbleSort` method begins by declaring three `int` variables to track the size of the collection, the step size, and the previously evaluated index. Following this, a `while` loop uses the `prev` and `step` values to define and search subsets of the collection for a range where the `key` could exist. If no acceptable subset is found, the method returns -1 indicating that the `key` cannot exist in this set. Otherwise, the value of `prev` and `step` identify the subset where the `key` might exist.

The next `while` loop examines each element within the subset to determine if it is less than the `key`. If no acceptable element is found, the method returns -1 indicating that the `key` cannot exist in this set. Otherwise, the value of `prev` identifies the best possible match for `key` in the subset.

Finally, the element at `prev` is compared to the `key`. If the two values match, then `prev` is returned. Otherwise, we reach the end of execution and -1 is returned:

```csharp
public int JumpSearch(int[] values, int key)
{
    int n = values.Length;
    int step = (int)Math.Sqrt(n);
    int prev = 0;

    while (values[Math.Min(step, n) - 1] < key)
    {
        prev = step;
        step += (int)Math.Floor(Math.Sqrt(n));
        if (prev >= n)
        {
            return -1;
        }
    }

    while (values[prev] < key)
    {
        prev++;
        if (prev == Math.Min(step, n))
        {
            return -1;
        }
    }

    if (values[prev] == key)
    {
        return prev;
    }
}
```

```
        return -1;
    }
```

Java

The Java implementation of each method is nearly identical in design to the C#
implementations, except for the name of the array `length` function.

```java
public int jumpSearch(int[] values, int key)
{
    int n = values.length;
    int step = (int)Math.sqrt(n);
    int prev = 0;

    while (values[Math.min(step, n) - 1] < key)
    {
        prev = step;
        step += (int)Math.floor(Math.sqrt(n));
        if (prev >= n)
        {
            return -1;
        }
    }

    while (values[prev] < key)
    {
        prev++;
        if (prev == Math.min(step, n))
        {
            return -1;
        }
    }

    if (values[prev] == key)
    {
        return prev;
    }

    return -1;
}
```

Objective-C

Since `NSArray` can only store objects, we need to cast our values to `NSNumber`, and when we evaluate the members we need to explicitly examine the `intValue`. Otherwise, this implementation is fundamentally the same as the C# or Java implementations.

```objectivec
-(NSInteger)jumpSearchArray:(NSMutableArray<NSNumber*>*)values forKey:
(NSInteger)key
{
    NSInteger n = [values count];
    NSInteger step = sqrt(n);
    NSInteger prev = 0;
    while ([values[(int)fmin(step, n)-1] intValue] < key)
    {
        prev = step;
        step += floor(sqrt(n));
        if (prev >= n)
        {
            return -1;
        }
    }
    while ([values[prev] intValue] < key)
    {
        prev++;
        if (prev == fmin(step, n))
        {
            return -1;
        }
    }
    if ([values[prev] intValue] == key)
    {
        return prev;
    }
    return -1;
}
```

Swift

Aside from from the extra casting of values returned from `sqrt()` and `floor()` methods, the functionality is fundamentally the same as its predecessors:

```swift
open func jumpSearch( values: [Int], key: Int) -> Int
{
    let n: Int = values.count
    var step: Int = Int(sqrt(Double(n)))
    var prev: Int = 0
    while values[min(step, n) - 1] < key
    {
```

```
            prev = step
            step = step + Int(floor(sqrt(Double(n))))
            if (prev >= n)
            {
                return -1
            }
        }
    while (values[prev] < key)
    {
        prev = prev + 1
        if (prev == min(step, n))
        {
            return -1
        }
    }
    if (values[prev] == key)
    {
        return prev
    }
    return -1
}
```

Summary

In this chapter, we examined several search algorithms. First, we looked at linear searching, or sequential searching. Linear searching is barely even an algorithm as your code is simply looping through the elements in a collection from left to right until a match is found. This approach is useful when working with very small collections, or with collections that have not been sorted, if for no other reason than it is easy to implement from a development point of view. However, when working with large sorted datasets, there are much better alternatives.

The next search algorithm we examined was the binary search. Binary search algorithms essentially divide-and-conquer the collection, halving the elements into smaller and smaller subsets of the original collection until a match is found or the list of possible matches has been exhausted. Whereas a linear search has an $O(n)$ complexity cost, a binary search pattern has a much improved $O(log(n))$ complexity cost. However, it is absolutely vital that a collection be properly sorted prior to running the binary search or the results will be meaningless.

Finally, we examined the jump search. Jump searches work by sequentially examining subsets of the collection that are each $\sqrt{n}$ in length where n is the total number of elements in the collection. Although somewhat more complex to implement, and with a worst case complexity of $O(n)$, the jump search has a vastly improved average cost complexity of $O(\sqrt{n})$ where n is the total number of elements in the collection.

Index

www.ingramcontent.com/pod-product-compliance
Lightning Source LLC
Chambersburg PA
CBHW062057050326
40690CB00016B/3123